Anke S. Biendarra
**Germans Going Global**

# Interdisciplinary German Cultural Studies

Edited by
Scott Denham, Irene Kacandes and
Jonathan Petropoulos

## Volume 12

Anke S. Biendarra

# Germans Going Global

Contemporary Literature and Cultural Globalization

**DE GRUYTER**

MIX
Papier aus verantwor-
tungsvollen Quellen
FSC
www.fsc.org    FSC® C016439

ISBN 978-3-11-048598-1
e-ISBN 978-3-11-028291-7
ISSN 1861-8030

**Library of Congress Cataloging-in-Publication Data**
A CIP catalog record for this book has been applied for at the Library of Congress.

**Bibliographic information published by the Deutsche Nationalbibliothek**
The Deutsche Nationalbibliothek lists this publication in the Deutsche Nationalbibliografie;
detailed bibliographic data are available in the Internet at http://dnb.dnb.de.

© 2012 Walter de Gruyter GmbH, Berlin/Boston
Cover image: ESA
Typesetting: Meta Systems GmbH, Wustermark
Printing: Hubert & Co. GmbH & Co. KG, Göttingen
∞ Printed on acid-free paper
Printed in Germany

www.degruyter.com

# Contents

————

For Robert
I love it when you sing to me
And you can sing me anything

# Acknowledgements

I would like to express my gratitude for the institutional support I received over the years while conceiving this project and completing the manuscript. The American Association of University Women (AAUW) granted me a yearlong American Postdoctoral Fellowship that provided me with crucial time free of teaching duties to write drafts of the first two chapters. The Dean's Office of the School of Humanities at the University of California, Irvine augmented my fellowship year. The Office of the Executive Vice Chancellor and the Academic Senate of the University of California, Irvine supported the writing of this book with various short-term grants. One of them allowed me to go to the *Deutsches Literaturarchiv* in Marbach a. N., where I read publications not available stateside. The International Center for Writing and Translation at UCI funded a trip to Berlin that allowed me to conduct interviews with some of the authors covered in this study. Thomas Meinecke, Antje Rávic Strubel, Gregor Hens, and Terézia Mora graciously allowed me to gain insight into their creative processes and enriched my research with their perspectives on the contemporary literary scene in Germany.

There are many people in German Studies and Germanistik whom I enjoyed meeting and whose research influenced this book, not all of whom I can list here. Apart from the many conference panels I had the pleasure to be part of, symposia in Luxembourg, Leeds, and Berlin in particular gave me insights and inspired me. Thank you to the organizers, Wilhelm Amann, Stuart Taberner and Lyn Marven, Johanna Bohley and Julia Schoell, and their respective institutions for inviting me and funding my stay.

A heartfelt thank you goes to my departmental colleagues, especially to John Smith and Gail Hart, for their guidance and professional wisdom. They both read many chapter drafts, and their feedback was nothing but helpful, constructive, and encouraging.

Working on this book with De Gruyter has been a very positive experience, and I thank my editor Manuela Gerlof for her truly enthusiastic support of this project from our first e-mail exchange. The careful and critical readings of the three editors of the series *Interdisciplinary German Cultural Studies*, Scott Denham, Irene Kacandes and Jonathan Petropoulos, made this a much better book. I am grateful to them, especially to Irene Kacandes who set the bar high with her rigorous scholarship and attention to detail.

My *Doktormutter* Sabine Wilke has become a friend over the years and deserves a special thank you for having been a wonderful mentor and an inspiring *Vorbild*. Katharina Gerstenberger, Imke Meyer, and Karin Bauer have supported my work for years in various ways, and I am grateful to them.

My friends in Germany and the U.S. have accompanied me on my path, showed interest in my research, discussed ideas and read drafts, or simply sustained me with conversations, outings, food, and positive energy. Thank you, Viktoria Harms, Rebeca Helfer, Raimund Hermes, Jeremy Lehnen, Laura Stahman, and Marnee Reiley.

I thank my families in Germany and the U.S.; especially my parents for fostering my love of literature from an early age and my sister Ulrike who has been an inspiration in her strength and tenacity.

Woven into this book is my love for Umbra who was her very own dog all along, enthusiastically licking books in what must have been her own pursuit of knowledge. She kept me company throughout the writing process, while Marxy provided happy breaks in the great California outdoors while I was revising the manuscript.

There are two people without whom writing this book would have been much more difficult. I feel much gratitude towards Leila Lehnen for being there for me while going through it also. Her critical mind, generosity, and kindness kept me oriented. And then there is Robert Plogman who stands taller than giants and outshines all the stars. His support and belief in me never waivered, which infused these pages in more ways than I can express. I am thankful for his love and friendship and cherish his sense of humor and comedic talent. His qualities prevailed through it all, and then some. This book is entirely for him.

Anke S. Biendarra                                                    Irvine, June 2012

# Introduction: Contemporary German Literature and Cultural Globalization

In his political picture book *Deutschland macht dicht* (2010, Germany Shuts Down) Dietmar Dath, born in 1970, presents a radical solution to the complex ramifications of a globalized world for Germany. The chancellor, advised by the irritable hologram ghost of famous economist Joseph Schumpeter, decides that the best way to negotiate the new world order will be to lock down the country, in order to strengthen its economic self-reliance and regulate migration, thereby protecting it from globalization:

> "If we do it ... hchhh...," grunted the chancellor, "of course it won't be for all times. More like in a mom-and-pop store, closed for taking inventory ... afterwards we can start to filter. The problem really is ... this unregulated in and out ... as the uncle from the bank said: we like the Vietnamese if the kids try hard, ethnic Germans from Russia are still acceptable, Eastern Europeans, Ukrainians, White Russians, fine by me, but please, no more Turks and Arabs ... Anyway, I am all for it. That we do it. All this partitioning off and cleaning up, first we have to get our own ducks in a row and then sort out who might later come back, all this trade and change, on the one hand immigrants, on the other export... The Monegenis Plan. Turn off the Internet. Great."[1]

Although Dath with his tongue-in-cheek humor might not be the best informant, the literary fantasy of sealing off the country from outside influences echoes sentiments of many Germans who have seen their spatial, political, and social environment undergo drastic changes over the past two decades in the aftermath of unification. A widespread ambivalence with regard to both Europeanization and globalization has been visible in German public discourse, the media, and politics and has gained further momentum with the worldwide economic crisis at the end of the first millennial decade and the failing of the economies of EU members such as Greece, Spain, and Ireland. While this

---

1 Unless otherwise noted, all translations from the German in this study are my own. "Wenn wir das machen ... hchhh"... grunzte der Kanzler, "dann natürlich nicht für immer. Eher wie beim Krämerladen, wegen Inventur geschlossen ... danach können wir dann filtern. Das Problem ist ... doch nur ... dieses unregelte Rein und Raus ... wie der Onkel von der Bank gesagt hat: Vietnamesen wollen wir gern, wenn sich die Kinder Mühe geben, Deutschrussen sind auch noch okay, Osteuropäer, Ukrainer, Weißrussen von mir aus, aber bitte keine Türken und Araber mehr. ... Also, jedenfalls, ich bin dafür. Daß man das macht. Dieses Abschotten und Aufräumen, erst mal den eigenen Laden in Schuß bringen und dann sortieren, wer später irgendwann wieder rein kann, den ganzen Handel und Wandel, einerseits Einwanderer, andererseits Export... Monogenis-Plan. Internet abschalten. Prima." 31.

ambivalence is an emotion Germans share with other Europeans, they have been especially affected by the changes brought about by globalization.

Sociologist Ulrich Beck, a prolific theorist of globalization, diagnosed a German "globalization shock" in recent years, pinpointing various distinct reasons for it (2000, 13–15). The most important one – which will be central to my discussion of neoliberal work literature in chapter three – is that globalization is primarily associated with the loss of jobs, rising unemployment, and the relocation of labor into low-wage economies. This is particularly significant because throughout the 1990s and well into the new millennium, Germany experienced mass unemployment despite economic growth, leading to it being labeled the "sick man of Europe." The fact that the tide has recently turned and the country seems to have escaped the global economic crisis relatively unscathed[2] does not change its long history of "high and sticky unemployment" since the 1970s, as economist Horst Siebert calls it (see 69–113). Neither does it alter the fact that unless new models of work are introduced, mass unemployment will remain one of the central problems for all Western economies.

The second point is that as a country that defines itself primarily through its economic successes – what Jürgen Habermas described as "D-Mark nationalism" after unification (i.e., a nationalism that is based on a strong economy and currency) – Germany has been feeling particularly threatened by the globalization of the world market seeping in from outside. One important example of this is the ongoing debate about Germany's role as a manufacturer and its ability to remain globally competitive ("Standortdebatte"), as are the mass protests ("Montagsdemonstrationen") that took place against the Hartz measures (i.e., government measures that institutionalize deep cuts in social welfare programs).[3] The famous "German model" that relies on balancing the markets and state interventions to link economic success with social justice became challenged by neoliberal free-market principles preeminent in the United States and the United Kingdom during the reign of Ronald Reagan and Margaret Thatcher.[4] Flexible work models, the disappearance of full-time jobs, the

---

2 As of May 2012, Germany had the lowest unemployment rate (6.7 %) since 1992 and experienced a robust growth rate of 3.7% in 2010 and 2.6% in the first quarter of 2011, respectively. This was the biggest growth in twenty years, leading the British paper *The Economist* to proclaim a "new German Wirtschaftswunder." "Angela in Wunderland: What Germany's Got Right, and What It Hasn't." February 3, 2011. (http://www.economist.com/node/18070170). See also Kulish. However, political scientist Ralph Jeremias challenges the notion of the current "job miracle."
3 See http://www.bundesweite-montagsdemo.com and http://de.wikipedia.org/wiki/Montagsdemonstrationen_gegen_Sozialabbau_2004#Literatur (March 25, 2012).
4 For a more detailed discussion see Taberner 2005. 1–24.

erosion of employee rights and welfare services are visible signs of this neoliberal turn. Third, social welfare states such as Germany and France are the losers of globalization in that national states have little control over worldwide economic development, but are still forced to deal with possible negative repercussions such as unemployment, poverty, and unregulated migration. Fourth, globalization has shaken the German self-conception as a homogenous, self-contained national entity. Although Germany is very much a global space, providing a home for people from many different cultures, this reality had long been obscured before the debate on globalization with its inherent potential for denationalization shed light on it. The most prominent sign of this was the often-reiterated political statement that Germany was not an immigration country; such rhetoric only began to change under the Red-Green coalition in 1998.

Finally, Beck argues that the shock of the globalization realization also ended the Germans' preoccupation with themselves (2000, 14). Indeed, for the better part of the 1990s, unification and the question of commonalities between East and West dominated the public discourse and fueled the reemergence of the nation. But the disappearance of socialism and GDR culture also led to an erasure of different life styles and gave free reign to the consumer ideologies inherent to globalization. One could argue that after the demise of the GDR and with the introduction of capitalism, all of Eastern Germany became a laboratory and prime example of globalization, undergoing in a matter of years a process that in Western Germany took decades. For example, thanks in part to the solidarity agreement (*Solidarpakt*) and controversial solidarity surcharge on the income tax (*Solidaritätszuschlag*), infrastructures were modernized and rebuilt in the five new *Länder*; by 2005 the German Telekom had established the globally most advanced telecommunications network in East Germany. The millennium thus served as a threshold after which globalizing factors came to the fore ever more forcefully: "In areas as diverse as economics, foreign policy and culture, the accelerating impact of globalization would make itself felt on a reunited Germany, recently extracted from its comfortable Cold-War seclusion and impelled into a new world order in which the free market reigned supreme" (Taberner 2004, 3).[5]

Broadening the commonly held view that the end of the Cold War and the opening of the Berlin Wall in 1989 are the key caesurae in all aspects of German society (von Oppen 1), September 11, 2001 certainly was another decisive

---

5 Some factors in these profound changes were the new Red-Green coalition and especially chancellor Gerhard Schröder's commitment to economic modernization, the rise of the New Economy and its reliance on new technologies, followed by its spectacular crash.

rupture. It forced the Germans to truly confront the complicated realities of a changing world, challenging them to acknowledge and deal with the contestations of globalization. The terrorist attacks served as forceful evidence of the world's interconnectedness: the United States as a nation was threatened by a post-national organization without an obvious location for retaliation, and one of the attacks targeted the *World Trade Center* as a symbol for capitalism and empire, thereby including all Western countries ("Wir sind eine Welt," proclaimed *Der Spiegel*, see Beste). The terrorist attacks and the subsequent events erased material boundaries of land and water as well as imaginary boundaries in cyberspace, and they provided the discomfiting experience of participating in an event that seemed unreal and cinematic in "real time" through an uncanny compression of time and space.

In recent years, issues of migration and immigration within both Germany and the European Union have become another aspect of the impact of globalizing factors, visible in the changes to German citizenship law in 2000 and the EU's adaptation of the Dublin Regulation to control immigration to the EU in 2003, respectively.[6]

If we agree with Beck that globality is "an unavoidable condition of human intercourse" (2000, 15) and that globalizing factors have contributed to the shaping of the Berlin Republic and German society, the question arises of what that means for contemporary culture, specifically for German-language literature and why it makes sense to devote a scholarly book to it. It has become a widely accepted position in German Studies that in the 1990s, Germany was in the process of negotiating competing versions of a new normality, which the literature of those years reflects (see Brockmann 1999, Taberner 2005). Around the millennium, the so-called "entertainment and event society" (*Erlebnisgesellschaft*) that Gerhard Schulze had established as the dominant sociological category of the 1990s, came to an end. Influenced by the events of September 11, 2001 and the changing political situation globally, cultural criticism diagnosed a "new seriousness,"[7] which was determined increasingly by globalizing influences on economic, political, and social factors. Economic insecurities, the unraveling of the social net, new social security legislation like the Hartz measures and the increasing numbers of workers in temporary, insecure, and underpaid jobs that lead to the new social group of the "Precar-

---

6 For the legal framework of the Dublin Regulation see the portal of the European Union: http://eur-lex.europa.eu/LexUriServ/LexUriServ.do?uri=CELEX:41997A0819(01):EN:NOT (June 1, 2011).

7 "Neue Ernsthaftigkeit" was the catchword in German. See Bürger and Leitgeb and the discussion between Wieland Freund, Martin Hielscher and Thomas Hettche.

iat" (see Standing) has inspired authors of a younger generation to thematize these social developments.

Even if the alleged "re-politicization" of German literature identified in the *Feuilleton* has much to do with a certain hype created by the media and functions as a self-fulfilling prophecy (see Thomas), we do witness a rising number of public attempts by younger authors to arrive at "shared paradigms for a literary discussion of political realities," as writers Norbert Niemann and Georg M. Oswald formulated in the introduction to the special issue of *Akzente* on "Politics" they edited in 2001. To be sure, most contemporary authors refuse to explicitly assume the role of public intellectual, and they do not want their texts to be received as a blueprint for political activism either. However, invoking political content and attempting to create an "aesthetic space of resonance"[8] through literary texts dealing with actual political and societal conflicts has become acceptable again. Consequently authors argue over what might be the appropriate aesthetic means to describe contemporary reality, as is visible in the debates discussed in chapter two of this book, including a second-round debate about a "relevant realism" that involved Juli Zeh, Robert Menasse, Thomas Hettche, and others.[9]

Younger authors now deal with topics that for years were controlled primarily by the contemporaries of the *Gruppe 47*. The literary publications that represent the rediscovering of social and political commitment by and large fall into two broad categories. The first, recently classified as "realistic memory literature" (Morgenroth and Viehöfer), is primarily concerned with the literary negotiation of the German pasts and thus participates in what Anne Fuchs calls "memory contests."[10] Over the last two decades, an array of literary texts has been published that offer an intense examination of both the National Socialist past and the Second World War, as well as the more recent GDR history, the legacy of the Red Army Faction and the ensuing "bleierne Zeit" of the 1970s.[11] Another interesting recent phenomenon are novels that explicitly

---

**8** "... einen ästhetischen Resonanzraum schaffen..." Ulrich Peltzer in conversation with Tanja Dückers on March 14, 2008 at the Leipzig Book Fair. http://www.mdr.de/mdr-figaro/literatur/ 5271119.html#absatz.10 (accessed June 25, 2008, no longer available online).

**9** The debate about "relevant realism" (*relevanter Realismus*) was about the appropriate aesthetic means that would allow contemporary German-language prose to articulate ethical standpoints. I will return to this debate in chapter two. See Martin R. Dean et al., as well as the responses by Andreas Maier, Juli Zeh, and Hans-Ulrich Treichel entitled "Der Roman schaut in fremde Zimmer hinein" in the same issue of *Die Zeit*.

**10** Fuchs suggests replacing the term "mastery of the past" (*Vergangenheitsbewältigung*) with "memory contests," which "involve retrospective imaginings that simultaneously articulate, question and investigate the normative self-image of previous generations" 179.

**11** Some of the many narratives dealing with the German pasts are Marcel Beyer's *Flughunde* (1995) and *Spione* (2000), Tanja Dückers's *Himmelskörper* (2003), Julia Franck's

thematize politics and the role of the state when confronted with grass-roots resistance.[12] This is accompanied by the articulation of a hedonistic, apolitical life style, as reflected in new German pop literature by Benjamin von Stuckrad-Barre, Alexa Hennig von Lange and others.

In addition, German-language narratives by transnational authors – such as Emine Sevgi Özdamar, Feridun Zaimoğlu, Herta Müller or Yoko Tawada – have experienced a growing interest in the literary public. While these and other transnational authors have added important voices and aesthetic influences, thereby redefining what contemporary German-speaking literature means in the twenty-first century, this study does not explicitly cover them. One reason is that my selection is limited to a specific group born between circa 1955 and 1975. Granted, authors such as Terézia Mora, Marica Bodrožić, and Saša Stanišić nominally belong to the cohort I am interested in, yet I chose to analyze their works in a different framework than the one applied here. Few of these writers would deny that their often-complicated life paths and experiences of displacement, revolution or war serve as a major source for their own story telling. In his anthology *Döner in Walhalla* (2000), Ilija Trojanow stresses that it is the multiplicity of interesting biographies that makes exciting texts possible, and Iranian-German Navid Kermani describes "existential strangeness" as a motif of his life and his writing (2005, 30). In order to do their texts justice, these writers are thus better considered in contexts such as European literature, literature of trauma, or post-communist literature, as Brigid Haines and others have argued.

The second major strand within the spectrum of contemporary literature – and the one that is at the heart of this study – articulates the conditions of global existence and contemporary realities. Narratives dealing with the neo-liberal work world, global travel, and the aftermath of 09/11 implicitly comment on contemporary debates on globalization, its socio-economic nature, impact, and the consequences for local culture. The analyses in *Germans Going Global* thus show that globalization, broadly conceptualized as Tomlinson's rapidly developing and ever-denser network of interconnections and interdependencies that characterize modern social life (2), has had far-reaching effects on Germany's cultural topography. This study examines the manner in which the impact of globalization has been experienced and discussed in German litera-

---

*Lagerfeuer* (2003) and *Die Mittagsfrau* (2007), Ingo Schulze's *Simple Storys* (1998) and *Neue Leben* (2005), Uwe Tellkamp's *Der Turm* (2008), and Eugen Ruge's *In Zeiten des abnehmenden Lichts* (2011). Leander Scholz's *Rosenfest* (2001) focuses on the legacy of the RAF, as do a number of German films in the aughts.

**12** For example, Ulrich Peltzer's *Teil der Lösung* (2007) and Michael Kumpfmüller's *Nachricht an alle* (2008).

ture from the late 1990s throughout the aughts, the first millennial decade.[13] Focusing primarily, though not exclusively, on German literature of the Federal Republic, I offer readings of a variety of cultural texts that can illuminate how the challenges globalization has posed for Germany over the last two decades have been manifested and reimagined in aesthetic production. Specifically, I evaluate the ways in which contemporary German writers respond to the pressures that globalizing factors impose on the concept of authorship, the individual and society, and what their aesthetic responses mean for identity construction in the Berlin Republic. The study aids in closing a lacuna since detailed analyses of the ramifications globalization entails for literary production are still few and far between. By focusing on the cultural production of roughly the last two decades, this study also provides a literary history of the present, if only a limited one. I hope that the scholarly snapshot I present of post-unification and millennial literary production inspires the reader to turn to the primary texts as well. Furthermore, by offering interpretations of a number of texts that have received little, if any, scholarly attention, it is my hope that these interesting authors will find a wider reception and be taught more frequently in university classrooms.

While globalization has become an important topic of discussion both in the public sphere and in the academy, it has come rather slowly to German Studies. Resistance by German historians notwithstanding, Germanists in Europe were the ones breaking ground on the topic of cultural globalization and the literary realm (see Schmeling, Taberner, Amann et al.). In recent years – approximately since 2005 – a growing interest has also been visible in the United States, as was first evidenced by a number of panels at conferences of professional scholarly organizations. Individual essays and collections (see Rechtien and von Oppen; von Dirke and Coury) slowly have supplemented earlier disciplinary reflections on German Studies and globalization.[14] While it must remain speculative why scholars have so far not examined this connection more closely, at least two explanations stand out.

First, the study of literature and globalization has been influenced by the example of English, due to the fact that it has developed into a transnational vernacular. English literature, as Paul Jay has observed in an influential early article, is nowadays defined less by a nation than by a language since writers from various cultural and ethnic backgrounds all over the world write in Eng-

---

**13** As such, it is in a way a continuation of Taberner's edited volume of 2004, which provided me with important impulses.
**14** See Volume 78 (2005) of *The German Quarterly* and its forum discussion of "German Studies and Globalization."

lish (33). Consequently, some of the models developed on the background of the specific British and U.S. histories of colonialism, migration, and displacement that might concern race, gender relations, and cultural hybridity do not map neatly onto the German context. Instead, they require modifications that take into account European cultural migrations (Trommler 241).

What Beck has pointed out for the discussion of globalization in the social sciences, namely that the experiential frame of national societies is increasingly moot (2002, 29), does apply to literature also, yet it is not easily transferred to a methodology. This brings us to a second significant reason for the absence of detailed studies. An analysis of German-language literature – or, for that matter, any literature *other than* the global lingua franca English – and globalization at first glance seems counterintuitive. The conventional structure of literary study is, of course, transparently nationalist and the critique of nationalism has coexisted comfortably with a continued nationalism in academic practice, as David Damrosch has pointed out (515). Despite the fact that interpretive methodological approaches such as deconstruction, New Historicism, and cultural studies have reconfigured the objects of literary study profoundly, national literary traditions remain a vital denominator. Literature can never entirely break free from a national context since it is written in a specific language, and its cultural references are embedded within it.[15] This is true even in the case of transnational writers such as Turkish-born Emine Sevgi Özdamar or Japanese-born Yoko Tawada who take their artistic influences from two distinct cultures, histories, and languages. If one follows this argument, dissolving the assumed tension between what constitutes a national literature and what constitutes globalization would require a comparative perspective that looked at different examples across, for instance, the European spectrum. As the cases of Özdamar and Tawada already signal, such a look would necessarily extend beyond Europe.

However, the solution to this methodological conundrum and the basis for *Germans Going Global* is the realization that the global and the local are intrinsically linked and cannot be divided. Roland Robertson's influential concept of glocalization, on which I rely heavily, contests that globalization is a process that overrides locality (1994) and instead proposes understanding the global in the everyday and in one's own life (2004, 98). The global and the local, homogenization and heterogeneity, singularity and plurality complement

---

**15** This statement pertains more to serious literature since there are some genres, such as young adult fiction (Harry Potter, vampire novels), crime fiction, and science fiction where national contexts are less important. One could venture to say that these are truly "global" genres.

each other in complex ways. When Anthony Giddens defines globalization as "the intensification of worldwide social relations which link distant localities in such a way that local happenings are shaped by events occurring many miles away and vice versa," he stresses that *"local transformation* is as much a part of globalization as the lateral extension of social connection across time and space" (1990, 64). And as Beck (2002, 23) and others have pointed out, it is impossible to think about globalization without referring to specific locales since it is narratively constructed at a local level, located in societies, political systems and interpersonal networks (Taberner 2004, 6). The local must be understood as an aspect of the global; thus I propose in this book that the relation between literature and globalization can best be illuminated if we read contemporary German-language literature as *glocal*. My subsequent interpretations will substantiate this position.

How globalization affects literature needs to be explored in specific national and local contexts. To ignore this aspect would also mean to ignore important local differences and alterity, as Russel Berman, himself a Germanist by training, has pointed out (2007). Within the discipline of literary and cultural studies, we instead need to understand literature as a universal process that nevertheless produces locally specific, as well as culturally hybrid forms (see Wilke 2008, 109). The disciplinary project that underlies this study is thus to describe and analyze, on the one hand, processes of gradual homogenization in German culture on a material and aesthetic level in the face of globalization, while on the other hand pointing to the critical potential inherent in contemporary narratives thematizing globalization.

This brings us to a brief survey of terms and historical discussions as they apply to this study. To be sure, globalization is one of the most widely used concepts in contemporary social, political, and academic discourse, "one of the markedly protean and thickly connotative words in our vocabulary" (Gupta 9), practically "a magic incantation," according to sociologist Zygmunt Bauman (1998, 1). As for its historic development, globalization is of course not a new concept that only appeared over the last two decades, even if the term really came into its own after the end of the Cold War. Trade routes crossed oceans long before Columbus discovered the West Indies, and global trade today is not much larger than it was a century ago. In this historical context, Peter Fäßler delineates an early phase of proto-globalization (1500–1840), followed by three distinct consolidating phases that were interrupted only by the disintegrative ruptures of the two World Wars and the global economic crisis of the late 1920s. He thus arrives at the following periodization of globalization: 1840–1914, 1945–1989, since 1990. This has proven useful in the conceptualization of this book, since I agree with Fäßler that the last phase of globalization has an unprecedented quality due to its spatial and social ramifications and the speed with which changes now occur, leaving the human being rather breathless and at a loss (153–54). Scholars in other disciplines generally share this evaluation: geographer David Harvey famously called it "time-space compression" (240); and Anthony Giddens contends that we should not depend on long historical continuities for clues to our own time and cultural condition (in Tomlinson, 43). Due to new electronic technologies and data transfers the last phase is in effect characterized by such a sense of simultaneity and interconnection that it has led Roland Robertson to speak of the concept of globalization as referring to "both the compression of the world and the intensification of consciousness of the world as a whole" (1992, 8). Like Harvey, he points out that globalization is so closely linked to the contours and the nature of (post)modernity that is refers primarily to the most recent developments. That globalization in Germany arrived in full force after unification explains my choice to limit this study to a discourse formation of German culture and literature that is confined with regards to the time and space of the last two decades.

For a long time the study of globalization was situated primarily in economics and political science, where it has been analyzed as a series of objective, material shifts linked to the increasing mobility of capital, the transnationalization of trade and production processes, the spread of neo-liberal policy norms, the decline of national autonomy, and a retreat from the practices of the Keynesian welfare state and social democracy (Rosamond 657). As the realization set in that all these factors also have far-reaching consequences for cultures, identities, and life-styles because the globalization of economic activity goes hand in hand with cultural transformation, this research was augmented by the study of *cultural globalization*, primarily situated in sociology and anthropology. Despite – or rather because of – the wide variety of disciplinary standpoints, the attempt to pinpoint the concept and discourse of globalization is like trying to nail a blancmange to the wall, as Beck puts it (2000, 20). This is undoubtedly due to the diffusion of the concept across different areas of contemporary life in different parts of the world. Since globalization needs to be recognized as a term that developed independently of literary studies, as a term that batters literature from *outside*, as Gupta has pointed out (6), it makes sense to further extend some of the concepts developed to understand globalization.

The effects of globalization reflect back on the literary field in numerous ways. In this study, I acknowledge this complex interrelatedness by analyzing both the more material as the well as the thematic and aesthetic sides of literary production. The main argument for the book's structure and the subjects chosen is that the connection between literature and globalization is apparent both in developments of the literary marketplace, in public debates about literary aesthetics, and in the aesthetic manner prose texts from the late 1990s through the first millennial decade narrate aspects linked topically to globalization. To this end, I combine close readings of contemporary fiction production with analyses of the ways in which authorship is constructed through old and new media. The decision to illuminate these various facets refracts the complexities of cultural globalization while at the same time acknowledging them, presenting a viable and innovative approach to literary analysis.

This study is firmly situated within a tradition of German Studies as cultural studies that reads texts as interventions in the social process. It shares a belief that has been formulated by various schools and theoreticians of culture, namely that aesthetic and social documents intervene in the material world through their form and embody and allegorize social tensions of historical moments in polyphonic ways (Kaes 213). Theodor W. Adorno, Leo Löwenthal and other scholars of the Frankfurt School emphasized the societal content of literary form, and in recent years cultural studies scholars such as Stuart Hall and social theorists such as Michel Foucault, Pierre Bourdieu, and Richard Sennett have expanded on this approach in other fields. They widened the framework to include analyses of the significance of institutional power and cultural capital. My study is indebted to them all, and I will refer back to their work where appropriate. As an intellectual endeavor that seeks to analyze the relationship between culture and society, identity and agency, the writings of the Birmingham School, especially Stuart Hall's, have been particularly instructive in the development of my thoughts on the subject.[16]

For instance, cultural studies theorists have pointed out that contemporary discourses allow for identity building. What this means for literary analysis is the opportunity to read literary texts as a unique mediator that transmits socioeconomic phenomena in altered form. It also implies being able to ignore the boundaries between different traditional genres and analyze texts that are generally understood as theoretical together with literary texts taken as autonomous artistic products that require interpretation. Within this perspective of cultural semiotics, they all have the same status as texts, meaning as cultural artifacts with an informative value regarding the culture they come from, while at the same time producing it (Posner 42).

---

**16** See for example Stuart Hall. "Cultural studies: two paradigms." *Media, Culture and Society* 2.1 (1980). My study is oriented by a definition of the discipline of cultural studies that can be described as "the study of the production, distribution, exchange and reception of textualised meaning," including "the practices that articulate them and that they articulate, … as well as texts 'in their own right'" (Milner 5).

This general approach is enhanced by the realization that global forces, institutions and structures always already organize the local. Consequently cultural analysis needs to take into account the politics of cultural production and consumption with due attention to the new globalized flows of power, people, and discourse (Szeman 204). This calls for a methodology that relies on a variety of disciplinary approaches concerning globalization, combining concepts developed in media studies with sociological analyses of globalization and political science analyses about the state of the Germany economy in the aughts.

Cultural texts are at the heart of my investigation, and I read them as interventions that are critical for the construction of cultural identities; I follow Irene Kacandes's suggestion that cultural objects need to be considered in relation to the society in which they were produced *and* in relation to the society in which the analysis takes place (11). By absorbing social changes and developments, literature gains a referentiality and relevance that extends beyond its mere content and presence. This is similarly true for intellectual debates, as they possess a substrate of reality that determines their respective content. The literary texts analyzed here are worldly ("welthaltig") in that they refract social realities in specific aesthetic formats, thereby affecting identity formation. Understanding discursive interventions of various kinds as assessments of cultural identities and as refractions of their wider context allows us to see forces of globalization at work in culture. The German literary scene is a particularly fruitful field for analysis since intellectuals and authors continue to play a crucial role in the public sphere. United Germany remains a country that defines itself through its cultural representation, and as the conditions of the latter change, so does the nation's identity.

The effects of globalization are particularly interesting to study in a younger generation of German-language writers. Up to the 1990s, established male writers such as Günter Grass, Martin Walser or Peter Handke – and the occasional female figure, such as Christa Wolf – served as models for public intellectuals and set the standard of quality for postwar German literature. Yet in the last two decades large numbers of younger female and male authors of various national and ethnic backgrounds have emerged. They have produced a wide and fascinating range of texts that often utilize innovative aesthetic formats. This generation – born between 1965 and 1975 and often called the *Generation Golf*, after the sporty Volkswagen model and the popular book of the same name by journalist Florian Illies – was the first to grow up with the accelerated effects of globalization. Like those who grew up in the shadow of the Nazi period or in the revolutionary 1960s, it makes sense to look at these authors as a separate group.[17] The members of this cohort mediate between the weight of the past German literary tradition and the spreading influences of (American) popular culture.

German-language fiction today is of interest to a public that extends beyond professional critics; it is being translated more frequently into other languages, and its authors often experience an unprecedented following, especially among younger readers. Literary critics and scholars alike are still searching for and test-ing evaluative criteria to account for these transformations. Anthropologist Arjun Appadurai's typology of the dimensions of globalization is useful for such an evaluation. Appadurai differentiates five different global cultural "flows," as the material and cognitive sites for which globalization has structural meaning. *Ethnoscapes* describe the landscapes of migrants, refugees, guest workers, tour-ists, and others who crisscross the globe and mark the unsettledness of our global world; *technoscapes* entail the global configuration of old and new tech-nology; *financescapes* encompass the disposition of global capital, such as stock exchanges; *mediascapes* produce and interlink large repertoires of globally dis-seminated images and narratives, in which the links between reality and fiction are often blurred (Appadurai 1996, 33–35). Audiences within these *mediascapes* construct imagined worlds, "image-centered, narrative-based accounts of strips of reality" (35). *Ideoscapes* also concern images but pertain more to the political realm – to state or opposition ideologies that have their roots in the Enlighten-ment worldview (36). One important dimension that invites an application of Appadurai's ideas to literary studies is that both electronic media and the move-ments of global migrants provide "new resources ... for the construction of imag-ined selves and imagined worlds" (3), enabling self-imagining as an everyday project. This is of particular significance for my readings in the first two chapters because self-fashioning and image building is central for contemporary author-ship. Appadurai's emphasis on the imagination as social practice understands individual imagination as a constitutive feature of modern subjectivity that is not just a source for fiction but also engenders new social practices, by which he means sites of individual agency as well as globally defined possibilities (31). Working with his notion of "disjunctural global flows" allows me to group the texts I am interested in into distinctive units that concern the role of the writer/intellectual in the public sphere, questions of authorship, work, mobility, and popular culture.

The first part of this study locates literary production within its socio-economic conditions. My premise is that concepts of authorship have under-

---

gone a paradigmatic shift in the late twentieth century, which we need to understand in order to fully appreciate the implications for a new generation of writers. These transformations are the results of various social and economic factors, which in turn are mediated by globalization. In a globalized editorial market, the desire for augmented profit margins, the shortening of production cycles, and the accelerated distribution of books influence modes of aesthetic production and reception. Electronic media such as the Internet have changed authorial construction by widening circulation, promoting popular forms of literary criticism, and creating iconic images of authors in the public sphere. More so than their predecessors, authors nowadays are part of a highly diversified public sphere dominated by economic interests. At least within the cohort of the *Generation Golf*, many writers are acutely aware of their position within the literary field and promote themselves and their work according to the rules dictated by the market place and the *Feuilleton*. Today's literary reception, especially that of younger authors, is thus driven in equal measure by economic concerns and by a globally inflected popular culture, making it a salient example of the impact of globalization.

Drawing on Appadurai's concept of *mediascape* as the landscape of images and stories, and *technoscape* as technology and its distribution, I explore in the first part of the book how global forces have impacted the production and material dissemination of literature and led to discussions in Germany's lively public sphere about the very significance of literary culture in a globalized world. More specifically, chapter one provides an overview of Germany's literary marketplace and its unique features, concentrating on some recent developments, such as international translations, licensing deals abroad, and the rising significance of literary agents.

Popular literary criticism and various media, especially the Internet, play catalytic roles by reducing complex content and offering labels that orient the reader. In this vein, I analyze the phenomenon of the literary *Fräuleinwunder*, the gendered categorization of female authors in the late 1990s, via an exemplary visual analysis of author photographs. I read the *Fräuleinwunder* as a salient instance of the promotional trendsetting techniques that make writers into literary commodities, which in a globalized environment entails a "celebrification" that, while not new, has become particularly powerful in today's media-dominated world.[18] I similarly analyze the meteoric rise of new German

---

18 "Celebrity, as a product of sophisticated mediation, relies on the way in which a famous person is both socially removed from the public and yet appears so familiar in all the intimate aspects of his or her personality as to be a part of our everyday lives. This curious mix of social distance and personal proximity is maintained by the 'celebrifying' media, which prioritize image over substance. Their coverage concerns the way in which a person

pop literature in the second half of the 1990s. While this genre is historically always already global because a worldwide popular culture infuses it with key images, points of reference and allusions, I show how pop literature has been localized into the specific context of post-unification Germany. I suggest that authorial presence in the public sphere can best be understood through the personal web sites of a number of authors as performative stagings of authorship.

Chapter two serves as a link and sets the stage for the literary interpretations later in the study. It provides an overview of the many debates between Germany's intellectuals, writers, and journalists about the future of German-language literature throughout the 1990s and into the new millennium. The leading question of this discourse is what role literature can still play in the globalized, post-industrial German society that despite Willy Brandt's projection is still not done "growing together." I first take up literary discourse dealing with realism, entertainment and "new readability" (*Neue Lesbarkeit*), highlighting the interconnectedness between debates *about* contemporary literature and literary texts that, while often neglected, are of tremendous importance for Germany and its public sphere. Second, I argue that these debates accompany paradigmatic changes in German-language literature and provide the underlying discourse to its globalization over the last two decades. Specifically, a return to realistic storytelling and the workaday world, as well as a focus on consumption and popular culture are advocated to make German literature more competitive internationally. The shift towards what I call the "authentic everyday" (*authentische Alltäglichkeit*) in prose fiction is a sign of an increasingly glocalized literature that, while not moving away from the German past entirely, seeks to process the realities of a newly unified country and the Berlin Republic. Critics and authors alike seek to align German-language literature with an internationalized literature that is potentially globally successful. I substantiate my claims by reading Ingo Schulze's *Simple Storys* (1998) and Elke Naters's novels *Königinnen* (1998, Queens) and *Lügen* (1999, Lies).

These readings also reveal the continued importance Germans assign to literature and the public discussion about it, which is a fact that American intellectuals usually admire and envy. It speaks against homogenizing tendencies globalization might foster in other arenas than the cultural one – in Germany intellectuals and authors still play a crucial role. Furthermore, literature continues to be viable despite prophecies of doom about the end of reading

---

represents public achievement, rather than offering an in-depth engagement with the achievement itself ..." Brown 75–76.

and the demise of the book. Competing media notwithstanding, my analyses affirm that united Germany remains a country defining itself through its cultural representation.

Chapters three, four, and five turn from the more material and external factors to extensive readings of a number of literary texts. What thereby comes to the fore is that globalization and German-language literature share certain features that make literature a useful analytic framework for the interpretation of globalization. Both are defined by the creation of virtual realms and the free and playful organization of time and space. Literature thus has the potential to reflect globalization in its themes as well as in its structures, especially due to its non-hierarchical, heterogeneous and polyvalent character (Linklater 71).

In my readings of prose texts however, I am not concerned with the tracing of globalization as a theme. Indeed, one reason to analyze literary representations is that the abstract phenomenon of globalization cannot appear *as such* but needs to be approached indirectly. The discourse of literature mirrors the social conditions and developments in the age of globalization but does not reflect on it in terms of mimetically accurate representation. Literature instead sets its own emphases and comments (mostly critically) on the observed processes.

My interpretations contextualize the trends and developments that the first two chapters have highlighted. Flexibility and mobility, two key concepts associated with globalization, provide the conceptual framework of these readings. With the help of a theoretical framework informed by scholars in economics, sociology, and anthropology, my close readings of narratives of work and unemployment in the New Economy and narratives of international travel, respectively, illustrate the modes in which effects of globalization have taken hold in literary aesthetics. They also reveal the tensions brought about by a globalized world and its ambiguous impact on the individual.

Chapter three aims at an overview of the literature of work in the aughts by assessing the renaissance of narratives dealing with work in the New Economy and its flip side, unemployment. A globalized work environment creates psychological fault lines in the individual and strains social bonds, thus threatening constructions of subjectivity. Rainer Merkel's *Das Jahr der Wunder* (2001, The Year of Wonders) and Joachim Bessing's *Wir Maschine* (2001, We Machine) debunk the world of advertising as a site where the individual loses any sense of self. The processes of capitalist normatization and the ways in which it produces over-disciplined bodies come to the fore in John von Düffel's *EGO* (2001) and Ernst-Wilhelm Händler's *Wenn wir sterben* (2002, When We Die). The materialist aesthetics of Kathrin Röggla's *wir schlafen nicht* (2004, We Don't Sleep) expose the normative power that the language and business practices of the consulting industry have developed in neoliberal society. Dealing with the devastating experience of being unemployed, both Jakob Hein's *Herr Jensen steigt aus* (2006, Herr Jensen Calls it Quits) and Annette Pehnt's *Mobbing* (2007, Harassment) focus on the question of how economic realities influence constructions of self, human relationships, and the individual's relation to the surrounding social and material world. Joachim Zelter's novel *Die Schule der Arbeitslosen* (2006, The School of the Unemployed) is read here as an openly political text that criticizes the ways in which the postindustrial society handles unemployment.

Over the past decade, the rise of texts dealing with global mobility in the form of travel has signaled an increasingly cosmopolitan cultural consciousness of German-language authors. My readings of Christian Kracht's *Der gelbe Bleistift* (2000, The Yellow Pencil), Judith Hermann's *Nichts als Gespenster* (2003, *Nothing But Ghosts*, 2007), Gregor Hens's *Transfer Lounge*, 2003 and *Matta verlässt seine Kinder* (2004, Matta Leaves His Children), Florian Illies's *Ortsgespräch* (2006, Local Call), and Sibylle Berg's *Die Fahrt* (2007, The Journey) reveal the tensions brought about by a globalized world and its ambiguous impact on identity constructions. While many of the fictional characters are distinctly transnational in their effortless maneuvering of global spaces, their relentless travel also conveys nostalgia for a bygone sense of place and a stable identity that the experience of globalization has called into question, maybe even eradicated. At the same time, the postmodern life strategies of these fictional global tourists point to the fragmentary and discontinuous nature of human relations in the global sphere and criticize (some implicitly, some explicitly) the social and economic inequities exacerbated by globalization.

In a coda to this study, I explore the genre of the literature of 09/11 as a second significant manifestation of narratives of mobility. While Anglo-American texts dealing with the terrorist attacks have been analyzed mostly in the framework of trauma literature, German-language prose displays a considerable psychological distance and takes a documentary approach working with a materialist aesthetics, as becomes evident in the accounts of Kathrin Röggla's *really ground zero* (2001) and Else Buschheuer's www.else-buschheuer.de. *Das New York Tagebuch* (2002, The New York Diary). In contrast, one later novel analyzed in juxtaposition to the documentary texts – Katharina Hacker's *Die Habenichtse* (2006, *The Have Nots*, 2007) uses the terrorist attacks as ominous background to illuminate the experience of globalization as an experience of surveillance, individual powerlessness, and border-defying violence.

# 1 Effects of Globalization on the Literary Marketplace and Contemporary Authorship

This chapter traces paradigmatic changes that authorship has undergone in the late twentieth century and early twenty-first century. In order to appreciate fully the implications for a new generation of writers, we need to take note that these transformations are the result of various social and economic factors. Sociological differences in generations, a diversified, multi-media literary industry, the influence of electronic media on the public sphere, changing media reception, and standardizing tendencies of global popular culture are all significant in the process of the construction of contemporary authorship. My analysis in this chapter will illuminate the first thesis of this book, namely that the nexus between literature and globalization is not only expressed in the content and aesthetics of literary texts, but also through the literary market. Second, the ways in which contemporary younger authors think of and present themselves in the public sphere refract references and allusions to a global consumerist popular culture.

The analysis of market aspects, books, and authors as "commodities" could, as Suman Gupta argues in his study *Globalization and Literature* (2009), help literary studies overcome a certain ingrained elitism that often prevents scholars from dealing with the material production of literature (157).[1] To this end, I will offer some observations on Germany's literary marketplace before turning to the question of how authorship is constructed in contemporary media. The most significant feature that sets Germany's publishing field apart from those in other European countries and the United States is that since the eighteenth century, Germany's literary field has been shaped by an active *Feuilleton*, i.e. the arts and leisure sections of newspapers, that provide a forum for public discussion, launch debates and create trends (see Todorov). Furthermore, the literary scene is characterized by the fostering of literary talent through countless prizes and contests, as well as television formats and professional writers' workshops. Many of these orchestrate literature as special events and propagate it as a learnable craft. In my analyses, I understand authors both as (self-performing) subjects and (managed) objects and make the following questions my guide: What aesthetic self-understanding do writers develop in such a literary field? What relationships do they establish

---

1 One should note that especially in the field of *Germanistik*, this insight is not new and already has led to interesting work, for example by Erhard Schütz, Thomas Wegmann, Stephan Porombka, Rolf Parr, and Klaus Bogdal.

in regard to their readers, reviewers, editors, and culture managers, whose interests determine their success or failure? How do the cultural imagination and cultural construction of authorship change in confrontation with visual and electronic media and the promotion of certain forms of popular literature and literary criticism? And finally, what is the relationship between the unique German situation and the wider development of global marketing?

## Distinctive Features of Germany's Literary Marketplace

Despite being heavily influenced by globalizing factors, Germany's literary marketplace has some unique features that make it different from those of other European countries and the United States. First, most recent statistics do not confirm popular fears that books are losing out to media of the electronic kind. In fact, sales figures have risen steadily in the last few years, especially due to the sale of popular fiction ("Belletristik").[2] The German book market is overall still healthy and quite variegated to the extent that it can support small, specialized presses and independent bookstores. The enormous numbers of new publications are the best indicator of this variety: in 2010, the last year for which the German Bookseller Association (*Börsenverband des Deutschen Buchhandels*) provides statistics, German publishing houses distributed 95,838 new books, 2.9% more than in the previous year.[3]

Günter Grass once called the approximately 4,000 bookstores in operation in Germany somewhat prosaically intellectual gas stations ("geistige Tankstellen"); they provide readers not only with the highest density of bookstores of any country but also, in comparison to most U.S. chain bookstores, with knowledgeable sales people, since bookseller ("Buchhändler") is still a profession requiring a formal apprenticeship that takes up to three years, depending on a person's educational background and schooling. Apart from fulfilling a guiding function for the customer, many bookstores in Germany also organize cultural events, such as authors' readings, long book nights and local book fairs (Rehm 83). Furthermore, German booksellers are able to order almost any book overnight; this structural characteristic sets Germany apart even from other European countries and allows small independent stores to survive, namely by offering a specialized, high-level service that guarantees the loyalty of many customers who make sure to shop only in their local bookstore.

---

2 In 2009, the German book industry made profits of about 9.7 billion Euros, 0.8% more than in 2008. http://www.boersenverein.de/de/158446/Wirtschaftszahlen/158286 (March 31, 2012).
3 http://www.boersenverein.de/de/158446/Wirtschaftszahlen/158286.

The main factor that preserves this relative variety is the German *Buchpreis-bindung*, literally "binding book prices," a law that obligates publishers and sellers to agree on fixed prices, thus preventing price dumping and unfair trade. It is founded on the conviction that books have a dual character as both cultural goods (*Kulturgut*) and economic goods (*Wirtschaftsgut*); according to this view, dealing in books while primarily abiding by economic criteria would not only lead to a diminishing of published titles and places that sell books but also constrain diversity of opinion in the literary public sphere. In comparison, many other countries do not have such a law. Switzerland abandoned the *Buchpreis-bindung* in March 2012 by popular vote after considerable strife (see http://www.buchpreisbindung-nein.ch). In the United Kingdom, the Net Book Agreement (NBA), established in 1957, was abandoned already in 1995, leading to more competition between bookstores and the rise of chains (see Feather 139–144). Furthermore, its absence has generally led to a market concentration both in publishing houses and the book trade in countries without such a law (Schenkel 89). In the United States, it has led to a reduction in the number of independent bookstores from 5,000 to 2,000 between 1991 and 2009 (Nisbet).

Translations predominate in the German book market, especially in the segments of fiction and non-fiction books. Since 1979, Germany has published 259,941 registered translations, making it the worldwide leader.[4] 75 percent of all bestselling books in Germany are translations, and the dominance of works translated from English – 48.6 percent in 2003, the numbers have risen slightly since – clearly indicates the realities of a globalized book market. Along the same lines, although the licensing of translations of German-language books is still a rather marginal segment, it rose by 30 percent in 2010[5], raising hopes that the international success of an author such as W.G. Sebald, which began with the publication of his novels in English by the small New Directions Press, might not remain an exception. In the fiction segment, 1027 licenses of German-language books were sold to foreign countries in 2010.[6]

In recent years, small independent presses such as KOOKbooks, founded by poet and editor Daniela Seel in 2003 (www.kookbooks.de) and Blumenbar, founded by journalist Wolfgang Farkas and bookseller Lars Birken-Bertsch in 2002 (www.blumenbar.de), have been the surprising success stories. KOOK-

---

**4** This is the figure as of April 1, 2012. See the UNESCO's *Index Translationum* (http://portal.unesco.org/culture/en/ev.php-URL_ID=7810&URL_DO=DO_TOPIC&URL_SECTION=201.html).
**5** In 2009 licensing was down by about 17.5% in comparison to 2008. In 2010, 8,191 licenses were sold to foreign countries; China rose to be the most important partner while Spain and Poland were in second and third place, respectively. http://www.boersen verein.de/de/portal/Wirtschaftszahlen/158286 (March 31, 2012).
**6** http://www.boersenverein.de/de/portal/Belletristik/189810.

books, for example, has not only been lavished with compliments by *Feuilleton* journalists and design prizes for the beauty of its books (see Thiel), but also an increasing number of its authors have garnered literary honors in the form of prizes and awards. These and other examples show that even in a globalized environment, it is possible to be viable both economically and aesthetically and survive in a highly competitive market.

Of course, the aforementioned examples cannot hide the fact that today's publishing industry is indeed dominated by very few global players. Advances in telecommunications technologies and more than two decades of deregulation in the industry have resulted in a global media system dominated by seven multinational corporations, namely Disney, AOL-Time Warner, Sony, News Corporation, Viacom, Vivendi, and Bertelsmann. They own the major U.S. film studios as well as all but one of the U.S. television networks; the few companies that control 80–85 percent of the global music market; the preponderance of satellite broadcasting worldwide; a significant percentage of book publishing and commercial magazine publishing; all or part of most of the commercial cable TV channels in the U.S. and worldwide; and a significant portion of European television (McCeshney 2). This concentrating trend is strong. Although smaller than Bertelsmann, the Stuttgart-based Georg von Holtzbrinck Publishing Group, which started as a modest book club in 1948, now also owns publishing companies worldwide, among them S. Fischer, Rowohlt, Kiepenheuer & Witsch in Germany, and Macmillan, Picador and St. Martin's Press in the United States and the United Kingdom. Given the intense competition among a few global players, market shares and profits are the leading principles by which such players operate, despite the fact that their wares are of the intellectual kind. The desire for larger profit margins and ever-shortening production cycles have turned literature into a marketable product and gained influence over the processes of literary production, distribution and criticism (see Feather 2003, esp. chapter two).

Literary agents who now play a significant role in the *Literaturbetrieb* might serve as indicators of these changes. Although the institution of the literary agency has existed since the nineteenth century, in its current form it developed in parallel with the globalizing economy. While literary agencies after the Second World War were mostly concentrated in Zurich and Munich and focused on international licensing and translations, since the mid-1990s there has been a significant increase in the numbers of agencies in Berlin that focus exclusively on contemporary German-language authors. This development has a direct connection to the increasing commercialization and globalization of the book market, concentration processes in the publishing landscape, and the changing role of the medium of the book in competition with other media offers. As market conditions changed, literary agents' roles were redefined, reinforcing the agents' position of power as mediators between authors and publishing houses, where managers are increasingly making the decisions instead of editors (Hager 219). Yet agents have also changed the way literature is discussed and handled through their often-aggressive lobbying practices that aim at receiving large advances for the represented authors. In an incisive *Spiegel* article in 2000, Suhrkamp's publishing manager Günter Berg and others criticized how negotiations about advances increasingly dominate the dialogue about a literary text: "Agents send us five pages and ask for an offer not under 25 000 Deutschmarks – but this is not how we do business."[7] Even if most authors still are more interested in stable relations with an editor than in large advances, it is not only an economic necessity, but also a matter of pride to be represented by a well-known, successful agency like Graf & Graf or Eggers & Landwehr, both located in Berlin (see Fischer).

## Authorship: Changed Paradigms

Intellectuals and writers often criticize the general economization of culture ("Ökonomisierung der Kultur"), as Erhard Schütz has called it (2002, 7). Instead they hang on to the ideal of an artist unaffected by the market and understandably express resentment when they find that their texts are increasingly handled like industrial products. Of course, generalizing statements such as this one are hard to quantify, but I have found this attitude in many of the writers I interviewed over the last fifteen years, among them Ingo Schulze, Maxim Biller, Marcel Beyer, Thomas Meinecke, Gregor Hens, and Terézia Mora.

However, even the conscious rejection of this economization, often coupled with the claim of recognizing only the demands of one's own language and literature, is already a label that again serves a particular variation of contemporary authorship, as Stephan Porombka points out (Clip Art, 227). Nevertheless, younger authors also see the creative opportunities that a multi-media literary marketplace offers as a *fait accompli* and an opportunity. Many are familiar with the rules of markets and media and manage to use them to their advantage due to their journalistic backgrounds (see Künzel 21). One might deduce here a dialectics of authenticity: since the meanings of mass-mediated images need to be negotiated constantly by readers, viewers, and consumers, authors are faced with the task of presenting themselves "authentically" as part of a marketing strategy.

---

7 "Die schicken dann fünf Seiten und wollen ein Angebot nicht unter 25 000 Mark – aber so kommt mit uns kein Geschäft zu Stande." Quoted in Wellershoff.

In a creative interpretation of the axiom formulated by Paul Watzlawick according to which one cannot *not* communicate, the following considerations assume that one cannot *not* stage oneself in the public sphere. Contemporary authorship is based on external operating rules that are dominated by the market and the media; within this system, the contemporary author is always trying to turn his or her "good side" toward the audience or the cameras (Porombka, Clip Art 226). If one accepts this basic assumption, it follows that the important issue is no longer to fundamentally question authorial self-staging by pointing to the nexus of authorship and genius that still holds sway in Germany; instead, it is important to discuss the how, in other words, the performative methods of staging authorship.

Authorship is constructed in and through various media, in literary and poetological texts, interviews, the arts and leisure sections and other print media, television, video clips, and last but not least, on the Internet. In this medium, authors and their works are represented in multiple forms. Many people use open content reference sites such as Wikipedia to quickly find basic information. Linked to commercial ventures such as Amazon, non-professional book reviews allow readers to enter into a dialogue with one another; they might also influence buying decisions. Literature and culture review sites addressing more specific interests have augmented offers available in print; professionally operated sites such as *Perlentaucher*, virtual literary salons (for instance, www.berlinerzimmer. de), online scholary forums (such as H-net), private and public weblogs (for an analysis, see Ernst) all orient readers and offer wide-ranging opportunities to obtain information or become involved in the discussion of literature. Web sites that are vetted by specialists – such as the one covering the oeuvre of W.G. Sebald (www.wgsebald.de) – make information more widely accessible in a virtual library. Finally, web sites such as J.K. Rowling's long-awaited *Pottermore* (www. pottermore.com) promise readers of various age groups to enhance the classic medium of the book with a more interactive experience.

Appearing in different formats, authorial staging on the Internet continues to evolve. The recent development of book clips, which publishing houses use increasingly for marketing purposes on their web sites, is a salient example. They might present a short reading by the author or a voice-over, combined with visual and audio material or animated graphics, to illustrate the narrated story artistically.[8] Book clips serve not only the purposes of commercialization, but also

---

**8** Two examples that have attracted much attention are the book clips for Christian Kracht's novel *Ich werde hier sein im Sonnenschein und im Schatten* from 2008 (http:// www.youtube.com/watch?v=KhqsTkg6yyM) and the animated clip for Kathrin Passig's and Sascha Lobo's nonfiction book *Dinge geregelt kriegen ohne einen Funken Selbstdisziplin*, also from 2008 (http://www.youtube.com/watch?v=YAlGk6NKZHI) [last access March 28, 2012].

operate to better an author's position within the literary field and boost his or her symbolic capital (Niefanger 2004, 87–88), by way of as interesting, funny, or artsy a performance as possible. Yet given how time-consuming and expensive the production of a book clip is, the author already needs to have a certain eminence in the literary sphere for a publishing house to even consider it.

In my understanding of cultural capital, I follow Pierre Bourdieu's definition of symbolic capital as "... economic or political capital that is disavowed, misrecognized and thereby recognized, hence legitimate, a 'credit' which, under certain conditions, and always in the long run, guarantees 'economic' profits" (1993, 75). Despite the different ways in which authorship is constructed through and in various media, the different formats are in my understanding all "cultural texts" that can be read as culturally coded sign systems, like a stage performance in a theater. With Gérard Genette, we can read these authorial stagings as a special form of paratext for a literary work. In Genette's understanding, paratexts are devices and contentions within and outside the book that mediate between text, author, and reader; titles, forewords and publisher's dust jacket form part of the book's private and public history. As epitexts – by which Genette understands paratexts that are external to the book itself and separate from the main text – different media formats contain "a more or less legitimate commentary" on literature in a narrower sense that appear "anywhere out of the book" (Genette 10, 328).

Taking such epitexts as examples, I analyze in this chapter two different formats of performative authorship, which are anchored in different primary media. The first is the traditional author photo, while the second format entails authorial constructions in the global medium of the World Wide Web. Both illuminate how cultural globalization is breaking open established concepts of authorial representation and understanding and what the performative stagings contribute to our understanding of contemporary authorship.

While it is difficult to imagine a truly "global author,"[9] the parameters of authorship have increasingly shifted in the late twentieth century.[10] The more

---

**9** One would first need to come to an understanding what "global authorship" might entail and where the dividing line would be to concepts of cosmopolitanism. One writer who spontaneously comes to mind, however, is Salman Rushdie who is Indian but, due to England's colonial history, also a British citizen. He thus belongs to (at least) two cultures, lives in various places, speaks multiple languages and is an internationally known intellectual whose work has been translated into many languages. Thematically, his literary and essayistic work focuses on central problems of globalization, such as post-colonialism, migration, and multiculturalism.

**10** There are lively discussions of these shifting parameters of authorship, both in the literary sphere and among scholars. See, for example, the contributions to an issue of the

that content-related and formal paradigms of market economies define the literary market, the more authors are forced to market their own books and themselves as commodities. Patronage-style relationships in which a publisher acts as a well-meaning benefactor for the artist as he or she battles writer's block – as was the case for *Suhrkamp's* editor Siegfried Unseld with authors Wolfgang Koeppen and Thomas Bernhard – may perhaps always have been unusual, but in a globalized market they seem virtually impossible. Nonetheless, the real and symbolic capital of the publishing house continues to influence the real and symbolic capital of the author. The venerable German publishing house Suhrkamp, for instance, is still associated with high literary culture, while Kiepenheuer & Witsch or Eichborn stand for popular literature, innovation, and subversion. A clear profile serves as an offer of identification to the public, and each respective publisher directs the author's reception in the media and the public sphere accordingly (Vaihinger 375).

If they want to achieve economic success, authors must diversify their own writing and be able to work in various sectors of the literary field. To be sure, much of this diversification happens out of sheer economic necessity. Katharina Hacker, for example, is frank in her admission that before winning the *German Book Prize* (a monetary award of 25,000 Euros) in 2006, she was often afraid of not being able to pay her rent.[11] However, many writers have recognized the changing parameters also as an opportunity and are skillfully using them to their own advantage. For instance, Antje Rávic Strubel, born in 1974 in Potsdam, is a model of productivity: in addition to literary texts, she publishes essayistic and editorial pieces, and she is also active as a literary translator for prominent contemporary U.S. author Joan Didion. Strubel travels a great deal, domestically as well as abroad, and she is accessible and professional when it comes to organizing her readings, like most authors of her generation. Thus she strategically places herself within a widely varied literary field, and her presence pays off both symbolically and economically in terms of high speaker's fees and literary prizes (see English). Furthermore, Strubel keeps close control over her public image, limiting the published photos of herself to those taken by her translator Zaia Alexander and carefully editing all state-

---

literary magazine *Literaturen*: "Schreiben jetzt. Wie Autoren auf dem Markt überleben" *Literaturen* 1/2 (2008), and Hartling.

**11** "Ich habe wirklich sehr lange so gelebt, dass ich gekämpft habe mit der Miete, und ich habe das als extrem belastend gefunden. Gerade die Miete. Mit allem anderen kann man ja umgehen, aber wenn man die Miete nicht mehr bezahlen kann, wird es wirklich problematisch." In Wojcik (radio feature).

ments before they are published.[12] While the latter is common practice in journalism, this strict management of a public persona also must be recognized as a form of self-staging.

In a differentiated public media arena, the desire for control is not surprising. After all, authors – just like politicians, actors, and musicians – are public figures within the media machinery, and are thus subject to a type of star culture that significantly shapes our perceptions (see Glass). Recent literary studies show that this global "celebrity culture" does not shy away from literary criticism, but in fact tends to steer the reception of books (see English and Frow). For authors themselves, this means being more present than ever in the public sphere and being forced to take part in forming public opinion if they want to effectively position themselves and their works in the media. This positioning takes various forms: Christian Kracht and Benjamin von Stuckrad-Barre, for instance, let themselves be interviewed on television in the *Harald Schmidt Show*, whereas the older generation had met with Gerhard Schröder at the German Chancellery to talk about the political situation in Afghanistan.

Authorial self-staging, which is associated with the build up of symbolic capital, is by no means a new phenomenon. The historical perspective provides the necessary depth of field. In the German context, the development started with the canonization of classical literature by Goethe, Schiller, Lessing, Herder, and Jean Paul in the eighteenth century and the ensuing cult of classical authors ("Klassikerverehrung"), which materialized among other things in public memorials. Authorial self-promotion was also common among Romantic writers (see Fang). With the advent of photography and the possibility of technical reproduction, authorial promotion gained a new quality, an aspect that Walter Benjamin commented on in his famous essay *The Work of Art in the Age of Mechanical Reproduction* (first published in French in 1936). Figures such as Stefan George and Bertolt Brecht managed to shape their public image and "stage their aura" (Bartels 30) by way of iconic photographs. Brecht's picture, taken by Konrad Reßler in 1927, in which he wears a leather coat and smokes a cigar, is only one well-known example (see Hans Harald Müller 79). Consider the cult status gained by *poetessa* Ingeborg Bachmann in the 1950s, which was promoted accordingly by her *Spiegel* cover photos. It provides another example for the role pictures have played in self staging, especially with regards to the part female authors played in Germany's literary scene post-World War Two.

Some conservative cultural critics find that the author photograph's ubiquity has displaced the moral, political and aesthetic authority of the author,

---

**12** Strubel rewrote large parts of our 2007 interview when I presented it to her for approval. To be sure, editing is common practice in journalism, but the intensity with which authors edit their own material varies widely.

and even literary criticism itself (for example Schärf, see also Grasskamp). The degree to which authors are transformed into literary stars today has a much different quality indeed. Technology not only allows for the worldwide distribution of goods, it also enhances the commodification of public figures. Photos concretize a tendency of the literary scene that manifested itself in the late 1990s: the author himself or herself increasingly takes the place of the text's aura, and its criticism is replaced by the "home story," i.e., the personal backstory, as novelist Thomas Hettche has called it in his essay "Nova Huta" from 2000. Younger authors in particular have become objects of identification, no longer admired for their intellectual brilliance or moral integrity, but because of their participation in the publicly staged "event culture" and their presence in the public awareness. Thomas Kraft has expressed this pointedly:

> In the 1990s, the sign of the times obviously has been mass culture. Popular formats run rampant, form trumps content, every function is supposed to be an "event," the author is a pop star one can touch; … the literary scene dances to the beat in houses built just for this purpose, new forms of events such as poetry slams serve subcultures and youth cultures, and the virus of commercialism infects them all.[13]

Young authors themselves then often use their popularity to perpetuate their own images, even if this sometimes happens with a degree of agony, as the following example illustrates.


## Showing the Authorial Self

The iconography of the author photograph generally functions to advertise an author and his or her newest publication. Different, for example, from lectures by an author on his or her poetics (*Poetikvorlesungen*), a photograph is a classic example of authorial presentation generated by the outside, namely the publishing house. Nevertheless, especially photographs taken by well known, professional photographers such as Isolde Ohlbaum or Renate von Mangoldt often reflect the self-understanding of the author.[14]

---

**13** "Die neunziger Jahre stehen offenkundig im Zeichen der Massenkultur. Der Boulevard greift um sich, die Form überlagert die Inhalte, jede Veranstaltung möglichst ein Event, der Autor ein Popstar zum Anfassen; … Der Betrieb tanzt dazu in eigens geschaffenen Häusern, neue Veranstaltungsformen wie Poetry Slams bedienen die Sub- und Jugendkulturen, der Bazillus Kommerz infiziert sie alle." Kraft 12.
**14** The photo gallery at the *Literarisches Colloquium Berlin* (LCB) assembles many examples in the famous author photographs of "Schriftstellergesichterforscherin" Isolde Ohlbaum, as writer Michael Krüger has called her.

In the fall of 1998, a single photograph appeared in the *Feuilleton* sections of all major German newspapers, and in reviews and advertisements. It showed the portrait of then twenty-eight-year-old Berlin writer Judith Hermann, an attractive young woman whose unusual physiognomy – large dark eyes, full lips, blond hair that was twisted into an old-fashioned bun – seemed to cast a spell over the onlooker.

Her gaze appeared lost in infinity and her fur-collar coat invited free associations of "the newly discovered wide-open spaces of the East, something Russian, open, mysterious."[15] The cover design of the book took up this line of association by showing a blurry cabin ("Datsche") against a dark-blue sky.

The iconic photo made a writer into a star of whom nobody had ever heard up to that point. Parallel to the publication of the photograph, Judith Hermann experienced an astonishing, unprecedented success with her first volume of short stories entitled *Sommerhaus, später* (*Summerhouse, later*, 2001). The enigmatic photograph accompanied almost every review of the book; and as for its critics, few neglected to mention how attractive the author was. Text and author image merged into one, making Hermann into a memorable brand. Thus anchored in the consciousness of potential readers, the photo lent Her-

Judith Hermann. © Renate von Mangoldt (1998)

---

**15** "…die neu aufgetauchten Weiten des Ostens, etwas Russisches, Offenes, Rätselhaftes," Böttiger 165.

mann the aura of a literary pop star.[16] Meanwhile, this marketing strategy has become common in the promotion of especially female writers; a fact to which I will return later in the chapter.

Hermann's example – whether strategically planned or the result of pure happenstance – illustrates how medially spread clichés are functionalized in the literary sphere. Many of the reviews claimed a congruence of image and literary text, in which Hermann's appearance and the topics and atmosphere of her stories matched perfectly, in turn again influencing their reception: "Inserted in the stories is the effigy of the author as a blonde Madonna, a face from bygone times that gazes at us from the book cover."[17] Critics also commented in detail on Hermann's biography, seemingly wanting to suggest to the reader that her upbringing in an artsy household in West Berlin and her literary talent were directly related. The somewhat unstable, yet exciting sounding past life of the author seemed to be saturated with authenticity: She was turned down by an acting school, had close ties to the famous Berlin *Volksbühne*, abandoned two courses of university study, toured for a year with the pop band *Poems for Leila*, attended the prestigious Axel Springer journalism school, did an internship at the now defunct German-language Jewish newspaper *Aufbau* in New York, and tended bar after the political turn (*Wende*) in Berlin's Prenzlauer Berg, before becoming a writer at long last.

To make the writer's biography and private life the spotlight is part of the strategies of tabloid journalism. Yet even for respectable newspapers and news magazines, economic and structural factors exacerbate the need to focus on personal details. Most are understaffed due to the ongoing newspaper crisis in Europe and the U.S. and research only a fraction of the material they publish. Instead they increasingly buy content from central sources such as news agencies, or they work with freelance writers who are paid meagerly.[18] The second

---

**16** "Die Lesungen mit Judith Hermann sind überfüllt. [Sie] sind, für eine beträchtliche Zielgruppe, ein Event. Sie hat etwas von einem literarischen Popstar. Es gibt eine bestimmt Zeichen- und Gebärdensprache, es gibt ein bestimmtes Outfit, das Zugehörigkeit schafft, ein atmosphärisches Einverständnis." Böttiger 165.

**17** "Eingelassen in die Geschichten ist auch das Bildnis der Autorin als blonde Madonna, ein Gesicht aus verflossener Zeit, das uns schon vom Buchumschlag anblickt." Köhler 2000, 87.

**18** "Anstatt zu verschlanken und unternehmerische Verantwortung und Kreativität an den Tag zu legen, werden Leute auf die Straße gesetzt. Ohne mit der Wimper zu zucken. Bei der Westdeutschen Zeitung, der FAZ, Gruner & Jahr, Südwestdeutsche Medienholding, Burda und wie alle die 'ehrenvollen' Namen heißen, die zu wenig bezahlen, aber alles kassieren wollen. ... Gleichzeitig wird immer mehr 'kostenloses' Material verwendet, um es in Geld umzuwandeln. Die angeblich 'journalistischen' Leistungen sind oft nur noch kaschierte PR, Recherchen und Kontrolle finden kaum noch statt, freie Mitarbeiter und auch fest angestellte werden ausgebeutet," writes freelance journalist Hardy Prothmann on his blog. "Die

factor is sociological and lies in the rise of a global celebrity culture that no longer applies exclusively to actors or starlets, but extends to almost anybody in the cultural realm – according to Joseph Epstein, even to academics![19] In his insightful essay "Celebrity Culture," Epstein suggests that (Anglo-American) culture values little more than money and celebrity, which has lead to fundamental changes in intellectual life in general. While these transformations might originate in the United States, a global popular culture distributed via global media formats has led to a similar development in Germany and elsewhere. For instance, the actors and actresses of *Bollywood* productions – the Hindi-language film industry based in Mumbai – possess enormous star power globally, which easily trumps that of their Hollywood counterparts, not least due to the films' global distribution and cross-cultural appeal (see Wadhwani).

Television and, more recently, the Internet wield enormous power over the literary public sphere. While broadcasts dealing with literary topics remain in the special interest category, more popular formats such as *Das Literarische Quartett* (The Literary Quartet; legendary since its inception in 1988, though discontinued in 2001)[20] or *Lesen!* (Reading!), moderated by the popular journalist Elke Heidenreich (who, after being let go by the ZDF, offered her show online until the end of 2009), managed to interest a broader public in contemporary literature.[21] Such shows – which are made possible by Germany's publicly funded broadcasting system and are unthinkable in a purely commercial television market such as that of the United States – have long existed in Germany. Nevertheless, even in literary broadcasts, the author persona and the topic of his or her book are the clear foci. In fact, the photogenic suitability ("Kameratauglichkeit") of the author is the most important criterion, as Hubert Winkels, himself a veteran of literary criticism in various media, has claimed in his analysis of literature formats on television (1995, 42). New (online) platforms, on the other hand, such as author clips or websites discussed later in the chapter, have transcended these considerations to some extent. Here,

---

blödsinnige Mär von der 'Kostenloskultur'." http://prothmann.posterous.com/ die-blodsinnige-mar-von-der-kostenloskultur. October 10, 2010.

**19** In U.S. academia, Joseph Epstein attributes celebrity status to scholars such as Henry Louis Gates, Cornel West or the late Eve Sedgewick.

**20** About the history of the *Literarisches Quartett*, see http://www.literaturkritik.de/reich-ranicki/index.php?content=http://www.literaturkritik.de/reich-ranicki/content_themen_litQuartett.html.

**21** "Dem 'Literarischen Quartett' [...] ist das Kunststück gelungen, die Literatur mit der schrecklichen Normalität zu versöhnen, indem er [Marcel Reich-Ranicki] das Bedürfnis des leistungs- und effizienzorientierten Konsumenten nach erwerbbarem Kulturbesitz bediente und den traurigen Rest freigab für das Wüten des gesunden Menschenverstands." Nentwich 2002.

performative and communicative aspects of authorship come to the forefront. While these formats do not presuppose that authors communicate directly with their readers, they provide the opportunity for such mediated exchanges, thereby undoubtedly changing authorial roles through new prospects of interaction.

Praise or rejection by professional TV critics has a direct and measurable impact on a book's commercial success, and the bookselling trade reacts accordingly by showcasing the reviewed books with special displays. Moreover, Winkels argues that the presentation of an author on these shows remains a clear marketing goal of publishers, because a significant and measurable increase in sales generally ensues. When Marcel Reich-Ranicki claimed on October 30, 1998 in *Das literarische Quartett* that Judith Hermann's success would be great, he thus knew that his public judgment might well be a self-fulfilling prophecy. Hermann acknowledged as much in 2003: "I do not want to deny the economic value of these literary television formats. Without this broadcast, the book would have never had this much success; one can actually prove that."[22] At the time however, the critic's praise unfortunately meant more harm than good for the writer's creativity, leading to a case of veritable writer's block. It took five years for Hermann to publish her long-awaited second book, *Nichts als Gespenster* (*Nothing But Ghosts*, 2005).

Much like her Eastern counterpart Ingo Schulze, Judith Hermann quickly became an ideal object of projection for the "literature of unification" genre. Having grown up in West Berlin but living in the then not yet gentrified Eastern neighborhood of Prenzlauer Berg, she figured as a sort of frontierswoman, representing not only a fresh version of German literature, but also the malleable and yet undefined concept of the culture of the "New Berlin." In fact, I want to argue that Hermann's close association with this changing city – both biographically as well as textually – connects to the very globalization of both the city of Berlin and, by symbolic extension, to the Berlin Republic, i.e. united Germany.

In the late 1990s both publishers and *Feuilleton* critics aimed to present contemporary German literature by young authors as being radically different from their predecessors: unencumbered by the German past and concerned with topics such as urban lifestyles, music, and popular culture, young, stylish and cheerful ("jung, schick und heiter"), as *Zeit* critic Richard Herzinger sarcastically put it. While a close reading of Hermann's prose reveals the

---

**22** "Ich will den literarischen Fernsehsendungen ihren markttechnischen Wert gar nicht absprechen, ohne diese Sendung hätte das Buch nie den Erfolg gehabt, man kann das ganz direkt nachweisen." In *FAZ* 2003.

tensions brought about by a globalized world, the marketing strategy that S. Fischer applied to her first book aimed to make her not only successful in German-speaking countries, but also a literary export hit ("Exportschlager"). Since her stories deal with universal themes – love, relationships, identity formation, and travel – they could be presented in a way that made them marketable to readers in many different contexts, spanning generational, gender, and even national divides. This is in part due to the globalized features of the stories. While most of them take place in Berlin, its localities and idiosyncrasies do not play a dominant role. To be sure, the bohemian characters – theater people, writers, painters, video artists and the groupies that cling to them – are tied closely to a metropolitan setting, but a city like London, New York or São Paulo could provide a similar backdrop for the stories (see Biendarra 2004).

The translation of *Sommerhaus, später* into seventeen languages and its German sale figures far exceeding 250,000 copies speak not only for the book's aesthetic quality. I maintain that they also prove the effectiveness of the described marketing strategies, to which literary critics such as Hellmuth Karasek, having attributed the "sound of a new generation" to Hermann's stories, lent professional gravitas. Authors like Hermann and Schulze became ambassadors for the culture of unified Germany and were sent around the globe by its main cultural institution, the Goethe Institute, to introduce this "new" literary culture to readers in other countries. Presumably, it was not only the renewed interest in Germany after unification but also the increased global visibility of German-language literature that motivated an established journal such as *The Chicago Review* in 2002 to publish a 350-page volume with translations of "New Writing in German."

Extending this argument to the larger context of the Berlin Republic and its globalization, it is no coincidence that Berlin once again became Germany's cultural center in the 1990s, attracting countless authors and artists, literary agents, and publishing houses; in 2010 even venerable publisher Suhrkamp finally gave up its longstanding ties to Frankfurt and took up residence on Prenzlauer Berg's Pappelallee. While the West Berliner Judith Hermann represented ideas of a globally marketable authorship, Berlin aimed to refashion itself in the 1990s as a (albeit small) "global city," building up its significance in the global art scene and in fashion, attracting television stations and media production companies and adding temples of consumerism with the glitzy shopping malls of Friedrichstrasse and Potsdamer Platz. While it has become clear that Berlin's structural problems – among them a lack of industry and the dismal state of the local economy – have prevented it so far from becoming a real economic, political, and cultural nodal point, as theorists such as Saskia

Sassen understand global cities, its refashioning undoubtedly has caused Berlin to become the cultural heart of united Germany and, alongside Paris and London, that of Europe. Promoted and supported by such diverse institutions as the Literary Colloquium Berlin (*Literarisches Colloquium Berlin*), the East Berlin artists' café Café Burger (*Kaffee Burger*) or House of the Cultures of the World (*Haus der Kulturen der Welt*) and countless informal reading venues ("Lesebühnen") and poetry slams, contemporary German-language literature has become a vital part of this cultural construction.

Hermann herself, however, repeatedly expressed her discomfort with the media frenzy she experienced. In her acceptance speech for the Sponsorship Award of the City of Bremen (*Bremer Förderpreis*) in Januar 1999 – the second literary prize she received – she questioned critically what expectations a literary debut fosters in the public sphere. Hermann maintains that once the author receives a second award, she must identify her aesthetic disposition and public persona. The acceptance speech measures

> ... whether the author can live up to the image that others have sketched of her, at least in the basic features. What is very important is that she reacts and reproduces and tries to imitate herself ... Now the reader does not have to read any more what the author has written, but the author has to write what the reader has read and what consequently is expressed in the honorific speech. When replying to it, the author has to prove, so to speak, with a new story that she really can produce the old stories, or, even better, surpass them – that she really is what people take her for. One wants to recognize her.[23]

Hermann's formulations of the demands made on the author read as a sort of categorical imperative and at the same time show her unwillingness to fulfill them. Her few poetological remarks reveal that in her writing she is less interested in working through her own experiences than "to escape an identity, however acknowledged it might be" in order to alienate herself from that which is secure and fixed to gain a fresh perspective: "I write to destroy my own history. Things stop when we name them. ... Do I write about myself, and if

---

23 "... ob der Autor dem Bild, das sich andere von ihm gemacht haben, zumindest in Grundzügen entsprechen kann, und zwar – das ist sehr wichtig – reagierend und reproduktiv, sich selbst imitierend. [...] Der Leser hat jetzt nicht mehr zu lesen, was der Autor geschrieben hat, sondern der Autor hat zu schreiben, was der Leser gelesen hat und was also in der Laudatio steht. In der Replik auf die Laudatio hat der Autor mit einer sozusagen neuen Geschichte unter Beweis zu stellen, dass er die alten Geschichten, so wie sie gelobt wurden, auch tatsächlich herstellen kann, besser noch überbieten – dass er also der ist, für den man ihn hält. Man will ihn erkennen. Man will ihn wieder erkennen." Hermann 1999, 34.

so, do I even want to know? I want to leave the answer to this question up to my stories."[24]

Judith Hermann's success illustrates that the cultural sphere is more and more oriented in line with economic principles. This economization of culture delineates the processes by which the language of the economy has infiltrated the literary field. In the late 1990s first-time authors were called the *New Economy* of the literary market, and books started to be designed and marketed for a specific target group. While there always had been best-seller lists, now sales figures became a true marker for a book's significance. This, in turn, has had far-reaching consequences for the public discourse about literature, which now is less dominated by serious critical reviews than by scandals and ephemerality (Bartmer 193–94). A self-perpetuating circle has ensued: One speaks about books and authors who are the subject of discussion, and they are being discussed because their respective sales figures have lifted them into the public's consciousness, as Bogdal puts it: "One could say pointedly that the significance of art does no longer depend on the 'stature' of the works, but on their position in the discursive space of literature."[25]

In order to sell books in the overflowing market place of the information society dominated by competing media, the literary market needs to create a desire that will lead to the purchase of its product. Increasingly, this happens by offering "ritual patterns of identification" to which the consumer feels attracted. New forms of the marketing of literature, such as the creation of labels, play a significant role here (see Niemann 160). As the result of a complicated media operation, in which literary criticism and television occupy important roles, trends are created.

## Fräuleinwunder

Another example of the late 1990s powerfully illustrates such trends. In March 1999, *Spiegel* literary critic Volker Hage proposed the term "Fräuleinwunder"[26]

---

**24** "Schreiben um die eigene Geschichte zu vernichten. Die Dinge hören auf, wenn man sie benennt. … Schreibe ich über mich und will ich das überhaupt wissen? Ich will die Antwort auf diese Frage meinen Geschichten überlassen." Hermann, 1999, 31 (Bremer Förderpreis).

**25** "Man könnte zugespitzt sagen, daß die Bedeutung von Kunst nicht mehr von der 'Größe' der Werke, sondern von ihrer Position im diskursiven Raum der Literatur abhängt." Bogdal 2004, 87.

**26** American soldiers had coined the term *Fräuleinwunder* after 1945, thereby expressing their admiration for the plucky women in postwar Germany. Following Hage's article, countless reviews in the *Feuilleton* sections used the word when dealing with female authors. The same holds true for discussions on television. See for example the TV show "Das Fräuleinwunder." *Literatur im Foyer*. Discussion with Zoe Jenny, Felicitas Hoppe, Karen

to describe various works by young female authors. Subsequently the word dominated the public discussion and even became a widely used category in literary studies (see Caemmerer). Hage used it as a collective denominator for "the young women who make sure that German literature is again a subject of discussion this spring." He claimed that these young women were less concerned with "the German question," the consequences of two German dictatorships, and preferred instead to thematize "eroticism and love." In so doing, Hage found that they were "less fussy" and told their stories "in a far less inhibited manner" than their male colleagues (245).

The journalist's use of the term *Fräuleinwunder* is problematic because it is at base a belittling one. Peter Graves initially showed how their grouping largely on the basis of gender was artificial. Adding to his criticism, let me point out a few more of the underlying issues. Hage implies in an avuncular manner that the authors in question – who, in reality, are well beyond a "Fräulein" age – are still immature, which makes the term's patronizing undertone most apparent. Consequently, the expression seems to suggest that one cannot hold their texts to the same high literary standards that apply to an Ingo Schulze or a Thomas Brussig. More troubling still, the labeling process pertains only to female authors while their male counterparts, instead of being categorized by others, get to fashion their own artistic profile. The *Fräuleinwunder* discussion reveals how a generation of middle-aged male critics seeks authors "for looks not books," as *The Times* formulated it (quoted in Graves, 206), thereby perpetuating a mode of criticism that is gendered and sexist. There were hardly any thematic or stylistic features shared by the female authors Hage chose for his review. The only common denominator of female authors such as Hermann, Alexa Hennig von Lange, Meike Wetzel or Malin Schwerdtfeger was their physical attractiveness. With the proclamation of belonging to the *Fräuleinwunder* category, female authors were subjected to an iconization and labeling that could not do justice to the aesthetic variety of their prose. Yet despite the ambivalence visible in Hermann's own statements, most female authors were aware that the trend Hage had fabricated helped their commercial success: "It would be naive to think that everything would be the same way if this media hype had never happened," as Julia Franck, now one of Germany's most successful writers, admitted in the year 2000.[27]

---

Duve et al. June 24, 1999. Mainz: Südwestdeutscher Rundfunk. Hage followed up with a second article six months later in which he claimed that the term *Fräuleinwunder* had become "almost proverbial."

**27** "Es wäre blind zu denken, es wäre alles genauso, wenn es den Medien-Hype nicht gegeben hätte." In Adorján and Karasek, W 1.

While my short discussion makes clear that *Fräuleinwunder* is a category that is difficult to employ analytically, it should nevertheless be noted that this trend exemplified the German variant of the global genre of "Chick Lit," pointing again to the way developments in Germany resemble larger trends in the international book market. *Chick Lit* is generally thought of as referring to fictional texts written by female authors that address issues of modern women, such as relationships, gender roles, and consumption, often in a humorous way (see Ferris and Young). In the UK, Helen Fielding's novel *Bridget Jones's Diary* (1996, inspired originally by Jane Austen's *Pride and Prejudice* and made into a popular movie) helped establish the category. In the U.S., Candace Bushnell's novel *Sex in the City* (1997) served as the genre's blueprint, as well as the source of the tremendously successful television series aired on HBO. Variants of *Chick Lit* exist in many other countries, such as Brazil and India (see Lakshmi). In Germany, prose by Ildikó von Kürthy (*Mondscheintarif*, 1999) or Hatice Akyün (*Einmal Hans mit scharfer Soße*, 2005) fit the established framework; the latter represents what Karin Yeşilada has called "Chick-Lit alla Turca."

My analysis so far has shown what iconization and labeling can mean for younger authors who might not be perfectly at ease with a differentiated public sphere because they feel that, while it is potentially economically lucrative, it ultimately misjudges their artistic works. Furthermore, we should ask whether the sketched developments influence the literary production itself, as Klaus-Michael Bogdal suggests. Specifically, Bogdal compares the contemporary literary space to "an *air conditioner*, which, through a system of functionally oriented and differently tempered corridors, delivers the desired aesthetic offerings of meaning to the various environments."[28] Authors who find themselves in this system are, according to Bogdal, all too aware of the need to actively seek out their readers in an individualistic society and adjust accordingly, both thematically and stylistically. Such conclusions are certainly useful in understanding the mechanism of the current literary field and the marketplace. However, they can be problematic with regard to the aesthetic analysis of literary texts since they confer functional processes of the literary market to literature itself, putting it a priori under suspicion of being ideologically questionable and thus reducing the texts' aesthetic value. Frequently, prose is read primarily as a social document of a generation or a societal stratum. Once the stratum disappears or specific references to brands and fashions lose their referential

---

**28** " … eine *Klimaanlage*, die durch ein funktional ausgerichtetes und unterschiedlich temperiertes System von 'Gängen' die verschiedenen Milieus mit den erwünschten ästhethischen Sinnangeboten beliefert." Bogdal 1998, 9, 21–23.

quality (as they invariably will), the texts themselves lose their aesthetic and cultural significance (Bartmer 202). Behind this argument lurks an understanding that equates literature not interested primarily in meaning, depth, and existential truth ("Bedeutung," "Tiefe" und "Wahrheit"), as *Zeit* critic Ulrich Greiner put it, with a lesser aesthetic and epistemological value.

## The Rise of New German Pop Literature

"dabei ist doch bekannt – sprich das pop-wort nicht aus!" Kathrin Röggla, *irres wetter*[29]

The critical reaction to the trend of "New German Pop literature" in the late 1990s illustrates the mistrust vis-à-vis a literature that is perceived as generational avowal rather than genuine work of art. My discussion of the pop literature phenomenon is more extensive for two reasons. Many of the authors analyzed in this book, such as Judith Hermann, Elke Naters, Joachim Bessing, Kathrin Röggla, and Sibylle Berg, were categorized in the late 1990s as "pop," yet the term was most often used by critics as a mere descriptive label, without an acknowledgement of its historical roots and thematic and aesthetic distinctiveness. But the differentiation of its qualities is necessary as a referential framework in order to understand the development of German-language prose over the last two decades. Furthermore, the rise of pop literature through many timely narratives is a salient example for globalizing tendencies in German-language literature that ultimately speak to its internationalization.

With Christian Kracht's novel *Faserland* (1995), which cleared the way for the advent of new German pop literature (see Biendarra 2002), formerly marginalized experiences of everyday life found their way into the literary mainstream. Subsequently, there were countless successors whose narratives of pop music, parties, life styles, shopping, sex, and drugs breathed new life into German prose and meant economic success especially for many first-time authors, such as Alexa Hennig von Lange (*Relax*, 1999), Benjamin von Stuckrad-Barre (*Soloalbum*, 1998), Elke Naters (*Königinnen* 1998), and Sarah Khan (*Gogo-Girl*, 1999), to name just a few. Despite the enthusiastic reception of a younger audience, professional critics in particular could hardly conceal their averseness towards a literature that narrates the hedonism and sparkling surfaces of a consumerist society, rejects intellectual depth, and does not parade any profound insights: "The nonaggression pact that the young literature of non-interference and détente has made with the world is a provocation. It is

---

29 "But everybody knows – don't utter the word 'pop'!"

an aesthetic, epistemological, and moral scandal that must upset anyone who believes in literature," blustered Iris Radisch in *Die Zeit*.[30]

One reason for such strongly worded renunciations is that late twentieth century pop literature no longer operates in the mode of resistance against the cultural establishment that was its trait in the 1960s and 1970s. Originating from the works of the American Beat and Underground generation, such as J.D. Salinger, Allen Ginsberg, and Jack Kerouac, and having a relative in the Pop Art of Andy Warhol and Robert Rauschenberg, pop soon became an international phenomenon, not least through music groups such as The Beatles and The Rolling Stones. After media theorist Leslie A. Fiedler had given it its name in 1968 in his Freiburg lecture "Close the Border, Bridge the Gap," poet Rolf Dieter Brinkmann introduced a German audience to pop, both through the translations of Beat generation poets in the *ACID* anthology and his own essays (for instance in *Der Film in Worten*, 1982). Subsequently, Brinkmann and other writers, such as Jörg Fauser, Hubert Fichte, Elfriede Jelinek and Hadayatullah Hübsch, negotiated topics such as sexual liberation, English-speaking internationality, the questioning of a protestant work ethic, minorities and their rights, and the rejection of institutions, hierarchies, and authorities in their literature (Diederichsen 273). Brinkmann's poetry, for example, protested against realistic modes of narration and advocated the importance of the workaday world and its phenomena.

New German pop literature – which pop theoretician Diedrich Diederich-sen has called "Pop II" in terminological and thematic differentiation to its predecessor "Pop I" – on the other hand, cannot break open established boundaries as Pop I did because it exists in a drastically altered cultural field. First, according to Diederichsen, the change from a public television culture to a privatized one in the late 1980s brought about a new type of public sphere that is closely related to pop. Characterized by novel formats such as talk shows and "edutainment," the contemporary media landscape seems open to democratic participation and plurality, while in reality it prevents the questioning of dominant ideologies and affirms societal consensus. The media have an amplifying position in this process. We can furthermore observe an increased permeability between new forms of public presentation in the media and known popular cultures, whereby both depend on and require each other. Even the smallest niche culture (such as *Star Trek* fans, for example) exists because

---

**30** "Der Nichtangriffspakt, den die junge Nichteinmischungs- und Entspannungsliteratur mit der Welt geschlossen hat, ist eine Provokation. Ein ästhetischer, erkenntnistheoretischer und moralischer Skandal, der jeden aufbringen muß, der an die Literatur [...] glaubt." Radisch 1999.

of mass entertainment, which respectively finds inspiration in the former (by creating a talk show about the so-called *Trekkies*, for example): "Even though they are not truly 'understood,' displayed and appreciated properly, phenomena that belong to an oppositional pop culture in the former sense are now making it into the new public sphere,"[31] finds Diederichsen.

This altered public sphere provides a relevant context for the evaluation of authors and works being labeled as new German pop literature. The inflationary use of the pop term means for Diederichsen that pop has degenerated into a diagnostic dummy term ("zeitdiagnostischer Dummy-Term," 274), in turn enabling literary criticism to establish a new label. Contemporary German prose – whose authors were almost all debutants – thus underwent a seemingly slip-proof categorization. Both the literature and its reception are structurally often characterized by socio-cultural identification, which undoubtedly explains the success with young readers. For instance, Florian Illies's book *Generation Golf* (1999) creates a nostalgic evaluation of growing up in the social stratum of the 1970s and 1980s West-German middle class. In an obvious remixing of elements from Nick Hornby's popular novel *High Fidelity* (1995), Stuckrad-Barre's *Soloalbum* (1998) recounts the familiar experience of a break-up of a twenty-something heterosexual couple. Through his rewriting of Hornby, the author seeks alignment with a globally successful English-language text, yet he also localizes the experiences of his male protagonist by giving him a specifically German context through the mention of German media, cultural phenomena such as soccer, and the description of youth and student cultures. Finally, Judith Hermann in *Sommerhaus, später* (1998) managed to attach a new perspective to the experience of living in bohemian post-*Wende* Berlin, before the city turned into the capital of the Berlin Republic. In so doing, younger authors attached a local flavor to a category of literature that is international by definition.

The labeling practice oriented potential consumers and reduced complex circumstances into one neat catchphrase, with the goal to attract especially a young, affluent audience. Similar to the *Fräuleinwunder* marketing strategy discussed earlier, the label of *New German Pop Literature* meant extraordinary economic success for publishing houses and authors, even if only for a short time period. The worldwide economic slump that followed September 11, 2001 and the general malaise of the publishing industry forced presses to redirect their attention to their trusted established authors instead of fostering more

---

**31** "Auch ohne 'verstanden', entfaltet und gewürdigt zu werden, schaffen es Phänomene, die eigentlich zur im alten Sinne oppositionellen Popkultur gehören, in die neue Öffentlichkeit." Diederichsen 277.

and more young talents whose manuscripts often had received lavish advances around the millennium (see Bartels). Kiepenheuer & Witsch, for example, paid almost two million Deutschmarks for the rights to eighteen-year old Benjamin Lebert's next three novels after his first book *Crazy* (1999) was an unexpected bestseller (Wellershoff).

Given the logic of indexing and labeling inherent to marketing strategies, the affiliation of literary texts with new German pop literature necessarily was quite arbitrary. In the late 1990s, almost every newspaper review or book blurb of a first-time author included a remark that one was about to read a pop text, to which the novels rarely lived up, especially since clear analytic criteria for evaluating went often missing. In the meantime, scholarly work has remedied this situation. Pop literature is taught and studied, and numerous analyses have been published in *Germanistik* as well as *Auslandsgermanistik* over the last decade. Johannes Ullmaier, for example, has developed a useful taxonomy of pop literature that shows that many of the texts share a number of thematic and aesthetic foci. I have chosen from Ullmaier what strikes me as the most important from a panorama of possible criteria.

First, the thematic foci of pop literature include: Renderings from the pop world (disco and concert visits; subculture, band and fan narratives); adolescence (first love, generational conflicts, etc.); youth cultures and subcultures (punks, skaters, etc.); a disavowal of the bourgeois norms, moving towards dandy, beatnik or avant-garde forms of existence; mobility, glamour, drugs, sexuality, ecstasy and excess. Second, the aesthetic foci entail the following: Moving away from linguistic standards of high literature towards slang and colloquialisms, everyday language, the language of the media; a recourse to different genres, preferred are science fiction, crime fiction, horror and pornography; an orientation towards pop-musical patterns, verses and lyrics that are reminiscent of DJ techniques; a recourse to modernist techniques, such as stream-of-consciousness, montage, and collage; an opening of the text towards integrated text/image ensembles, avant-garde typography, integrated text/ music ensembles, and finally the transgression of genres, the mixing of genres, and multimediality (Ullmaier 2001, 16–18).

Many of the texts of the authors analyzed in this study employ one or more of these features. However, this characterization is necessarily so generalized that it is akin to the "passe-partout function" of pop that Diederichsen criticized. Yet it is almost impossible to refrain from generalizations since the popularity and longevity of the pop term are due in part to its tautological qualities: Something is popular because it is popular, banal songs express how banal most pop music is, etc. (Mertens 213). Writer Rainald Goetz has described the qualities of pop memorably when he attributed its fascination to the freedom of dealing with everything that pops ("alles was knallt") in order to withstand the "BIG SINN:" "We need even more stimuli, even more advertisements speed cars fashion hedonism pop and more pop."[32] The indeterminacy and morphing tendencies that characterize pop became even more prominent around the millennium, due to the societal generalization of pop experiences.

Consequently, in analyzing reviews of popular literary criticism and press materials of publishing houses, we come to realize that the labeling of authors as *New German Pop Literature* actually has less to do with thematic or formal features of their texts than with the specific relation between an author and his or her work, which can be activated without any specific textual reference. Consequently, Ullmaier's taxonomy of pop literature covers in a third category this specific connection, which includes the following points: Mere author popularity as measured by sales, a continuous presence in various media, emphatic popularity with a wide, preferably young audience; promotional patterns borrowed from the pop music world, such as making an author into a star, attractiveness, image, outfit, styling; a pop cultural orientation in the design and titling of books and in their marketing; the pop cultural maximization of synergies following the motto "from the book to the movie to the interview," this includes adhering to the conventions of the respective format (the most favored of which is the novel, with short sentences, dialogical style, and a well-organized plot), and finally, the youth or youthfulness of the author (Ullmaier 16).

To be sure, the public presence of young authors in the media plays a significant role in their success. Through the construction of pop images, authors truly seemed to become congruent with their books, even more so than critics had claimed for the *Fräuleinwunder* trend. For instance, Benjamin von Stuckrad-Barre and Christian Kracht entrenched their public personae as dandies by posing in expensive suits in an ad for the clothing store Peek & Cloppenburg (see Philippi and Schmidt), thus seeking to corroborate the arrogance towards the social mainstream that their fictional characters in *Faserland* and *Soloalbum* displayed as well. Furthermore, they published a transcript of a conversational marathon that the two of them, together with authors Alexander von Schönburg, Eckhart Nickel, and Joachim Bessing, had staged at the Berlin Hotel Adlon in 1999 that quickly became infamous. Under the title *Tristesse Royale* (Grand Melancholy), the five men conversed for three days about Germany, fashion, trends, politics, and literature. The book functioned by the principle that reality is what the media attest it to be and thus staged an

---

**32** "Wir brauchen noch mehr Reize, noch viel mehr Werbung Tempo Autos Modehedonismen Pop und noch mal Pop." Goetz. "Subito" 21.

ongoing, sometimes absurd dialogue about popular culture that was supposed to show a moral genre view of a generation ("Sittenbild einer Generation").[33] According to Kracht, critics unanimously savaged *Tristesse Royale* in 140 reviews (2000), yet their scorn granted the five authors an enormous media presence that they had consciously created. When asked about the fact that the protocol came out at the same time as his second book, *Livealbum* (1999), Stuckrad-Barre ironically commented on his strategy: "Since our publishers refuse to placard our images onto billboards and do not book commercials at the cinema or on TV, in which top models pose with our books, we have to take other measures to communicate to the reader that he or she is allowed to spend money on us again."[34]

The global popular culture that Adorno and Horkheimer had condemned so vehemently in *The Dialectic of the Enlightenment* has become a reality impossible to escape. My discussion of new German pop literature provides evidence for how its rise has led to paradigmatic shifts in the ways that authors and their texts are packaged and marketed. Undoubtedly the pop trend has added to a larger readership interested in contemporary literature – Antje Rávic Strubel and Thomas Kraft, among others, have spoken of a boom – and thus illustrates strategies with which literature can counteract its own marginalization. When we interpret new German pop literature of the millennium, we should be mindful of these changes and hold the texts to the catalogue of features described above. Especially important is that contemporary German-language literature exists within a field characterized by structural changes, such as an altered and globalized media landscape, which in turn influences both the literary reception and production and the presentation of writers.

## Fashioning the Authorial Self on the World Wide Web

As a global medium *par excellence*, the new driving medium of the twenty-first century plays a decisive role in the developments outlined above. Statistically speaking, the use of the Internet has increased exponentially over the last

---

**33** Bessing, Joachim. *Tristesse Royale. Das popkulturelle Quintett mit Joachim Bessing, Christian Kracht, Eckhart Nickel, Alexander v. Schönburg und Benjamin v. Stuckrad-Barre.* Berlin: Ullstein, 1999. Here 11.
**34** "Da sich unsere Verlag weigern, Bauzäune mit uns zu plakatieren, und sie auch keine Werbespots im Kino oder Fernsehen buchen, in denen Topmodels mit unseren Büchern posieren, müssen wir zu anderen Mitteln greifen, um dem Leser zu übermitteln: Es darf wieder gekauft werden." In Philippi and Schmidt, 3.

decade. The development followed similar paths in Germany and the United States, but more people use online services in the U.S. In 2005, the average rate of Internet use in Germany was 63.5 percent and in 2008 it was 65.8 percent (42.7 million adults).[35] In contrast, a study by the *Pew Internet and American Life Project* in 2006 determined that 73 percent of the adults in the United States (about 147 million adults) browse the Web. The study also showed that Americans see the Internet as a positive influence on their lives; they believe that the medium significantly improves their access to information in the areas of leisure, work, shopping and health. In 2010, these views manifested themselves further. Today, about 90 percent of adults in the United States are online. While younger users primarily use the Web to maintain social contacts and for entertainment, people age 33 and older are more likely to use the Internet to search for information, write and receive emails, and shop.[36]

The Internet is both simultaneous and outside of time (topicality); it overcomes geographic distances and national borders (transnationality); and due to its universal accessibility, it is a democratic medium that can be used to distribute information and establish community (interactivity). As Arjun Appadurai showed in his relevant globalization study, this leads to the creation of imaginary worlds, new identity formations, and the development of alternatives to national and political ways of thinking. While Appadurai has stressed mostly the positive sides of electronic media, there are also much more pessimistic voices who find that the Internet undermines community, limits social action, and enables corporations to control our subconscious (see Poster). The exploding field of digital humanities has examined, among other aspects, how the Internet has developed since the 1950s and how it has changed the balance of power between the individual and the state (see Ryan), and how meaning is mediated and changes online (see Lovink). This research is, of course, extremely varied and ongoing.

In terms of authorial construction, the Internet is a popular medium of expression that can reach a large audience and that facilitates and encourages innovative forms of authorial self-representation. In addition to the authors'

---

**35** Schneller and Faeling. The 2008 numbers come from the *ARD/ZDF Online-Studie 2008*: http://www.daserste.de/service/studie.asp.

**36** The use of the Internet has risen considerably in older people since 2005, but generational differences remain statistically significant. While 89% of all 18 to 24-year-olds are online, only 45% of 70 to 75-year-olds are. See http://www.pewinternet.org/Reports/2009/Generations-Online-in-2009.aspx. The *Pew Internet and American Life Project* is an independent "fact tank," dealing, among other things, with the influence of the Internet on American society. It regularly conducts large statistical surveys, all of which can be found online at http://www.pewinternet.org.

personal web sites discussed subsequently, publishers' web sites and commercial providers (such as Amazon) provide information about authors, marketing them and their literary products to a potentially global public. Literature and culture review sites such as *Perlentaucher* in Germany and *Arts and Letters Daily* or *Slate* in the U.S. affect popularity and book sales and shape cultural discussions through their online forums. Here, creativity is limited only by technology, but even these limits are constantly being expanded, as we can see from the development of new formats like Weblogs, clips from author interviews, and book trailers.

In addition to the democratic forms of accessibility already mentioned, the Web is characterized by a de-localized environment and disintermediation – in other words, the loss of the middleman, who plays an important role in the traditional publishing and newspaper business (Shapiro 133–141, 188–192). Disintermediation also occurs in terms of the literary field, since the Internet places literature in a modified procedural and communicative framework: increasingly, it is becoming a collective text that anyone can potentially help write. In certain formats, such as the weblog (or blog), this plays a decisive role.

We can distinguish various basic forms of Internet authorship. Corresponding more closely to traditional concepts are examples of internet literature (for instance, Matthias Politycki's novel *Marietta* and Rainald Goetz's online journal *Abfall für alle*), as well as collaborative co-writing projects (e.g. NULL, Forum der Dreizehn, am pool[37]), with which authors in Germany experimented in the late 1990s. Shortly after each project had been completed in book form, the online versions disappeared from the Web. The second basic form involves texts that are produced and distributed exclusively on the Internet. They make use of the networking aspect and the technical possibilities inherent to the medium, subvert the linearity of traditional narrative, and are "hypertextual, interactive and multimedia-based." (Simanowski 14) The two forms have different goals and their own target audiences.

A third type of authorship in which the Web is primarily used as a medium for the self-representation of oneself and one's works is important to the literary-sociological center of my argument here. In this context, Kerstin Paulsen has differentiated between a) externally generated approaches, for instance

---

37 *Null* was only intended to be online for a year as an experiment. *am pool* on the other hand, edited by Elke Naters and Sven Lager, was discontinued due to a lack of interest by the contributors. *Forum der 13* has existed since 1999 and is still operational, although it differs considerably from the original platform, see http://www.forum-der-13.de (last access April 2, 2012).

web sites provided by publishing houses that present advertisings for books, text samples, or information on book tours, and b) self-staged individual representations (259). This differentiation, which is functional in and of itself, must nonetheless be problematized. First, it seems to implicitly equate the Web presence qua personal web site with "direct" authorship, thereby overlooking the fact that even authors' personal web sites are usually filtered through technical personnel such as programmers or web designers. Thus supposedly authentic presentations are already a priori disrupted. Furthermore, the boundaries between the two categories are mutable, since every author is entitled to voice his opinion about the ways he or she is represented by the publishing house, in the service of creating a positive public image.

What can a personal author web site typically offer? In a rather basic article, Luigi Ghezzi suggests that it (1) represents a window display in which the literary works can be shown, (2) offers a conduit for reviews, articles and essays, and (3) provides a place for communication between the author and the readers, including many different possibilities for experimentation (Ghezzi 40). I observe four additional functions. Also central is (4) the aspect of creative self-expression online, which can be guided not just by the internal rules of the literary market, but also by one's own desires and aesthetic ideas. Creating a virtual presence in the public realm goes hand in hand with the possibility of (5) increasing the experiential quality of literature for the audience – by including external links, using flash animation and embedding visual materials in the form of slide shows or audio files and video clips. In summary, a convincing web site can transform an author's biography and works into an ongoing narrative project that serves less to promote direct book sales than (6) to help establish or stabilize an image (Porombka 2005, 151). By way of contrast, it is also possible to use the medium in a critical way. In addition to literary texts, editorial pieces and public appearances, a personal web site can provide a forum for authorial representation that counteracts the machinery of the literary industry. Thus the Web presence allows authors to (7) regain agency, or at least a form of self-determination.

## Personal Web Sites as a Medium of Authorial Self-Representation

A comparison of the web sites of various German-language authors allows us to note differences in their self-marketing approaches and to experience the range of inherent possibilities. These are due in part to variations in their respective approaches to electronic media, which are significantly shaped by cultural influences. However, if one opens the perspective across national boundaries, it becomes apparent that these differences clearly have something to do with the literary genre in which the authors are primarily active. Metaphorically speaking, the differences can be described as a leap from Authorship 1.0 to Authorship 2.0, i.e. from Web 1.0 to Web 2.0.[38] According to my thesis, only by completing the move to Authorship 2.0 can a successful internet presence be built up that functionalizes the possibilities of the Web and uses them to develop symbolic capital. A comparison with contemporary American author Stephenie Meyer will make this clearer.

I formally investigated approximately thirty personal web sites, i.e., sites not maintained by publishing houses, of contemporary authors in Germany, Austria, Switzerland, and the United States. My primary analytical criteria were interactivity, graphics and animation, the integration of other material from different media (i.e., aspects of intermediality) and the use of hyperlinks. If one analyzes the web sites of German-speaking authors, it quickly becomes clear that many underutilize the medium. Most mainstream, well-known authors use their site as a "business card" that *informs* readers in a professional manner, without truly *animating* them. If authors have a personal web site at all – the overall online presence remains relatively marginal – they see it primarily as a container for storing basic information about the person and the works, without providing insight into their personal interests or social and political involvement. Elfriede Jelinek's web site (http://www.elfriedejelinek. com) represents an extreme end of the spectrum. Since 2007 Jelinek has been publishing her texts exclusively online, in order to guarantee a democratic form of distribution that is accessible to everyone (see her interview with Gropps). However, there is no biographical information about Jelinek to be found there and citing the texts is expressly prohibited, which undermines the author's egalitarian claim.

Generally, however, web sites contain professional quasi-résumés for which Peter Stamm's site is a good example, http://www.peterstamm.ch, information about new releases and reading tours, text excerpts, interviews, and author photos that can be downloaded free of charge. As is visible from the web site credits, professional web designers build most of the sites, even if the authors are responsible for the contents.

---

**38** 'Web 2.0' is a useful conceptual term that serves as an umbrella for a new generation of internet applications, such as blogs, wikis, and social networking sites such as Facebook and Twitter. These applications grew out of the "participatory web" and offer the user both interactive services and the possibility to better control his/her own data. See the web site of Tim O'Reilly, who popularized the term; also Fox and Madden.

Interestingly, in most cases there is congruence between the graphic implementation of the page and the author's public persona; this confirms that many web sites do place an emphasis on the abovementioned function of stabilizing the image. For instance, Ingo Schulze's home page (http://www.ingo schulze.com) evokes the image of an old-fashioned author by depicting a realistic image of a typewriter – an impression reinforced by Schulze's black and white portrait by celebrity photographer Jim Rakete. In contrast, Sybille Berg (http://www.sibylleberg.ch, a visually interesting, yet technically somewhat counterintuitive web site) presents the dark, eccentric personality commonly attributed to the author: on the home page, users find a graphic representation of a traditional modern house, perched on a cliff above a roiling ink-black sea. The cryptic links to the rooms – which include every station from the nursery to the deathbed – represent areas of Berg's life and work. Flash animation creates an eerie glow in each room of the graphic as the user clicks on it.

Overall, projects with interesting contents and aesthetics are currently still in the minority among German-language authors. What the web sites lack in terms of their implementation are aspects that distinguish the Web and make it an innovative medium. Interactivity, dialogicity, graphic innovations, animations, intermediality and additional links placed by the author are all generally neglected. This wastes an opportunity to use the personal web site for more than just informational purposes; it could establish an added aesthetic value that reflects upon both the literary products and the identity of the author, creating a particular aura for both, as Porombka has suggested (2002, 20). The web pages of Daniel Kehlmann (www.kehlmann.com) and Thomas Glavinic (www.thomas-glavinic.de) show what a successful web presence looks like, especially with regards to the technical possibilities of embedding audio clips and podcasts (for an in-depth analysis, see Schoell).

Alexa Hennig von Lange's web site illustrates some of the problems contemporary authors seem to have with the creative use of the Web. Hennig von Lange was born in 1973 in Hannover. While she started writing early, her public career began when she was twenty-one years old and worked as a model and moderator for a children's television show. In the context of the rise of *New German Pop Literature*, her first novel *Relax* (1997) made her known instantly on the literary scene, and she has since been the subject of numerous literary analyses (for example, Mehrfort). Hennig von Lange has written a number of novels after *Relax*, many of which are in the category of young adult fiction, plays, and journalistic pieces. She also moderates a radio show.

Hennig von Lange's web page shares certain similarities with Stephenie Meyer's site, which I will discuss next. More important than various biographical similarities between the two women – both were born in 1973 and have more traditional views regarding gender roles and family, which affect their choice of topics (see Hennig von Lange 2006, and Mensing) – are the congruencies in their professional profiles. Hennig von Lange and Meyer both are prolific writers who published several novels within a short period of time.[39] In addition to attracting a large community of readers and keeping them interested, their productivity also ensures that their publishers provide extensive marketing measures. They have also received much attention in many different media and are visible in the public sphere. Although the boundaries between youth and adult fiction are fluid and arbitrary, for the German as well as the American market[40], Hennig von Lange's and Meyer's books, with their focus on adolescent problems, certainly also intersect in terms of content. Despite the very different staging of each web site, they confirm that an internet presence seems to be more important for authors who might be considered commercial fiction writers and young adult writers than it is for authors of serious fiction – an aspect to which I will return later.

Alexa Hennig von Lange has maintained her own web site since 2002. The initial site – linked to her first publisher, Rogner und Bernhard – has now been transformed into a personal site with her own domain name (http://www.alexahennigvonlange.de).[41] As with most German authors, this is a professionally designed site that is not updated by the author herself, which is apparent from the web site credits. In her self-representation, Hennig von Lange still relies on the image often circulated in the media of herself as the "Spice Girl of literature," a nickname coined by fellow author Joachim Lottmann in a sexist newspaper feature – the young, attractive female author who confidently controls her own public image, much like an Anglo-American pop star. In keeping with this theme, photos of Hennig von Lange dominate her web site. On the home page one encounters a photograph that is not uninteresting and effec-

---

**39** See "Immer auf dem Sprung. Gleich drei Bücher von ihr sind in diesem Monat erschienen: Workaholic Alexa Hennig von Lange wartet nicht, bis sie die Muse küsst, sondern schreibt, bis es dampft." Interview mit Stefan Hauck. *Buchjournal*, February 16, 2009 (http://buchjournal.buchhandel.de/307438/). Alexa von Lange published a tetralogy whose hero is a teenager named Lelle: *Ich habe einfach Glück* (Rogner und Bernhard, 2001), *Erste Liebe* (Rowohlt 2004), *Leute, ich fühle mich leicht* (cbj Verlag 2008), *Leute, mein Herz glüht* (cbj Verlag 2009). Her most recent novel *Leichte Turbulenzen* (C. Bertelsmann, 2011), however, is not in the category of young adult fiction. Neither is Stephenie Meyer's latest science fiction novel *The Host* (Little, Brown & Company, 2008).
**40** The categorization as "young adult fiction" is usually related primarily to marketing aspects. Stephenie Meyer's publisher Little, Brown & Company used the trend of gothic fiction with a strong female hero to market Meyer's first book *Twilight* in this particular market segment. See Rabb.
**41** Older versions of web sites can be found here: http://web.archive.org.

tively highlights her external traits – in particular, her famous red curls. Clicking on further pages reveals that that photo is part of a visual essay by Swiss photographer Walter Pfeiffer, who staged the ending of Hennig von Lange's novel *Risiko* (2007), using six photos with the author in the main role. In addition, her image is shown on the covers of most of her books, which can of course be seen on the web site and immediately purchased from Amazon with another click. The link to Hennig von Lange's biography presents no fewer than forty photos in the form of a colorful collage, which makes the text of the biography all but disappear.

This image policy conflating the author with the text performs various functions. First, the use of the photographs, which focus exclusively on staging Alexa Hennig von Lange, effectively implements the basic rules of brand marketing, highlighting similar aspects as in the earlier example of Judith Hermann. The most important goal here is to create a public identity in which the consumer automatically identifies a brand with a certain logo, as is the case in company branding, only in this case the logo is the face of the author. Text and image flow into one another and become one inseparable product. The resulting, sometimes excessive media presence of contemporary authors causes even serious readers to assume that literary figures reveal something about the author as a private individual.[42] This presumably increases interest in the novels and results in higher sales figures as well as greater identification by readers with the "product" Alexa Hennig von Lange. In light of her novels this identification is essential since they largely deal with the problems of young women.

Ultimately, the dominance of the photos demonstrates that literature is part of contemporary visual culture and that a book is simply one of many media products. This contrasts with authorial online self-portrayals in which the presentation of the literary texts is the central focus and epitexts such as author photos are limited to a single image. The use of but one photo thus serves to authenticate literature as a consciously traditional counter-model to other media; in addition to Ingo Schulze's site, mentioned above, another example can be found on Terézia Mora's web site (http://www.tereziamora.de).

To be sure, Alexa Hennig von Lange's web site does take advantage of the multi-media possibilities inherent to the Internet, yet all integrated media remain limited to visually staging her identity. In addition to the photos, there

---

**42** One could study this after the publication of Christian Kracht's first novel *Faserland* in 1995, when even fellow literary writers such as Matthias Poliycki confused the separate categories of author and narrator: "Ein Bürschlein [...] bereist Deutschland [...] Das Bürschlein heißt Christian Kracht." *Taz* (2000).

are links to three YouTube videos. Two of these show Hennig von Lange during appearances on the *Harald Schmidt Show* in 2001, where she coquettishly responds to Schmidt's sexual innuendos and thereby essentially supports her own objectification. There is almost no mention of her artistic projects. The fact that the Hennig von Lange site continues to link to these videos over a decade later illustrates the persistence of the Spice Girl narrative project and the author's interest in maintaining and confirming this public image.

Von Lange's many novels are referenced through links to book-jacket-style summaries, each accompanied by a cover photo. However, the literary texts themselves are not the main focus; they are placed on equal footing with the visual texts. To date, Hennig von Lange has also made little use of the medium's interactive qualities. Although she is one of the few authors one can contact directly by email, the typical five-day response time lags defeats the simultaneous potential of the medium.

## Authorship 2.0: Stephenie Meyer

In contrast, American best-seller author Stephenie Meyer makes creative use of many of the possibilities offered by the Internet. This seems to directly correlate to the author's own media usage when she calls the Web a significant part of her day-to-day reality. By her own admission, it is "indispensable" both as a research tool and a communication medium: "At home, I really am online every waking minute" (in Dallach).

In this sense, Meyer is representative of a lifestyle in which the use of the Internet is an integral component of the individual's daily life and thus his or her own identity. While the Web was initially part of the working world for many people (company communications, finding information, professional networking), it has increasingly become a medium used for entertainment (gaming, movies, music), transnational and cross-continental communications (email, Skyping) and social networking (instant messaging, MySpace, Facebook, Flickr, Twitter, and other social media applications). These tendencies are strongly supported by technical innovations. In the last few years, for instance, technologies that disconnect the networking process from computers and transfer it to mobile data services (such as smartphones, e-readers, and tablets) have given even more impetus to the tendency of leading a completely networked life in which one can be online all day long regardless of location. Initial studies on the long-term psychological and neurological effects of these developments demonstrate the much-discussed concept of the media revolution (see Carr) and in many ways they confirm the theories of Marshall McLuhan, who believed that media sources are not passive information channels but in fact alter our thought processes.

One could say that Meyer is the American answer to the United Kingdom's literary superstar J. K. Rowling. Completely unknown in literary circles a few years ago, she is now leading the international bestseller lists and is one of the richest women in the UK. Similarly to Hennig von Lange, Meyer became famous in the category "young adult fiction" with her vampire tetralogy, a morbid modern version of *Romeo and Juliet*.[43] Having sold 40 million books by 2008, Meyer might be on her way to dethroning Rowling as the most successful author of all times, at least if one believes the sales figures in the American press.[44] Despite the obvious aesthetic weaknesses of her writing and her rather Victorian understanding of gender issues, the cultural significance of bestselling authors like her and Rowling has been confirmed officially. In a study from 2009, the *National Endowment for the Humanities* found that the continuous decline of reading fiction in the U.S., which had lasted a quarter of a century, finally had been reversed.[45]

Meyer has made excellent use of the ubiquity of the Internet. Her ability to draw continuously more readers – both youths and adults – has much to do with her ability to forge personal contacts with her audience, thereby creating a loyal following of fans, which she built up through her Internet presence in the beginning of her career (see Carpenter). Her official web site http://www.stepheniemeyer.com is unusual in many ways and an interesting example of the Web's use as a successful medium of communication. Like many other web sites by U.S. authors, the site is not connected to Meyer's publishing house Little, Brown & Company. Instead the author runs it herself as a sort of family business. Her husband Cristiaan 'Pancho' Meyer uses his own photographs to frame each respective page. While photos of Picacho Peak point to Meyer's place of residence in Phoenix, AZ, photos of the rain forest in Forks, WA indicate the setting of the vampire novels. Meyer's official web master is her brother Seth, a student of optometry and an autodidact in web design.[46]

---

**43** *Twilight* (2005), *New Moon* (2006), *Eclipse* (2007), *Breaking Dawn* (2008) were all published by Brown, Little & Co, New York/Boston. In Germany, the series is similarly successful, but has been published under much more playful titles directed at a younger public: *Bis(s) zum Morgengrauen, Bis(s) zur Mittagsstunde, Bis(s) zum Abendrot* (all 2008), *Bis(s) zum Ende der Nacht* (2009).
**44** "Stephenie Meyers By The Numbers." *Publishers Weekly*, May 12, 2008. http://www.publishersweekly.com/article/CA6559505.html.
**45** National Endowment for the Humanities. *Reading on the Rise.* January 12, 2009. http://graphics8.nytimes.com/packages/pdf/books/ReadingReport.pdf.
**46** Meyer stressed the importance of the operation being manageable in order for her to deal with her fame: "It's a small business for me still. I mean, people don't understand; it's

Accordingly, the web site is technically fairly simple; the use of graphic elements is minimal and there is no animation.

The decisive difference is that an authorial concept more oriented towards the reader than outward self-presentation underlies Meyer's web site. Its primary function is to inform visitors to the site; consequently it convenes the most up-to-date information from the vampire universe. It is updated regularly by Meyer herself (who signs her posts casually with "Steph") and Seth, her brother and Webmaster. The avid reader fan will find all kinds of material that might be interesting – updates about the *Twilight* movies, new publications, links to projects the author sponsors, and new, unofficial photos of her that do not seem to have been altered in Photoshop. Because of linked recommendations to books and CDs, the blog also gives insight into Meyer's interests and likes, while reports from meeting fans on book tours or fundraisers illustrate her professional activities.

The general impression of the web site is that it attempts to counteract Meyer's extraordinary commercial success by providing non-commercialized content. She presents herself as someone who has remained down-to-earth despite her status as a literary superstar; an author who is primarily obliged to her fans.[47] The website supports this impression with the post of an unofficial humorous biography, the direct address of the readers ("Hey guys"), personal thank-you notes ("Thanks, Cassandra! You rock!"), and the correction of rumors and gossip ("There's been a lot of worry and speculation on the boards lately and I want to let you know what's going on"). This attempt to show her readers an unedited version of herself accords with Meyer's presumed value system as a practicing Mormon. The upholding of social and Christian values is not only communicated in her books,[48] but also stage-managed for the reader on the Web site.

With regard to cultural imagination and identity, Meyer's online narrative project reflects conservative, all-American values. Her literary success, which takes a back seat to the presentation of the real-life person, is congruent with the ideals of American individualism and the pursuit of happiness. For example, Meyer has stressed that she wrote the *Twilight* series primarily out of her

---

just a little family thing. I couldn't deal with it if I didn't keep it small. It freaks me out." In Sullivan.

**47** J. K. Rowling, on the other hand, is well known for suing readers whose admiration for Harry Potter might mean infringement upon her copyright. See Eligon.

**48** The tension between youthful desire and sexual abstinence is the main topic driving the plot of the *Twilight* series. The relationship between Bella and vampire Edward is only possible because they abstain in order to control Edward's blood lust, even though this changes in the last book, *Breaking Dawn*.

love for writing without economic success being her primary motivation. Her private life seems largely unchanged; she continues to live in Phoenix, AZ where her three sons determine her daily routine and emphasizes that she only writes at night after the children have gone to bed. Various portraits show Meyer as a down-to-earth "family manager" whose literary ambition takes a back seat to familial needs.

In effect, Stephenie Meyer has created an online presence in which public image and self-representation are meant to overlap. She functionalizes the inherent qualities of the Internet in various ways: the links emphasize multi-media aspects, and her site exploits the medium's intercommunicative possibilities. Meyer's self-representation creates a sense of authenticity, which is an essential requirement for the success of contemporary literature,[49] an aspect that I will come back to in the next chapter. An author's effect in the literary arena often has less to do with the quality of the literary texts than with his or her circulation in the respective cultural area and personal appearances in various media formats, as Dirk Niefanger has shown in a study on different literary periods from the late 1800s to contemporary pop literature (2002, 526). Contemporary authors with well-developed media skills – this includes both Stephenie Meyer and Alexa Hennig von Lange – skillfully functionalize the gray area between staging and authenticity. In this way, they use their personal web sites to communicate information that increases and cements their symbolic (and thereby also their economic) capital.

In his remarks on the literary profession, Stephan Porombka has stated that in Germany, online publications are still suspected of being "part of a great deal of noise created mainly by dilettantes."[50] While he does exempt innovative web sites from this suspicion, his observation may hint at German-speaking authors' reasons for neglecting the creative possibilities of this medium and using their own web sites – if they exist at all – primarily as a container and marketing medium. These authors seem to attach little conscious significance to the symbolic capital created through Web activity.

However, a distinction must be made here between writers who are generally considered part of high literary culture ("ernsthafte Literatur") and those who are perceived as writers of young adult literature or commercial fiction. Authors in the last two categories, regardless of country of origin or residence, have recognized the significance of the Internet; through interesting, sometimes technically sophisticated web sites, they use those sites not just as a

---

**49** Kathrin Blumenkamp has shown this, also using the example of Hennig von Lange.
**50** "…Teil eines großen, zumeist von Dilettanten erzeugten Rauschens." Stephan Porombka. "Schriftstellerberuf." *Handbuch Literaturwissenschaft*, 289.

platform for themselves and their work, but also as a forum for communicating directly with their readers. In addition to Hennig von Lange and Meyer, the same applies to J.K. Rowling (www.jkrowling.com) whose new interactive website *Pottermore* (www.pottermore.com) launched in April 2012, and to the U.S.-based author of the *Inkheart* (*Tintenwelt*) trilogy, Cornelia Funke (www.corneliafunke.de). Certainly a key point is the target audience of younger readers who see the Internet as their own medium, using it without a second thought and expecting authors to maintain an active Web presence. Clearly, the differences in the individual web sites described here are in large part dependent upon the genre in which the authors are most active. It is also significant that both young adult literature and commercial fiction researched here are global genres that work in many different languages and on different continents; what is true for Stephenie Meyer and her vampire novels also works for the Harry Potter phenomenon and crime fiction such as Stieg Larsson's *Millennium Triology*. For serious literature, this universal translatability and transnational quality is much more limited, as the comparatively low numbers of translations of German-language prose suggest.

Furthermore, in addition to the statistical differences in Internet use cited above, cultural differences between Germany and the United States come into play. Although these are difficult to quantify without generalizing in an inadmissible fashion, two examples from the field of political culture show that in the United States, the Web is much more likely to be used as a medium not only to provide information, but also to organize people and to inspire them. Since 2000, the grass-roots organization MoveOn.org (www.MoveOn.org), which in 1998 consisted mainly of e-mail communications and now uses the internet as its central platform, has raised millions of dollars in donations for Democratic Party candidates. The second example is, of course, Barack Obama – himself a bestselling author! – whom *Newsweek* magazine dubbed "President 2.0" because of his unprecedented use of the Web during the first election. Beginning in 2007, Obama deployed his web site, www.barackobama.com, to inform the public of his goals, raise donations and rally a legendary number of voters ("an army," Lyons and Stone in *Newsweek*). The web site now plays an important role in his reelection campaign in 2012. In addition, Obama used social networking sites like Facebook and MySpace, and continues to maintain a presence on both as the President of the United States. The fact that his electoral success is directly linked with his use of the Internet is now widely acknowledged, and has been confirmed by many analyses (for instance, Schifferes). The President's success story in turn lends credibility to the medium, which he was the first to use to its fullest potential. Thus Americans have less trouble seeing the Internet not only as an entertainment medium, but also as a source of credible information. In comparison, certain prejudices against the Web still exist in Germany, especially against blog journalism. This might be due to the fact that 99% of all 500,000 German-language bloggers write about apolitical, innocuous topics such as their hobbies.[51]

The ideas presented here illustrate through different examples authorial approaches to self-representation and the construction of authorship. They also show that both photographs and the Internet ultimately transcend national boundaries and erase differences. In individual cases, American authors may be making more use of the technical possibilities of the Web, moving toward a concept of authorship that is increasingly focused on direct communication with the readers. However, in the end it is probably only a matter of time before German-speaking authors, too, become more comfortable using the Internet as a multimedia communication tool.

---

**51** This is according to information from the blogger conference re:publica, April 1–3, 2009 in Berlin. See also the conversation about new media between Henryk M. Broder and Thierry Chavel that focuses on the differences between Germany and the U.S., in Miersch.

# 2 Globalizing German Literature: Literary Debates around the Millennium

The 1990s were not only the decade of unification and the subsequent collapse of Communist regimes throughout Eastern Europe, but also the years in which globalizing factors in the form of new technologies and media, consumerism, and ever-expanding mass culture began to take hold in the nascent Berlin Republic. This chapter characterizes the nineties as a time of a cultural battle ("Kulturkampf") waged mostly in the *Feuilleton* sections of Germany's leading newspapers. In the first decade after unification multiple debates about writers, their political responsibility, their social roles and their aesthetic contributions, carried out with perseverance, enthusiasm, and bitterness, moved Germany's cultural landscape. An older generation of authors, such as Christa Wolf, Günter Grass, Botho Strauß or Martin Walser and their respective critics were involved in publicly staged discussions that concerned issues of political responsibility as well as the question of how one could assess the role that a "gesamtdeutsche," a united German literature should play after the fall of the Wall.[1] The first part of the chapter briefly recalls these important debates, which highlight the differences to the emerging authors, to whom the second part is devoted.

Younger writers, editors and *Feuilleton* critics were less concerned with the political implications of literature than with the potential and significance it can hold in a globalized, highly differentiated media landscape. Their contributions concerned questions such as the following: How, that is, by what means can contemporary German literature interest the reader in its tales of the Here and Now? Which specific qualities can prevent prose from becoming marginalized in the competition of various media, such as with visual culture and the Internet? What aesthetic innovations does new German literature bring about? At the end of the 1990s, these discussions merged with those concerning the unprecedented success of the *Fräuleinwunder*, the diatribes on new German pop literature, and novel literary forms like hyper-fiction.

Here I want to highlight a few strands of the intricate debates that took place in the first decade after unification and tease out the main issues that were at stake. What becomes apparent is that the generational divide informs two distinct standpoints. Older, more established authors continue to occupy

---

1 The controversies concerning Prenzlauer Berg writers and their activities for the Stasi that focused primarily on Sascha Anderson (1991), and Botho Strauss' essay *Anschwellender Bocksgesang* (*Der Spiegel* 6:1993) that provided intellectuals of the New Right with arguments also belong on this long list.

a position of moral authority and intellectual responsibility in the public sphere that guides their self-understanding; younger authors generally – implicitly or explicitly – reject this role. Instead they increasingly refer to concepts of "authenticity" when delineating their own aesthetic practices. Writers like Maxim Biller and Matthias Politycki, on whom I focus, represent a sort of middle position where authenticity still possesses the inherent qualities that Martin Heidegger described as authenticity ("Eigentlichkeit"), which includes the idea of a commitment to aesthetics that are grounded in shared values and morals. Other writers, mostly those categorized under the label of new German pop literature, understand authenticity primarily as mimetic practice. I characterize this position as a turn towards the authentic narration of workaday life ("authentische Alltäglichkeit").

Although the discussions among younger writers covered a wide range of topics, one of the recurrent questions was how literature could compete with newer offerings such as digital media and cinema. An aesthetic strategy emerged as the remedy to ensure the survival of the "slow" medium, literature. Critics ascertained that with the help of an innovative realism, entertainment ("Unterhaltsamkeit") and an unfettered storytelling ("neue Erzählbarkeit") could be achieved even in so-called "serious" literature (E-Literatur, i.e., "ernsthafte" Literatur). The recurring emphasis on realistic narration provides the most important common thread of the discourse among younger authors, which leads me to summarize all these discussions henceforth under the heading "debate on realism" ("Realismusstreit").

The significance of this discourse is visible in its effect on the intellectual climate in united Germany and the consequences that arose for the literary field in particular. A closer analysis allows a mapping of the interconnectedness between debates about literature and literature itself, which heretofore has been neglected in literary studies. This mapping illustrates how debates on realism accompanied paradigmatic changes in German-language literature of the 1990s and provided the underlying discourse to its globalization. Writers and critics (mostly of the so-called generation of 1978, i.e., the generation between the 1968ers and a younger *Generation Golf*) recognized that in order to remain significant in a globalizing literary marketplace, German-language literature needed to revamp its themes and its aesthetics. A return to realistic storytelling and a focus on the workaday world, consumption, and phenomena of popular culture were advocated as means to foster said competitiveness. Emerging authors were most successful at introducing new voices into literature with considerable economic success, leading editors to speak of a reversal of predominant trends ("Trendwende"): "Never before have there been so many debuts, never before have young authors created such an interest in the media and especially the readers. Advances and editions attest to a new optimism."[2] At the same time, many writers felt uneasy about their role in a globalizing literary market place. Attempts to position themselves favorably in the public eye through the debates and to engage in strategies of self-marketing attested to this incertitude. As my analyses in chapter one have shown, these strategies proved to be effective methods of dealing with globalizing factors.

## Debates among Older Intellectuals

In order to characterize these issues and their development in the first decade of the Berlin Republic, it will be helpful to set up a contrasting perspective that highlights the differences to a younger generation discussed thereafter. My intention is not to offer a detailed reading of these debates among older writers and intellectuals since countless scholars have analyzed them already. Instead, I want to highlight the underlying themes of the role of literature, memory, and intellectual responsibility as the foremost concerns of an older generation. The central point for them was the question of whether or how the process of unification could be advanced through a shared language and literature. The continuous call by literary critics throughout the 1990s for a Vereinigungsroman / Berlin-Roman / Wenderoman, i.e., a German novel that would narrate the *Wende* and the tremendous political and social changes the East was experiencing exemplifies this claim. It was primarily guided by hopes that an East German author finally would present a West German audience with an "authentic" rendering of the late GDR.[3] Interestingly, the accolades for and criticism of two monumental novels, Uwe Tellkamp's *Der Turm* (2008, The Tower) and Eugen Ruge's *In Zeiten des abnehmenden Lichts* (2011, In Times of Waning Light), both of which deal with life in the GDR, show that this topos is still operational twenty years after unification (see Weidermann 28).

The debate about the late Christa Wolf and *Was bleibt* (*What Remains*) was the foremost example of a focus on unification. In 1989 Wolf published her short text that described one day in the life of a female author being surveyed by the *Stasi*, the GDR's secret police. It is a close study of the writer's morale under stress – a sequence of fear, depression and nervous crisis ensues. Wolf

---

2 "Nie zuvor hat es so viele Debüts gegeben, nie zuvor haben junge Autoren ein solches Medien- und vor allem Leserinteresse geweckt. Die Vorschüsse und Auflagen der Verlage belegen einen neuen Optimismus." Becker and Janetzki 7.

3 On a social level the wish for the ultimate *Wenderoman* was motivated by the ignorance of most West Germans of their eastern counterparts, despite the lip service paid to the cause of national unity before 1989. See Durrani xii.

had written the text in the summer of 1979, but never published it in the GDR. Her failure to do so at least during the GDR's last phase, which was characterized by an overall relaxation of socialist and aesthetic doctrine (see Emmerich 2005, 396–418), became the starting point for criticism after she did publish it. It soon developed into a major public dispute, leading to what has been documented as the "new German literary controversy" ("Neuer Deutscher Literaturstreit," see Deiritz and Kraus and Anz 1995 for its documentation). The contributions of critics – most of them representing leading West German newspapers like *Frankfurter Allgemeine Zeitung* and *Die Zeit* – resembled a crusade, with only few voices in favor of Wolf. They quickly moved her from the category of resister to that of a writer asserting the implicit superiority of the GDR's political system, and derisively called her a state poet ("Staatsdichterin").[4] According to the critics, Wolf's literary production had not – as Western literary criticism claimed before the fall of the Wall – undermined the system, but ultimately reaffirmed it. Her critics supported this view by pointing out that Wolf was a loyal party member of the SED until the official end of the GDR in 1990. From the beginning, they used political, not aesthetic categories to discredit her.

Consequently the debate revolved around much more than only the role of a writer and her political responsibility in the GDR. Wolf functioned as a stand-in and scapegoat for most East German intellectuals, and the real narrative of the debate surrounding her book was to establish a hegemonic discourse concerning the issue of how to read GDR literature after the failure of the state (see Grunenberg). With the breakdown of the communist regime, the leftist intellectual criticism of the Federal Republic was supposed to come to an end as well. Furthermore, critics not only judged GDR literature, but GDR politics as a whole, since both were inseparably intertwined in the socialist state (see Jurek Becker). The indictment of Wolf's work was therefore an indictment of the GDR and its culture.

In the fall of 1990 the debate over Wolf took a new turn. She was no longer at the center of attention but critics now discussed postwar German literature in its entirety, debating questions like aesthetics and morals, literature and social commitment. In hindsight, one can identify an implicit agenda behind the contributions, which was to prove the superiority of West German literature

---

**4** The experience was traumatic for Wolf. In her first novel in seventeen years *Stadt der Engel oder The Overcoat of Dr. Freud* (2010) she recalled the aftermath of the debate, her experience in Los Angeles in 1992 while on a Getty Fellowship, and the attempt to come to terms with the end of the GDR and her own role in the process.

over the East and its aesthetic backwardness.[5] Ulrich Greiner developed in 1990 the term dispositional aesthetics ("Gesinnungsästhetik") and defined it as follows: "It does not allow for art to have its own, genuine qualities but always follows a purpose: either it makes a stand for bourgeois moral values, for a class position, humanitarian goals or most recently against the ecological apocalypse." Greiner's article was a follow-up to a contribution by Frank Schirrmacher who proclaimed "the end of the literature of the FRG." He lamented that intellectuals since World War Two had assumed the role of a national consciousness and concerned themselves too much with questions that should be left to politicians and political scientists (1990).

Ultimately, both Schirrmacher and Greiner called for a literature close to a pure *l'art pour l'art* concept. Although the former did not even mention Christa Wolf's name in this second article, it was no coincidence that he attacked Walter Jens and Günter Grass, since both authors had defended Wolf earlier. The discourse on Christa Wolf thus entailed a criticism of all those intellectuals who did not eagerly promote unification but rather promoted alternatives. While the majority of the population in East and West in the fall of 1989 embraced the idea of unification and felt reasonably comfortable with it, many German writers did not share these sentiments: "Political autonomy versus the sell-out of moral values: that was the alternative offered to the demonstrating masses by East German intellectuals" (7), as Sabine Wilke put it in 1997. Many intellectuals were looking for a so-called third way ("dritter Weg") and tried to promote the idea of a different sort of socialism with a human face (Brockmann 1996). The pace of the unification process and rapid changes – such as the influx and lobbying of East German citizens by West German political parties or the dismantling of state industries by the *Treuhand-anstalt*, the privatization and state holding company that was tasked to dismantle and privatize East German state businesses, rendered the ideals of writers and intellectuals increasingly obsolete. The societal functions they had had in the GDR disintegrated in the unification process. Just like the rest of the population, East German writers were faced with the challenges of a democratic multi-media society where books were no longer the exclusive public place for arguments and debate, as had been the case in the GDR. Many found their economic livelihood threatened and grappled with the loss of their former role as artists who had helped grow and sustain the ideals of socialism.

The second important issue that underlies discussions in the first half of the 1990s is the attempt to establish a new national literature ("Nationallitera-

---

**5** Iris Radisch's articles from 1994 and 2000 are salient examples for the attempt to establish this discursive hegemony, even in the new millennium.

tur") that could anticipate and lead the way to an inner unity of the two German states. The historic model for this idea lies of course in the 19th century, especially in the writings of *Junges Deutschland* (Young Germany), as well as in the parallels to the founding of the German Reich in 1871 (see Pape). Günter de Bruyn, for example, an East German author who was neither as enthusiastically for unification as Martin Walser (cf. 1990, 1994) nor as acrimoniously opposed to it as Günter Grass, advocated the idea of a cultural nation ("Kulturnation") as a guarantor for supranational sovereignty (in Brandt). Consciously positioning his argument in a line of tradition that referenced Johann Gottfried Herder, Friedrich Schiller, and Jean Paul, he asserted that the Germans would find their solidarity and unity not in a state, but in culture:

> To take the existence of a culture nation, to which one belongs whether one wants to or not, as a basis seems more honest and objective to me than the talk about national emotions that supposedly move the masses or supposedly do not. The notion of a cultural nation ... metapolitically, in a manner of speaking ... means that the Germans belong together because of their culture and history, but it does not say anything about borders, constitutional principles and rights of sovereignty.[6]

The discussion about Günter Grass and his novel *Ein weites Feld* (1995, *Too Far Afield*, 2000) in 1995 illustrates the complexities of this issue. Grass, one of the most prominent critics of the rapidly paced unification process who expressed his opinions in numerous essays and articles (1990), was the western example of a type of criticism leveled primarily against easterners, for example Christa Wolf. Grass opted for a confederation model of the two German states and denounced unification as a destructive act of western colonization. The main reason for his stark resistance lay in his historical perspective; due to its responsibility for the Holocaust and two World Wars, Germany, according to Grass, should be prevented from ever existing as a unified nation state again. Since his political opposition was well known, the publication of his novel *Ein weites Feld* caused another uproar. The popular critic Marcel Reich-Ranicki, famous for his blunt criticism, instigated this reactipon by writing an open letter to Grass in the *Spiegel*, in which he savaged the book (the cover shows Reich-Ranicki tearing it to pieces), and once again the public divided into various camps (documented in Negt). Grass's text is the literary

---

6 "Von der Existenz einer deutschen Kulturnation auszugehen, zu der man gehört, ob man will oder nicht, scheint mir ehrlicher und objektiver als das Reden von nationalen Gefühlen, die die Massen angeblich bewegen oder auch angeblich nicht. Der Begriff der Kulturnation ..., sozusagen metapolitisch ... sagt aus, daß die Deutschen, durch Kultur und Geschichte bedingt, zusammengehören, aber über Grenzen, Verfassungsgrundsätze und Souveränitätsrechte sagt er nichts." De Bruyn 19.

attempt to thoroughly reflect on the recent changes in Germany by drawing a parallel between the foundation of the German nation state in 1871 and the unification process of 1989. The text can be read as an allegory for the German nation's utopian wish for unity but does not gloss over the ruptures of German history. The tension between Buchenwald and Weimar, which constitutes a central principle of narrative construction in Grass's work, is always present.

In light of the political and social necessity of making unification a success, Grass's ongoing critical reflection of Germany's past was one reason why he was heavily criticized for his novel. In the 1990s prominent figures in the intellectual and political sphere began to question Germany's on-going attempts to come to terms with its history after 1945. Calls for a "normalization" became louder, stressing that Germany had left its special path ("Sonderweg"), freed itself through forty years of stable democracy from the shadows of the past and established, in Jürgen Habermas's words, an institutional patriotism ("Verfassungspatriotismus") built on democratic institutions (see Hohendahl 1994, Taberner 2005). While this was a completely valid observation, many who at the time favored the forging of an identity whose common denominator would be the successful unification seemed oblivious to the fact that the controversy about cultural memory, normalcy and remembrance could not be relegated to the margins because it continues to shape the meta-narrative of German identity, as Assmann and Frevert have shown (1999).

This brings us to the third issue at stake, namely questions of memory and remembrance. The question of German responsibility that had been discussed fervently during the historians' debate (*Historikerstreit*) in the late 1980s (see Peter) was taken up again in 1998 in the Walser-Bubis debate. In his acceptance speech for the Peace Prize of the German Booksellers Association (*Friedenspreis des deutschen Buchhandels*), Walser declared that he was tired of seeing the Holocaust as the one and only evaluative standard in German politics and culture. In reflecting on the ways in which the Holocaust was remembered in Germany, he rejected the role of moral leader commonly associated with intellectuals as empty, pompous, and comical ("leer, pompös, komisch," 1998, 13). Chastising the media for their constant representation of our shame ("Dauerpräsentation unserer Schande"), Walser accused them of instrumentalizing the obligation to keep the past alive. He suggested that it should be left to the individual to deal with the memory of the Holocaust since conscience could not be delegated willfully to certain causes. His insistence on the right to remember in his own personal way led him to call the planned Holocaust memorial in Berlin – completed in 2005 after a design by Peter Eisenman – a failure that would turn the center of the capital into a nightmare made of concrete monumentalizing Germany's disgrace (Walser 20).

Walser's speech caused a major indignation that led to a heated discussion in the media throughout the fall of 1998. His main antagonist was Ignatz Bubis, at the time president of the Central Committee of Jews in Germany who died shortly afterward in 1999. Bubis, politicians, and intellectuals alike were appalled by the statements Walser had made in his speech, especially because as a writer, his language and utterances were necessarily under closer scrutiny than those of a regular person. Bubis accused Walser of being an "intellectual arsonist" who provided the political right with arguments that might further facilitate a subliminal anti-Semitism and intellectual chauvinism in united Germany (47). Similarly, Reich-Ranicki passed judgment on Walser on account of his vague, misleading language, which had failed the public (41). After three months of Walser's refusing to relent despite being criticized from all sides,[7] Frank Schirrmacher managed to bring the two adversaries together on December 12, 1998 for an open discussion, which was documented two days later in the FAZ. Bubis took back his accusation of "intellectual arsonist," but still scolded Walser for having opened a door for those who so far did not dare to voice publicly their agreement that the past should be forgotten. Walser, on the other hand, insisted that this discussion was overdue. Despite a seemingly conciliatory ending, the only agreement to which the two men came was that an appropriate language for coming to terms with the past had yet to be found.

If one takes seriously Walser's claim of intending to voice his opinion with poetic means as a private citizen, without being aware of the political implications of doing so in a major public speech, one must accuse him of political naïveté and criticize that he did not take seriously, or apparently even recognize, his responsibility as a public intellectual. Instead, he aligned himself with the stabilizing discourse of normalization that according to Edward Said is ill-advised for any critical intellectual.[8] Walser obviously underestimated the symbolism of public memorials because he mistook memory – in the sense of bearing in mind historical time (*memento*) – with mere recollection. Aleida Assmann differentiated the two in the terms memory ("Gedächtnis") and remembrance ("Erinnerung," 1999). Bubis, on the other hand, understood the speech as an attempt to revoke a public memory that according to Walser had

---

7 The debate is documented in Schirrmacher 1999.
8 "[Intellectuals] are either against the prevailing norms or, in some basically accommodating way, they exist to provide 'order and continuity in public life.' My opinion is that only the first of these two possibilities is truly the modern intellectual's role [...] precisely because the dominant norms are today so intimately connected to (because commanded at the top by) the nation, which is always triumphalist, always in a position of authority, always exacting loyalty and subservience rather than intellectual investigation and re-examination [...]." Said 36–37.

never been convincing in the first place. Yet maintaining the memory of the Shoah continues to be the determinant prerequisite for Jewish life in Germany because the global Jewish community must be able to rely on the country's willingness to acknowledge and accept responsibility. Atonement is only possible when based on a collective acknowledgment and public remembrance, as the debate about the Memorial for the Murdered Jews of Europe showed (see Knischweski and Spittler). Renouncing this fact more than fifty years after the Holocaust, like Walser did, would indeed have represented a paradigmatic shift in German-Jewish relations.

Wolf's, Grass's and Walser's self-understanding is indebted to the idea of a traditional, "universal intellectual" who feels able and required to take a position towards contemporary problems and voices an opinion without letting himself be co-opted by the public (Foucault 1980, 126). This identity necessarily includes an individual positioning vis-à-vis the nation. It has its roots in the experience of World War Two and the consolidation of the two German states in the 1950s when writers became "a kind of national superego, chastising and seeking to punish the nation for its crimes" (Brockmann 1999, 12). Come of age in this tradition led older authors like Wolf, Grass, and Walser to accept the intellectual responsibility a united Germany requires, including the attempt to reestablish a shared cultural identity. As we have seen, such constructions are closely linked to the concept of coming to terms with the past, which was valid on both sides of the Wall and the respective literatures: in the GDR antifascism provided one of the founding myths of the state, in the FRG the Holocaust became a dominant theme, at least after 1968.

What further links the debates about Wolf, Grass and Walser are issues of cultural hegemony in united Germany. Ulrich Greiner, literary critic for *Die Zeit* famously declared in 1990: "Who determines what was also determines what will be." Talking about the past – be it the personal history and morals of a writer, the literary interpretation of the concept of a German nation or the coming to terms with the past – defines it at the same time as it shapes the future. This power play concerned not only the role of intellectuals in a unified Germany, but also the future of German literature.

## "... ist alles so schön bunt hier:" Debates on Contemporary Realism

The conspicuous absence of younger authors and critics from the debates sketched above points to the continuing dominance of an older generation in the public sphere. Yet the silence of younger authors is not only due to the generational aspects already mentioned, but also to paradigmatic changes in the role and function assigned to intellectuals and writers in the public sphere that have to do with globalizing factors and commodification. In a world characterized by highly differentiated media spheres, the former role of the intellectual as moral opinion leader is challenged by a constant amplification of texts, images, and statements that are a priori suspect of being plagiarized. For any intellectual, public appearances as well as colleagues and their opinions become increasingly important, leading to "the age of the critics, debates about debates, the increasing self-referentiality of discourses" (49), as Thomas Macho points out. Younger authors, most of whom also work journalistically and often have been socialized in different media careers, are all too aware of these changes and have learned to use them to their advantage. Many accept that literature is but one medium among many that no longer holds a special cachet or privileged rank. Consequently, younger authors seldom believe that they have an intellectual monopoly or that their work entails the moral duty to assume a leading societal role. In fact, most authors explicitly reject the role of spokesperson, not least because they were socialized with and have come to dislike the "Grass-Walser-Handke-dominance" (Maxim Biller) that the West German media still support.

For Moritz Baßler and others, the literature of the cultural landscape up to the 1980s was shaped primarily by shame, coming-to-terms, attempts at problematization, and ethical statements:

> A sophisticated literature did not exhibit its assertions so that it was decipherable for everyone; it was complex, required study and rewarded with an unveiling of its meaning. The reader was a hunter of hidden implications.[9]

Debates of the 1990s among younger authors challenged the widely held belief – embodied in the so-called *Suhrkamp* culture – that German-language literature was difficult to read, hermetic, and boring. Contesting this notion and disproving it, not least through the texts of new German pop literature, significantly raised awareness about contemporary literature in the public sphere and enabled the publication of a tremendous number of texts by younger first-time authors. The economic success that followed promoted the translation and export of literary products, giving German-language literature a raised profile in a globalized literary marketplace. Thus the debates helped to

---

**9** "Die bessere Literatur trug ihre Aussagen natürlich nicht so vor sich her, daß sie für alle sofort lesbar gewesen wären; sie war schwierig, erforderte schwierige Lektüren und belohnte diese mit der Preisgabe ihres Sinns. Der Leser war ein Jäger der verborgenen Bedeutungen." Baßler 14.

validate the importance of literature, even in a differentiated media landscape. Furthermore, they showed that the discussion about literary issues continues to be a vital component of a country that defines itself through its cultural production, especially in the formative years following unification.

The discourse in question also added new perspectives to the skepticism of the culture industry that the Frankfurt School had analyzed and the generation of 1968 had supported. While literature concerned with the noble project of critical enlightenment had dominated German literature, the debates of the 1990s directed attention for the first time to a new multiplicity of voices, not least to non-native, transnational writers of German-language literature who, while previously rather marginalized, have been illustrating the true cultural diversity of the unified Germany (see Hielscher).

I argue that the discussion about realism encouraged prose that narrated the workaday world in a realistic fashion and thematized the changes brought about by unification and the ensuing normalization of Germany, as well as the effect that globalization has had on identity constructions. This is most visible in the shift towards lifestyle themes and an aesthetic of consumption that primarily comes to the fore in new German pop literature. It linked texts to trends and developments that also exist in other national contexts, thereby blurring the demarcations of national literatures and making German-language literature more international and global.

The following readings show the complex interconnectedness between literature and literary criticism that has always shaped Germany's cultural landscape. Yet with the rise of the Internet, blogs, and wikis, the significance of the *Feuilleton* as a forum of public debate and agenda setter has diminished. The debates that constitute the *Realismusstreit* in the latter years of the 1990s are thus also attempts by literary critics to regain interpretational power. Nevertheless, the connection between literature and its criticism needs to be closely scrutinized in order to appreciate the development of contemporary literature and recent literary trends. To this end, the next part of the chapter offers the reader an overview of some of the debates that constitute the *Realismusstreit*, and places the discussions in their historical context. My reading clearly demonstrates how different these issues are from the concerns of older authors. I focus on Maxim Biller and Matthias Politycki, two of the most outspoken authors who comment eloquently and fervently on the state of contemporary literature in numerous essays.[10] While their positions differ in the details, both are nevertheless representatives of the position that a writer's

---

**10** Other contributions to the debate are documented in Döring (1995) and Köhler and Moritz (1998).

authenticity is linked to his or her moral authority. They emphasize the necessity to revive contemporary prose by establishing guidelines, even aesthetic programs for writing entertaining, realistic prose. They direct their recommendations at their own generation of German authors whose sense of belonging they want to strengthen, in order to break the dominance of an older generation of intellectuals.

The last part of the chapter zooms in on the micro level of two specific prose texts and illustrates some of the aesthetic changes that mirror the debates. Ingo Schulze and Elke Naters serve as examples for the range of writers that emerged in the late 1990s and added new narrative and aesthetic forms to contemporary literature. While Schulze's novel *Simple Storys* (1998) demonstrates the significance of realistic writing for the evaluation of the aftermath of unification, Naters's novels *Königinnen* (1998) and *Lügen* (1999) show the turn towards lifestyle themes and an aesthetic of consumption that became prevalent in the late 1990s.

Frank Schirrmacher was the first to lament the desolate state of literature in 1989. One month before the Wall came down, Schirrmacher declared young German authors to be untalented. Far away from the big cities that were once home to literary modernity, they have withdrawn into the desert of their own sensibilities. They only narrate what they know best: themselves, or, in other words, the inability to narrate, and they upgrade their tales with an exuberant rhetoric that is supposed to secure intellectually what has failed artistically. The prose of these newcomers who, to Schirrmacher's dismay, are subsidized heavily by grants and literary prizes is, according to him, indistinguishable and almost automated: "'It' writes, and it always writes the same way."[11] Schirrmacher's wholesale condemnation of literature was not remarkable because of its accuracy – many critics opposed his appraisal passionately – but because it reiterated a common feeling that dominated discussions in the early 1990s. German literature was seen as atrophied, boring, and non-contemporary; and its critics especially bemoaned its incapacity to depict the experience of metropolitan living in a global city. The call for a postwar Berlin novel that could rival Alfred Döblin's *Berlin Alexanderplatz* (1929) was, of course, a direct reaction to the fall of the Wall and the aforementioned attempt to establish a new national literature that could aid in making the two Germanys grow together as one and overcoming the oft-cited "Mauer im Kopf," the psychological wall between Easterners and Westerners.

Schirrmacher's contribution is only the prelude to the larger discourse on realism, in which one can differentiate two different factions. On the one hand,

---

11 "'Es' schreibt, und es schreibt immer gleich." In Köhler and Moritz 16.

there are the representatives of a largely conservative, or, to use a more euphemistic term, "idealistic" cultural criticism, such as Schirrmacher, Ulrich Greiner or Karl Heinz Bohrer. Their referential framework is literary modernism; the texts they prefer are hermetic, self-reflective, and weighty; and a text's worth increases exponentially with the hermeneutic difficulties the reader might experience, as Hielscher put it in 1996 (Köhler and Moritz, 158–159). In the value system of these critics, literature has *a priori* a higher significance than other media because it is not transient – like a television broadcast – but of a timeless and hence "eternal" quality. Consequently, this faction hardly acknowledges the fact that the old medium has to compete with other entertainment offerings in an increasingly complex and differentiated public sphere. Undoubtedly, this attitude is rooted in an elitism governed by a certain haughtiness, which equates especially the electronic media with intellectual feeble-mindedness (Sprang 59–60).

Critics such as Jochen Hörisch, Uwe Wittstock, and Martin Hielscher, on the other hand, argue that a German *Sonderweg*, a special path since 1945 rooted in an obsession with politics and morality prevented the adoption of postmodernist impulses originating in the United States. They further claim that the failure of postmodernism to take root in Germany in the 1980s has left the country with an atrophied, unexciting and non-contemporary literature. Although they echo in this regard the evaluation of more conservative voices, these critics are much more realistic when it comes to contemporary literature. While they acknowledge that it has become marginalized in the public sphere, they seek to stress its specific qualities, which will allow it to compete with other, "sexier" media. Their common belief is that contemporary prose will entertain its reader just as much as visual culture if it possesses multiplicity and playfulness; realism, entertainment ("Unterhaltsamkeit") and a new readability ("Neue Lesbarkeit") are the qualities that literary texts should possess to spellbind their audience, as Wittstock formulates it. On the premise that literature is entertaining and readable, it will satisfy the intellect as well as the imagination of its readers, just like postmodern American literature does. If successful, this new program would allow a change of literary paradigms und assert postmodern aesthetics in Germany.

It is important to note that many of the contributors who put forth these arguments are professional editors who know the literary marketplace and are used to making decisions that are not only based on aesthetic but also on economic considerations.[12] Consequently, other critics accused Hielscher and

---

12 At the time, Martin Hielscher was editor for Kiepenheuer & Witsch and Uwe Wittstock was editor for Fischer Verlage.

Wittstock on the grounds that their pleas to render contemporary literature more attractive were little more than thinly veiled attempts to make it more streamlined and thus marketable (for instance, Vormweg).

Maxim Biller, born in 1960 in Prague into a family of Czech-Russian Jews, immigrated with his family at the age of ten to Munich where he lived until his move to Berlin in 2001. He has published a number of short story and prose collections, among them *Wenn ich einmal reich und tot bin* (1990), *Harlem Holocaust* (1998) and *Deutschbuch* (2001).[13] He was the first writer to proclaim and analyze the supposed deficiencies of contemporary literature in depth. In agreement with Schirrmacher, he argued in 1991 in a manifesto against an academic literature that mainly narrates how narration has become impossible. Biller complained that life, reality, and the will to communicate had been driven out of German literature by a false understanding of the avant-garde. The resulting literary canon is, as Biller put it, about as sensuous as a city map of Kiel (1991, 64). The dismayed reader reacts to this development by turning to television, cinema, and magazines. To counter this development, Biller pleaded that the contemporary author should take his or her material from reality and employ journalistic techniques to write about the existential questions, emulating writers like Joseph Roth, Erich Kästner or Friedrich Torberg. These questions must be determined by the here and now, yet always tied to a historical perspective, more specifically the German past. As a Jewish refugee from Prague, much of whose family suffered and perished in the Holocaust, Biller had, in his own words, the luck that provided him with material ("stoffspendendes Glück") to find the determining factors for his writing in his own biography, stylizing himself into a paradigm of excellence that was supposed to lend him a special position within the literary landscape (Schlaffer). According to him, German literature is boring because his own generation leads lives that are void of existential conflict and valid experiences (1991, 65). In order to reach their audience, texts need an interesting subject matter as well as substance. If the writer is to take his or her material from reality, then realistic forms of narration naturally become the first choice to guarantee aesthetic success for text and author: Writers should narrate stories written by life and attempt to poeticize the language that we speak today (in Gächter); literature must show "why the world is such a rotten pile of manure and at the same time, the most beautiful thing we can imagine."[14]

---

**13** Biller's reputation in Germany's literary landscape is that of an *enfant terrible*, see Stein. His novel *Ezra* (2003) caused a judicial scandal because his former partner sued him for violating her personal rights. All copies of the book were subsequently confiscated and remain banned from being sold.

**14** "… warum die Welt so ein verrotteter Misthaufen ist und zugleich das Schönste, Herrlichste, was wir uns vorstellen können." Biller 1991, 70.

Biller also set out to establish a new set of morals in German literature, which he stressed most fervently in his speech at a writers' convention in Tutzing in the year 2000. In his opening lecture, "A Cowardly Country, A Feeble Literature: On the Difficulties Of Telling the Truth" ("Feige das Land, schlapp die Literatur: Über die Schwierigkeiten beim Sagen der Wahrheit"), Biller, taking an ironic bow to Peter Handke, staged a fifty-minute assault on the audience whose main accusation was the unhistorical aestheticism of contemporary German literature. Under the long reign of Helmut Kohl, the Germans have turned into a people of egotistical, neurotic cowards who are driven exclusively by their wish to "feel good." According to Biller, this political culture of cowardice has direct repercussions on the cultural sphere. The general lack in moral standards produces indifferent intellectuals and bad books. Texts that move the reader and change his or her perception of the world do not exist; German literature is "Schlappschwanzliteratur," a feeble, flaccid literature characterized by "the incapacity to dream of morals, to want, to hate, to love."[15] This inability of German authors to write within a framework of moral values is, according to Biller, not only an ethical but also an aesthetic problem, because moral imagination, which has to go hand in hand with narrating reality as violently as it presents itself, is the premise of every great author; is it his or her ability for poetry.

Biller's appeal for a biographically motivated realism, intellectually framed by a set of morals whose referential system is the German past, intersect in many points with the arguments of his colleague Matthias Politycki who was born in 1955 in Karlsruhe and studied German philology in Munich, where he also received his doctorate.[16] Politicky presented his ideas in numerous essays over the course of the 1990s, which were published in *Die Farbe der Vokale. Von der Literatur, den 78ern und dem Gequake satter Frösche* (1998, The Color of Vowels: Of Literature, The Generation of 78 and the Calling of Satiated Frogs). In this collection Politycki, just like Biller, sought to answer the core question at the heart of the debate: To what degree should literature be referential of the world and – equally important – how can it interest the reader in its tales?

In response to these questions, Politycki drafted a program for his colleagues of the "generation of 78." They were born between 1955 and 1965 and

---

**15** "Schlappschwanzliteratur … charakterisiert von der Unfähigkeit, von Moral zu träumen, zu wollen, zu hassen, zu lieben." Biller 2000, 47.
**16** Matthias Politicky has published widely from poetry to prose, including the novels *Weiberroman* (1997) and the sequel *Ein Mann von vierzig Jahren* (2000).

thus hold an in-between position between the 68ers and the *Generation Golf*.[17] They do not fit the generational criteria developed by the sociology of the twentieth century since, in the words of sociologist Karl Mannheim, they did not experience a formative event of great significance ("ein generationsstiftendes Großereignis," see Erhart). To be sure, one could argue that such an experience would have been growing up and coming to terms with the terrorism of the Red Army Faction in the 1970s and 1980s. This, however, played absolutely no role in any of the discussions. Instead Politicky characterized his cohort as an individualistic group who lack a shared political perspective or conviction (1996, 60).

According to Politycki, the assertion of postmodern aesthetics in German literature was hindered historically by the major influence of German critics and academics for whom the aesthetic merit of a text was directly proportional to its degree of "Verquastheit," i.e. the difficulty to understand or interpret it. Politycki calls passionately on German authors to fight this attitude. First, they need to learn how to write well, which requires them to adopt a more professional attitude and the self-understanding that they provide a service to their readers. Second, writers should strive to lend their texts polyvalence, which would allow the reader to approach prose in a consumerist fashion for mere entertainment, as well as enjoy its constructedness and complexity for the more ambitious reader. In summary, contemporary authors should produce texts that comply with the concept of *Neue Lesbarkeit*, a new readability that is fun and entertaining for the reader, yet nevertheless challenges him or her to crack the aesthetic codes of the text ("Kalbfleisch mit Reis," 1997).

Although Politycki claims that his program is completely new, he bases his suggestions on a rather traditional understanding. He advocates that following a given concept of production aesthetics will be the safe road to success and to a bestseller. Although he is a trained *Germanist* himself, it does not seem to occur to him that the principle of literature produced with a didactic goal in mind runs counter to the very idea of postmodern aesthetics in all its fragmentation and multiplicity. Instead he goes so far as to suggest that a literary interest group modeled after the *Gruppe 47* could monitor the application of the program (in Krause).

It is no coincidence that the peak of Politycki's activism intersected with the rise and economic success of authors belonging to new German pop litera-

---

17 Politicky bases his characterization on *Spiegel* copy editor Reinhard Mohr's book *Zaungäste. Die Generation, die nach der Revolte kam* (1992). Mohr criticizes their inability to develop generational criteria that would allow a clear demarcation to the generation of 1968. Sociologist Heinz Bude subsequently renamed this cohort and analyzed it in his book *Generation Berlin* (2001).

ture and the so-called *Fräuleinwunder*. After 1995 – more specifically, with the likes of Christian Kracht's *Faserland* (1995) and Judith Hermann's *Sommerhaus, später* (1998) – the public interest centered on unknown young authors who were quickly labeled by critics as pop and subsequently hailed for the thematic and aesthetic innovations they brought to contemporary literature, as I noted in the first chapter. Politycki watches this development with skepticism because these authors do not care about anything anymore, "least of at all about the question what differentiates a piece of paper full of scribbles from a literary text."[18] According to him, pop literature does nothing more than to satisfy the reader's desire for triviality; its lack of a pedagogical impetus leads to what he calls "BigMäc literature" (8) that holds as little surprise and suspense as a cardboard box prepared by McDonalds.

At first glance, Politycki's strong disapproval – which Biller does not share – is rather surprising since many of the young authors write entertaining, realistic prose that fulfills most all of the former's demands. Yet his uneasiness has its underlying reason in their refusal to fill the shoes of the politically and morally engaged German intellectual of the postwar tradition. This became apparent in many conversations I have had with different writers since 1995. Authors as diverse as Thomas Meinecke, Felicitas Hoppe or Marcel Beyer instead seek to deconstruct the myth of the author who has no other choice but to be an artist, whose writing stems from an inner drive and a true calling. As Meinecke puts it somewhat provocatively, "I don't have to write to keep myself from going crazy" (in Lenz and Pütz, 150). For Politycki and Biller, on the other hand, a good text is inextricably linked to the persona of its author. He or she has to bring the sum of his or her own life to the artistic product to lend it passion and credibility; following in effect the German tradition of the poetic genius, which Politycki alludes to when he says that literature originates from an existential need. It is only logical then that he, in accord with Biller, called for moral integrity, "an author must be more than the sum of his books, he needs a standpoint, a set of moral values … and a politically conscious attitude towards the world: in short, he needs all the things that the representatives of the entertainment culture lack."[19]

Both Politycki and Biller positioned their essays strategically in the *Feuilleton* sections of the leading German newspapers, which brought the attention

---

**18** "… am allerwenigsten um die Frage, was ein vollgeschwalltes Stück Papier von einem literarischen Text unterscheidet." "Kalbfleisch mit Reis," 1997, 6.
**19** "Ein Autor muss mehr sein als die Summe seiner Bücher, er muss einen Standpunkt haben, eine Moral … und eine politisch reflektierte Stellung zur Welt: eben all das, was den Vertretern der Spaßkultur notorisch abgeht." 2001.

of a broader public to their controversial statements. Interestingly and not coincidentally, they launched their articles at the same time that their own new literary texts appeared. This is obvious with Politycki's *Weiberroman* (1997), as well as with Biller's novel *Die Tochter* (2000), which appeared parallel to his provocative speech in Tutzing. Both use their somewhat ambiguous roles as writers and journalists to perpetuate and distribute their own intellectual products, be it essays or prose texts. Thus they assist and promote the intertwining and confusion of various cultural fields, which Pierre Bourdieu (1991) and Edward Said (1996) have identified as problematic in their assessment of the intellectual in his or her societal functions. However, to position oneself in the public sphere, to set a controversial agenda, to talk and be talked about is an important characteristic of a younger generation of intellectual actors in the 1990s. It is the logical result of the differentiation of the public sphere and the economic pressures of a globalized literary marketplace, and both Biller and Politycki are very accomplished in dealing with those aspects, adding another example to the paradigmatic changes of authorship that chapter one analyzed. As the latter put it in an interview: "... you have to see yourself as a market commodity – only then will you be successful in the age of advertisement."[20]

## *Authentische Alltäglichkeit:* Turning Towards a Literature of the Authentic Everyday

"Ist das alles, was das Leben fragt/Kommst du mit in den Alltag?"[21]
Blumfeld, *Old Nobody* (1999)

Despite Politycki's bashing of some of his younger colleagues, his and Biller's ideas clearly represent an attempt to put a stop to the lamentations about the mediocrity of German prose and to redirect the reader's attention back to the countless interesting texts that appeared in the 1990s. Writers like Ingo Schulze, Daniel Kehlmann, Karen Duve, Tanja Dückers, Marcel Beyer, Julia Franck, and Inka Parei, to name just a few, present realistic narratives about everyday life with well-structured plots; all of which makes them interesting for readers, critics, and scholars alike. The multitudes of newly published texts by young German authors, as well as their unprecedented critical and economic success at home and abroad, speak for a sea change during the late 1990s into the new millennium.

---

**20** "... man muß sich als Markenartikel verstehen – erst dann wird man im Zeitalter der Werbung Erfolg haben." In Agnes Müller, 23.
**21** "Is this all that life asks of you – will you follow me into the workaday world?"

The theme of realistic writing runs as a thread through the second set of literary debates illustrated. Yet to speak of a renaissance of narration ("Wiederkehr des Erzählens") in the 1990s, as many critics did, is also a tactical maneuver of literary criticism to draw the attention of a large audience. To declare narrative literature dead one year justifies the attempt to revive it fervently a few years later, and in times of the ongoing newspaper crisis, finding controversial topics for the culture section is all the more important. From the perspective of literary history, the assertion of a complete break with the tradition of realistic writing is unsupportable. Even at the peak of experimental prose in the 1970s authors narrated realistically like Günther Wallraff [*Industriereportagen*, 1970] or in the vein of New Subjectivity like Karin Struck [*Klassenliebe*, 1973]. In the 1980s the presence of an entertaining, realistically narrated and – highly successful – prose became ever more prevalent. Authors like Patrick Süskind [*Das Parfum*, 1985], Christoph Ransmeyer [*Die letzte Welt*, 1988] or Robert Schneider [*Schlafes Bruder*, 1992] playfully employed and developed the modernist tradition, as Nikolaus Förster has shown in his comprehensive study *Die Wiederkehr des Erzählens* (1999). Those who bemoaned the absence of realistic writing in the 1980s and celebrate its resurgence in the mid 1990s exposed their unwillingness to take note of the many realistically narrated texts. More importantly, they also revealed a limited understanding of what realism can imply.

Given the long German tradition of realistic writing, which of course harks back to the literary periods of Naturalism and Realism, it seems fruitful not to speak here of a "new realism," but to characterize the changes around the millennium instead as "authentische Alltäglichkeit," a turn towards the realistic mimesis of workaday life. In East and West Germany, "authenticity" becomes the new, positively coded criterion to describe and measure how prose is more referential of the surrounding world. East German authors of a younger generation continue to be preoccupied primarily with life in the GDR and the ramifications of unification as Thomas Brussig's *Helden wie wir* (1995), Jakob Hein's *Mein erstes T-shirt* (2001), and Antje Rávic Strubel's *Tupolew 134* (2004) illustrate. In the West, prose with a focus on the (Nazi) past continues to play an important role as well, as in Marcel Beyer's *Flughunde* (1995). Yet if we recall the debates about Wolf, Grass, and Walser, a significant change in focus become obvious. This shift is signified in the renderings of popular culture (music, concerts, band stories), adolescence (generational conflicts, relationships, first love), subcultures, the distancing from the bourgeois norm towards Dandyism and a bohemian life style, as well as mobility, glamour, drugs, sexual experiences, and excess, as is evident in Rainald Goetz's *Rave* (1998), Alexa Hennig von Lange's *Relax* (1997) or Benjamin von Stuckrad-Barre's *Soloalbum*

(1998). The framework of realistic writing not only illuminates the themes summarized here, but also the narrative strategies.

The prose texts of Ingo Schulze from the East and Elke Naters from the West can illustrate these developments. Neither started writing until after unification and both profited from the debates analyzed in this chapter and experienced remarkable success in their wake. With his second book *Simple Storys* Schulze became a veritable shooting star of the German literary scene at the Leipzig Book Fair in 1998 (see Böttiger 168) and is now doubtlessly one of the most important and well-known contemporary writers of a younger generation, both in German-speaking countries and internationally. To date, *Simple Storys* was translated into no fewer than twenty-three languages, among them Arabic, Korean, and Mandarin Chinese, thus globalizing the text.[22] Elke Naters never reached Schulze's fame but emerged in the late 1990s as a representative of both the *Fräuleinwunder* and the trend of new German pop literature.

Their relatively high profile notwithstanding, the decision to analyze their prose is a conceptual one. My argument is that Schulze and Naters both are representatives of a glocalized literature that refracts the global in the local. The term glocalization, coined originally by sociologist Roland Robertson in 1994, implies that the processes of globalization promote concepts such as home, community, and locality in the first place. The local thus is not opposed to the global, but an aspect of it. Schulze's and Naters's respective novels are inflected with aesthetic choices, both formal and thematic, that have links to global forms of story telling, as the following textual analyses will show. Yet at the same time their texts are firmly located within the Berlin Republic and keep the horizon of the German past – in Schulze's case the memory of the GDR – alive, thus giving a local twist through the inscription of signifiers of Germanness, as Andrew Plowman has argued (49), albeit in the context of other texts. In order to flesh out this thesis, the guiding question of the following analyses is how one East German and one West German author employ realistic forms of narration and what role the workaday world and authenticity play in their prose.

## Ingo Schulze's *Simple Storys* (1998)

Ingo Schulze was born in 1962 in Dresden, where he also grew up. After the mandatory military service in the NVA (national people's army), he studied

---

22 According to information from Berlin Verlag's licensing department via e-mail, August 2010.

classical philology and German philology in Jena, and then worked in the theater as a dramaturg. In 1988 Schulze founded and managed a newspaper in Altenburg (Thuringia), an experience that made its way into at least two of his novels.[23] His second, breakthrough novel *Simple Storys* (1998) marks a turning point in literature of the 1990s. According to many critics, it was the first novel of reunification that truly deserved the name. More importantly and somewhat paradoxically, it cleared the way for a reinvigoration of the short story, which had been less favored throughout the 1980s.

*Simple Storys* is set in Altenburg and spans the post-unification years from 1990 to 1997. It is structured by twenty-nine episodes, which are numbered as chapters. Each has its own title, with an added *argumentum*:

> Chapter 5 – Migratory Birds: Lydia tells about Dr. Barbara Holitzschek, who claims that she's run over a badger. A long conversation about animals. The scene of the accident. A puzzling ending with no badger.[24]

According to the rules of classical poetics, an *argumentum* is supposed to summarize and illuminate the plot, thereby orienting the reader (Rädle). In Schulze's text, however, the structural element reveals very little about the true constellation of the protagonists and the narrative, which effectively counteracts its function. Dr. Holitzschek, for example, has run over not a badger but the cyclist Andrea Meurer, wife and mother of other characters; and the non-existent badger is by no means the central element, as the argumentum suggests. In *Simple Storys* the *argumentum* thus not only works as a means to create suspense; it also mirrors the fragmented understanding that the characters themselves have of their world.

Frequent changes in the narrative perspective shape the text. There is no central character; instead, we find multiple first person or personal narrators. In the first chapter, for example, Renate Meurer tells the story of a package tour she took with her husband Ernst to Italy in February of 1990. On this trip, the couple encounters Dieter Schubert, a former teacher whom Ernst, then a member of the SED and the principal at Schubert's school, had fired during GDR times. The reader, however, does not learn about the circumstances of Schubert's dismissal until page 222. Only then does his bizarre behavior in

---

**23** The experience as manager of a newspaper plays a role in *33 Augenblicke des Glücks* (1995), *Neue Leben* (2005), and in some of the stories in *Handy* (2007).
**24** Quoted after *Simple Stories*, the English edition translated by John E. Woods, viii. "Kapitel 5 – Zugvögel: Lydia erzählt von Dr. Barbara Holitzschek, die behauptet, einen Dachs überfahren zu haben. Ein langes Gespräch über Tiere. Die Unfallstelle. Rätselhaftes Ende ohne Dachs." *Simple Storys*. Inhaltsverzeichnis.

Chapter One start to make sense: apparently rattled by his encounter with Ernst, he had climbed the cathedral in Perugia and hurled insults at Ernst from this lofty height, calling him "the big shot in the green anorak" (9), ("der Bonze im grünen Anorak," 21).

Deliberate omissions are another common component of *Simple Storys*. Frequent allusions in the beginning of the text condense into hypotheses later, often at a point when other speakers unwillingly explain them. The reader who appreciates all chapters separately will find that the particular segments in Schulze's text do indeed work as short stories, or even as novellas: most entail an unprecedented event ("eine unerhörte Begebenheit"), as Goethe called it, that knocks an individual off his or her track. Nevertheless, the single stories only truly make sense in their entirety, when the fragments begin to form a bigger mosaic, as in the above example of Dieter insulting Ernst.

The total number of protagonists amounts to between thirty and forty, depending on whom one considers central. This easily overtaxes the reader. Some, like *Zeit* critic Ulrich Greiner, suggested that an index would have made it easier to keep track of all the characters and their interdependencies (1998). Yet his suggestion misapprehends the governing idea behind Schulze's text. His characters are representative of the distinct time and culture of the years from 1990 to 1997, and his complex social network and its realistic depictions are not an end in themselves but point to Schulze's project, which is to construct an "archive of the present moment," as Moritz Baßler has called it (esp. 82–90).

As the blurb on the inside cover of the novel informs us, the author consciously employs the tradition of the American short story, as written by Ernest Hemingway, Richard Ford or Raymond Carver. Referring back to the poetics of Alfred Döblin, Schulze explains in his poetological writings how for him each book requires a certain literary style, which needs to emanate from the fabric of the respective text (2000; see also Biendarra and Wilke 1999). In *Simple Storys* however, Schulze uses not so much the narrative techniques of Carver as the filmic elements of their adaptation by American director Robert Altman. Whereas Altman's film *Short Cuts* (1993) presents the social network of life among different social classes in the American metropolis Los Angeles, Schulze transposes the movie's principle into literature in order to create a realistic tableau of the small town Altenburg in the historic post-*Wende* depression of the 1990s. He thereby globalizes the phenomenon of being on the periphery of a wealthy capitalist society.

In Altman's film the viewer easily recognizes the characters because of their physiognomy, their neighborhood or their jobs. What works automatically in film through a visual identification process takes hermeneutical effort and concentration on the reader's part in the complex literary universe of *Simple Storys*. Schulze holds the multitude of life stories together and organizes the threads of competing narratives by narrating visually, which allows the reader to transform language into ideas and images immediately (Roth). It works so well that German ethnographers at the University of Cologne used Schulze's network for a so-called network analysis. They were able to prove their hypothesis that certain realistic novels lend themselves to this type of investigation because they pose similar tasks as the interpretation of specific ethnographic case studies. Interestingly, the ethnographers concluded from their network analysis that the narrated world in *Simple Storys* was just as realistic as the real one (Schweizer and Schnegg).[25]

Schulze's project of building an archive requires a realism that can record the smallest details. These facets generally encapsulate clues about the bigger picture, i.e. the social realities of freshly united Germany and the conquest of the East through Western consumer goods:

> He squeezes toothpaste from the red Elmex tube onto their toothbrushes, fills a glass with warm water, lays her brush across the top, and begins to brush his teeth. 'Beauty Cosmetic – Pads Naturelle', he reads on the package hanging beside the basin. 'Double pads of pure cotton, soft as a blossom, easy on the skin, multilayered, never shred.' (132)[26]

Just like the deliberate misspelling of the English title *Simple Storys* keeps (East) German idosyncracies present and reveals the continuing implementation of English (and "Denglish") into the German language, the narration of realistic details in this scene comments on the rapid influx of western goods and the puzzlement of East Germans about some of them in the early period of unification. Furthermore, we can read it an ironic commentary on the globalizing western influence. The presumably "simple" stories narrated here illustrate that nothing the characters experience is actually easy. Although they now have free access to consumer goods and the ability to travel, which were the two privileges most citizens of the GDR sorely missed before 1989, their realities are continuously reshaped by strange experiences and new challenges. Globalization is revealing the chasm of interpersonal relationships for the inhabitants of Altenburg.

---

**25** The file is no longer available online. See the reproduction in Baßler 86–87.

**26** "Auf beide Zahnbürsten drückt er Pasta aus der roten Elmex-Tube, füllt ein Glas mit Wasser, legt ihre Bürste darüber und beginnt, sich die Zähne zu putzen. 'Beauty Cosmetic – Pads Naturelle', liest er dabei auf der Packung, die neben dem Becken hängt. 'Doppelkissen aus hautfreundlicher, blütenzarter reiner Baumwolle, mehrlagig, flusenfrei.'" *Simple Storys* 148.

Schulze's narrative technique depicts the outer and inner states of his characters and their environment visually and realistically without psychologizing them. The narration of certain types illustrates the winners and losers of unification: former Stasi officials who have managed to retain their secure positions, Western entrepreneurs who take advantage of the Eastern unfamiliarity with capitalism, women who lose their jobs and struggle to come to terms with the ensuing loss of self-worth, and dark-skinned foreigners who are chased through the streets of Altenburg by skinheads. The author does not need to denounce the injustices of unification openly. The distinctive "Schulzerealismus" (Jürgen Roth) reveals them subtly through language, as in the following example where a word of the GDR vocabulary becomes more and more foreign to the Easterners the further the Westernization of the East progresses:

> "Dispatcher," Raffael says. "Dispatcher, dispatcher," he repeats, "dispatcher, dispatcher." He says it faster and faster, until the syllables are disconnected and sound as strange and meaningless to him as they do to most people when he answers "dispatcher" to the question of what he used to do ... He had once believed "dispatcher" was one of the few job designations used worldwide. At least West Germans ought to understand it. The word was English, after all. "Dispatcherdispatcher." (82)[27]

Schulze's *Simple Storys* are representative of a form of realistic narration that creates an archive of the present moment. The novel is but one of the many literary examples of the late 1990s that illustrate the attempt of East German writers to come to terms with the aftermath of unification. Whereas authors such as Thomas Brussig in *Sonnenallee* (1999), Jana Hensel in *Zonenkinder* (2002) or Claudia Rusch in *Meine freie deutsche Jugend* (2003) present more ideological constructions of Easternness, Schulze's approach is based on a visceral understanding of the former GDR. In so doing, *Simple Storys* cuts across many oppositions, such as modern/postmodern, filmic/literary, global/local, and abstract form/realistic description, to name just a few. The novel also covers many different layers of the past – events in the GDR, the *Wende* and its immediate aftermath, as well as post-unification, and keeps them present through subtle allusions and deliberate omissions. Yet it avoids more traditional modes of coming to terms with the past ("Vergangenheitsbewälti-

---

27 «Dispatcher», sagt Raffael. «Dispatcher, Dispatcher», wiederholt er, «Dispatcher, Dispatcher.» Immer schneller spricht er, damit sich die Silben voneinander lösen, bis sie auch für ihn fremd und sinnlos klingen, wie für die meisten, denen Raffael auf die Frage nach seinem früheren Beruf mit «Dispatcher» antwortet. ... Früher hatte er geglaubt, «Dispatcher» sei eine der wenigen Berufsbezeichnungen, die auf der ganzen Welt gebraucht wurden. Zumindest die Westdeutschen mußten es verstehen. Es war doch englisch. «Dispatcherdispatcher.» (98).

gung") that rely on a realistic depiction of the GDR, such as Julia Franck's *Lagerfeuer* (2003, Campfire) or a discussion of the relation between victim/perpetrator in the Third Reich that we encounter in Bernhard Schlink's *Der Vorleser* (1995, *The Reader*). Through his literary utilization of the American tradition in the form of realism, short story, and filmic rendering, Schulze puts the experience of his Altenburg characters into a global context and raises its status by showing points of connection between East Germans and other communities.

## Elke Naters's *Königinnen* (1998) and *Lügen* (1999)

Broadening the arguments made so far, we can now see that the literary controversies of the late 1990s and the discourse on realism in particular played a much bigger role in the critical and economic success of young authors, especially those from the West, than has previously been acknowledged. The discourse supported and initiated the changes in Germany's literary field laid out earlier, that is the shift from the tradition of the project of critical enlightenment, in which literature is functionalized to advance the development of an educated public governed by moral and humanistic values, to a literature more concerned with everyday life and an aesthetic of consumption (which is not to suggest that the latter cannot achieve that for which the former explicitly stands).

The case of Elke Naters, born in 1963 in Munich, supports this assertion. She originally was a seamstress and studied fine arts photography in Berlin before discovering writing as her primary talent. Apart from the novels discussed here, she has published a number of other books, including the text/photo collage *G.L.A.M.* (2001, Glamour), the novels *Mau Mau* (2002, Go Fish) and *Justyna* (2006, Justyna) and, with her husband Sven Lager, *Durst, Hunger, Müde* (2004, Thirsty, Hungry, Tired) and *Was wir von der Liebe verstehen* (2008, What We Understand About Love). Naters is one of the many female authors who have profited directly from the attention that ensued from the literary debates and who owe at least part of their success to the marketing machine that was driving literary trends in the second half of the 1990s. Like Judith Hermann, Julia Franck, Karen Duve, Zoe Jenny, Maike Wetzel, Alexa Hennig von Lange and others, Naters was marketed originally as part of the *Fräuleinwunder* phenomenon, the German variant of the global genre of *Chick Lit*. Her books have been translated into a number of languages, and around the millennium Naters was a frequent presence at literary events where she was introduced to the audience as one of the important voices of young German literature.

An example of the kind of new author we saw in chapter one, her success derives in part from the marketing of her books and the construction of her public persona. First, Naters used to publish with Kiepenheuer & Witsch, which under the editorship of Martin Hielscher and Kerstin Gleba in the 1990s promoted many literary newcomers (such as Christian Kracht and Benjamin von Stuckrad-Barre) and focused on new German pop literature. KiWi thereby capitalized on a line of tradition that it had begun in the 1960s under editor and author Dieter Wellershoff who promoted pop authors such as Rolf Dieter Brinkmann.[28] Naters's prose was thus positioned in a larger network of other successful authors, which steered the reception of her texts in the 1990s. A second reason for Naters's visibility is her commitment to publishing prose online, which was in its exploratory stages in the late 1990s. With her author husband Sven Lager, Naters started the writing platform www.ampool.de whose texts were published in book form by KiWi in 2001. Naters's pioneering activity aided in her labeling as a "pop author" since she positioned herself in the multimedia context so typical of pop literature.

The main reason for Naters's success, however, is the choice of her subjects. Her first two novels *Königinnen* and *Lügen*, published in 1998 and 1999 respectively, are set in 1990s Berlin and assign a much bigger role to the Berlin locale than comparable texts by other authors (such as Judith Hermann in *Sommerhaus, später*, 1998 or Julia Franck in *Bauchlandung*, 2000, see Biendarra 2004). They enabled the rest of the Republic to gain a glimpse of the thriving cultural milieus of the new capital and, in the context of the relocation of the German government to the city in 1998, assisted the literary and cultural construction of the new Berlin Republic. Furthermore, Naters's novels illustrate that literature can never be global per se. It naturally remains inflected with locality since it is published in a national language and often deals with issues that are specific to its local and national setting. Even in the adaptation of global brand names and consumerism, Naters's novels show "the ways in which cultural products are locally consumed, locally read, and transformed in the process,"(Held et al. 373) which leads me to characterize her writing as another example of glocal literature.

In the 1980s, i.e. before the pop trend, the explosion of the Internet in Germany, and the veritable Berlin hype, Naters's first two novels might have appeared in a series such as the now-defunct *Die Frau in der Gesellschaft* (Woman in Society) by Fischer. From 1986, this series published some very successful, though no longer overtly feminist novels, such as Eva Heller's *Beim*

---

**28** A recent anthology edited by Kerstin Gleba and Eckhard Schumacher aids in the construction of this line of tradition at KiWi. See also Smith-Prei.

*nächsten Mann wird alles anders* (1987; *With the Next Man Everything Will Be Different*, 1992) and Hera Lind's best-seller *Das Superweib* (*The Super Broad*, 1994), both of which bear a certain resemblance to Naters's two novels (see Karolle-Berg and Skow). They too are conventionally narrated stories about the workaday world of white female German 30-somethings and their interpersonal relationships. Yet Naters complements the popular desire for *authentische Alltäglichkeit* and *Neue Lesbarkeit* by transforming the experiences of women into sketches that depict everyday life and its details so vividly that they gain an almost photo-realistic quality. It is hence not surprising that the depiction of straightforward experiences and the simplicity of Naters's prose was the point that prompted many critics to rave about her subject matter as well as her style (for example, Krumbholz). Aesthetic shortcomings, such as the erroneous syntax, have been perceived not as stylistic flaws but as indicators of an authentic and unedited writing style that increases the immediacy of her texts.

In *Königinnen*, Naters tells the story of two female characters, Gloria and Marie, both thirty years old, who are best friends and at the same time beloved enemies. Gloria envies Marie's freedom as a single woman, while Marie resents Gloria for having a partner and children. Naters doubles the perspective by splitting the narrative voice between the two protagonists who tell about their rather mundane existence in alternating chapters. The subject matters of their reports are their ongoing problems with the opposite sex, frustrating late night adventures in the bar scene of West Berlin's Schöneberg neighborhood, shopping sprees, and fashion questions. The characters' realizations about their lives that they candidly share with the reader seldom amount to more than truisms, but nevertheless invite instantaneous identification: "The only things always worth spending money on are shoes. Anything else you can get cheaply if you have taste and patience. ... And when you wear good shoes, everything else also looks as if you bought it at Helmut Lang. And not at H&M."[29]

Naters's sentences are short; she loves paratactic constructions. The spontaneous, seemingly unedited language mirrors the brief attention spans of the protagonists and does not overburden the reader's concentration, leading *Der Spiegel* to suggest that her novels read like the magazine *Bunte* at the hairdresser.[30] More importantly, it supports the aesthetic project of a pop novel,

---

**29** "Das einzige, für das es sich immer lohnt, viel Geld auszugeben, sind Schuhe. Alles andere kann man mit Geschmack und Geduld genauso billig erstehen. ... Und wenn man gute Schuhe trägt, dann sieht alles andere auch gleich aus, als wäre es von Helmut Lang. Und nicht von H&M." *Königinnen* 9.
**30** Quoted after the blurb of *Lügen*.

which, as Katharina Rutschky argues, has its predecessor in a novel like Goethe's *Werther*. The goal here is the simulation of immediacy. In *Königinnen*, this is exemplified in aspects such as the colloquialisms of the often-anglicized prose ("Ich nehme eine Dusche", 9; the literal translation of "I am taking a shower" is not idiomatic in German), which anchor the events firmly in the 1990s and in the specific social stratum of Berlin's hipster scene and promote the reader's recognition.

The same holds true for the vigorous consumer fetishism and materialism of the protagonists. In *Königinnen* and *Lügen* respectively, shopping becomes the salvation that allows the women to deal with life's frustrations. When their daily grind weighs too heavily on them, they go on a shopping spree, preferably in Berlin's high-end department store *KaDeWe* (Department Store of the West), the epitome of Western consumerism. Even if they are unable to pay their rent because they have already spent their monthly welfare checks, Marie's platinum credit card affords them the fantasy of leading a glamorous life, which makes them feel like the queens of the novels' title (27). In Naters's world, money can (and does) buy happiness. Shopping is depicted as an activity bestowing a level of satisfaction upon the characters that human interactions and work do not grant. The prominent product fetishism, displayed in the recurring enumeration of name brands, has the sensual, erotic quality that Marie's and Gloria's love relationships decidedly lack (Schmelcher). Consequently, their male life partners remain pale and nebulous. Information about Lorenz, Gloria's partner and father to one of her two children, is restricted to the facts that he works in a bike shop, has a Swedish grandmother, and is a good father. Wolfgang Schäfer, who releases Marie from her ongoing search for Mr. Right, also remains a shadowy character. In both her novels, Naters constructs an exclusively female cosmos, in which men are demoted to mere accessories whose primary function is to take care of the children and shop for groceries.

Despite the fact that Naters's novels appear to create a monument to female friendship, the author does not romanticize it. This sets her texts apart from Matthias Politycki's novels, *Weiberroman* (1997, The Broad's Novel), and the sequel, *Ein Mann von vierzig Jahren* (2000, A Man of Forty), whose basis is the sentimental invocation of male loyalty and buddydom. Instead, Marie and Gloria, as well as the main characters Augusta und Be in *Lügen*, unmask themselves through the egotism, jealousy, and resentment they feel towards each other, providing the conflicts of the respective novels. The amusing glimpses into the complicated dynamics of female relationships furthermore explain the success of Naters's first two novels and debunk clichéd notions of female solidarity.

Naters's ironic style however, at least in *Königinnen*, does not fully succeed in unmasking the women's persistent fixation on the other sex, the importance of physical attractiveness or their mindless enjoyment of consumerism as dictated by social norms. The author transforms certain proverbial female qualities into veritable clichés without showing how they are determined by societal expectations and hence socially constructed. In this regard, she reproduces and validates the conventional postulate of innate gender differences and renders the narrated female cosmos a formulaic world. Even Marie's fantasies seem void of original qualities but are instead reminiscent of the streamlined consumer aesthetic of TV ads, albeit an ironic and thus redeeming reading might also be possible.

> All of a sudden a basket on a string would dangle in front of my window. I would not be able to trust my eyes. I would open the window, and there'd be roses in the basket, red ones, and a bottle of champagne. I'd look up, right into HIS grinning face. On the upper right, he'd have a tooth missing and he'd have been living above me for years without me noticing him.[31]

Although *Königinnen* does not offer a salient commentary on the social reality of women in the late 1990s, the superficiality Naters parades on a thematic and aesthetic level is actually programmatic. By displaying a narrative form of realism that functionalizes both the surface and consumerism as creative principles, the characters' isolation and inability to communicate fully materialize. This in turn promotes the reader's critical reflection on the melancholic and ultimately failed attempts of a young generation to establish meaningful identities and is thus indeed a commentary on life in the Berlin Republic.

At first glance, *Lügen* (1999, Lies) seems to be the mere continuation of *Königinnen*, telling the story of the two girlfriends Augusta and Barbara, also called Be, in Berlin. This time, the plot is narrated entirely from Augusta's perspective. Due to an unfulfilled life as a student who is half-heartedly attempting to finish a masters thesis, her thoughts center exclusively on the life of her "frenemy," Be. She seems to possess everything Augusta lacks – a husband and children, as well as a certain authority in all walks of life.

Naters's second novel is formally and aesthetically more convincing than the first. Here the superficiality of the descriptions becomes the structural and aesthetic means to unnerve the reader who cannot help but attribute the pre-

---

**31** "Auf einmal würde ein Korb an einer Schnur vor meinem Fenster baumeln. Ich würde meinen Augen nicht trauen. Ich würde das Fenster aufmachen, und in dem Korb wären Rosen, rote, und eine Flasche Champagner. Ich würde nach oben schauen, direkt in SEIN grinsendes Gesicht hinein. Oben links hätte er eine Zahnlücke und würde schon Jahre über mir wohnen, ohne daß ich ihn bemerkt hätte." *Königinnen* 40.

tentiousness to the main character. Augusta, however, reveals herself to be an entirely unreliable narrator, since Be only exists through her projections and thus turns out to be doubly fictitious. Augusta's own life, on the other hand, is revealed as a negation of Be's life so that the narrative about Be becomes a gigantic maneuver to distract Augusta as well as the reader from the loneliness that permeates the novel (Krumbholz). In making the surface the ruling aesthetic principle, Augusta's isolation and inability to communicate reveal her narration as a melancholic attempt to establish a sense of self. *Lügen* thus gains a hermeneutic surplus by transcending the mere narration of female friendships to a different level. Naters leaves behind the bourgeois heterosexual cosmos she previously described when Be's surprising coming out and her new love for Petra become the focus of Augusta's verbal attacks and aggressive insecurities. In turn, Be's confession that she has fallen in love with a woman and her wish to reorganize her life finally force the depressed Augusta to develop strategies for mastering her own existence.

Naters's novels are a pivotal example of the shift towards lifestyle themes and aesthetics of the surface that many other texts of the late 1990s illustrate as well. In *Sommerhaus später* (1998, *Summerhouse Later*), for example, Judith Hermann sprinkles a carefully measured dose of pop-cultural accessories onto her texts that lend the timeless realism of her prose a contemporary aura and provide the possibility of identification for the reader. Christian Kracht's novel *Faserland* (1995) shows the world soberly as a Vanity Fair that offers the characters no possibility of establishing a stable concept of subjectivity (see Biendarra 2002).

One important reason for these new forms of literature is the generational change from postwar and post-1968 authors to the *Generation Golf*. While its members profited from the relaxation of social traditions achieved by the generation of 1968, they were born too late to participate in its political utopia (see Anz 2001). Consequently, as Andrew Plowman has put it succinctly, "they were left stranded in the no man's land of their private self-absorption" (53). For example, in Florian Illies's bestseller *Generation Golf* (2000) or David Wagner's novel *Meine nachtblaue Hose* (2000, My Night Blue Trousers), the emptiness of present-day society manifests itself in waxing nostalgic about their childhood in West Germany of the 1980s and the consumer products, clothes, and TV shows of this era.

Changes brought about by globalization provide an even more significant explanation for this shift. The fetishization of lifestyle themes and the consumption of both German and wider international brands and commodities, as illustrated in Naters's novels, construct Germany as a normal Western consumer society, in which the weight of German history that influenced the self-conception of previous generations so tremendously, has lost its immediate urgency. It is thus no coincidence that the movement towards *authentische Alltäglichkeit*, i.e., the authentic narration of workaday life in these texts is complemented by a prominent shift towards an aesthetic of consumption, which in turn relates to trends on the international book market. If popular cultural forms are mobilized as markers of the consumer's lifestyle choices, they also signal an aesthetic stance in which texts are posited as commodities that point to the anticipated mode of their own consumption (Plowman 54).

The variety of voices, themes, and narrative strategies that this chapter has highlighted shows that the old medium literature held its ground in the German media and event society of the late 1990s. Moreover, critical debates and a growing readership increased the attention paid to a new generation of writers and helped along their critical and economic success. The interconnectedness between literary debates and literature itself illustrates how intellectual and literary debates influenced cultural production in united Germany. In summary, one could say that the debate on realism and the focus on *authentische Alltäglichkeit* shifted the emphasis from the Horatian principle of *prodesse*, education, which might have been overstated in German literature up to the late 1980s, to that of *delectare*, entertaining the reader.

The ensuing effects have internationalized contemporary German-language literature. Realistic narration and an emphasis on consumption, which were the primary examples of this chapter, add to the authenticity of this prose and provide linkages to international literature concerned with similar themes and aesthetic strategies. Moving towards a new ordinariness might have been troublesome to some who asserted that younger writers of the *Generation Golf* were tangled up in the entertainment society ("Spaßgesellschaft") and lacked historical or political awareness. Yet their literary texts narrate social realities of a younger generation in the nascent Berlin Republic and assess and refigure experiences in post-unification Germany in their own way. They are significant as cultural and aesthetic interventions because they probe critically the antagonisms in post-unification Germany as well as the chasms of interpersonal relationships in a globalized society; concepts that continue to determine the construction of cultural identities in the Berlin Republic.

# 3 Brave New Work World: Narratives of the New Economy

"All that is solid melts into air." (The Communist Manifesto)

Work and labor are central markers of identity for the individual and play a significant role in human self-understanding and identity construction. While this insight is not limited to western societies such as Germany or the United States, work here tends to take on a complicated meaning. For better or worse, having money – which for most of us implies having to earn it first – is the precondition for participation in capitalist consumer society, yet the significance of work extends far beyond economic inevitability. Not only do most people spend the bulk of their waking hours in the workplace, they define themselves in relationship to it. Having meaningful work is of primary importance to the individual worker and contributes significantly to the experience of a happy and rewarding life. Being out of work or unemployed prohibits this kind of economic participation and quickly leads to alienation from society, which is mirrored in the fact that the unemployed generally have no lobbying power and are marginalized and looked down upon (see Lützeler, *Merkur* 1998).

Over the course of the last two centuries, work and ideas about it underwent significant changes. It became a central economic and anthropological category in the 19th century, as is visible in the semantic changes from 'molestia' (troublesomeness, annoyance) to 'opus' (productive work) (Vogl 337). The modern work world, as we know it, has been constituted in a historical progression dominated by a variety of factors. The development of the monetary system, different phases of industrialization, an expansion of the service sector, and the continuous automatization, specialization, and rationalization of (office) work all play their respective role here. Yet especially the last point has complicated the relationship between work and identity. In the Industrial Age, the use of machines still went hand in hand with mass human labor, whereas in the current "Age of Access" (Rifkin xv) intelligent machines increasingly have replaced human labor in agriculture, manufacturing, and the service sector. Robotization and computerization have led to a technological revolution whose backdrop is the ever-increasing scarcity of work. New consumer habits such as shopping and banking online have dashed initial hopes that the service industry could be an important growth factor. The industrialization of the service sector instead has validated theorists such as Jeremy Rifkin, who predicted in *The End of Work* that the automatization of the service industry would eliminate millions of jobs and lead to a decline in purchasing power (2004 Introduction, x-xliv). These and other factors have brought about a veritable disappearance of work not only in Western societies, making it one of the foremost problems of the globalized world and a challenge to the political economy of all industrialized countries.

A study such as this one can only sketch broadly the complexities of the interplay between globalization, the economy and the labor market.[1] Yet it must not ignore the large body of research that points to the increasing interdependency between economics and culture discussed, for instance, in the work of sociologist John Urry: "Economic and symbolic processes are more than ever interlaced and interarticulated; that is ... the economy is increasingly culturally inflected and ... culture is more and more economically inflected" (Lash and Urry 64). Literature is a central medium of the reflection and construction of cultural subjectivity and integrates it into the public discourse. Paradigmatic changes in the economy shape society and leave traces in the material authors use.[2]

In effect, linguistic and social modifications as mediated in the modern work world are so formative that writers whose chief concern is language cannot escape them. After all, they really are prototypes of the "flexible individual" (Richard Sennett) the globalized work world favors, and flexibility and mobility are of great significance to them: While their primary occupation might be novelist, many also write stage plays, screen plays, poetry, and essays. Most also work journalistically, spend a good part of their time applying for fellowships and prizes, participate in public readings, discussions, and appear on television. Interviews I conducted with Thomas Meinecke, Antje Rávic Strubel, Gregor Hens, and Terézia Mora in 2008 confirm the assumption that today's writers need to be multitaskers in order to survive.[3] Modern authorship requires perpetual mobility: Authors must travel on book tours organized by their publishing houses, are paid by cultural institutions such as the Goethe Institute to represent German-speaking culture in far-away lands, and seek positions as writers-in-residence in German cities and on college campuses abroad. John von Düffel speaks of a traveling circus ("Reisezirkus"): "One is a traveling salesman on one's own account, and as such one

---

1 There is an abundance of research that details the interplay between globalization, the economy and the labor market, See Hoffmann, for instance.
2 Richard Gray shows in *Money Matters. Economics and the German Cultural Imagination* how German aesthetic theory and artistic practice are connected in the 18th and 19th century.
3 Exact references to these interviews can be found in the works cited section.

really has to be professional."[4] The commitment that contemporary authors have to their work fits the demands of late capitalism, where professional duties and play bleed into each other: People work at the office, the café, or at home and can be reached 24/7 through e-mail on laptops or smart phones. Consequently many contemporary work narratives reflect the growing importance that concepts such as "information" and ideas hold and highlight problems that new conditions of work cause for the individual in the age of hyper-capitalism.

Much of the post-millennial aesthetic production demonstrates how painfully aware German-speaking artists are of the negative side of global capitalism, echoing Heiner Müller's assessment that the phantom of a free market society finally replaced the ghost of communism (233). This is especially true for the focus of this chapter, i.e., narratives dealing with the advertising and consulting business, two sectors of the New Economy that flourished with the rise of neoliberalism. Joachim Bessing's *Wir Maschine* (2001, We Machine) and Rainer Merkel's *Das Jahr der Wunder* (2001, The Year of Wonders) debunk the world of advertising as a site in which the individual loses any sense of self and identity. The processes of capitalist normatization and the ways in which it produces over-disciplined bodies come to the fore in John von Düffel's *EGO* (2001). The materialist aesthetics of Kathrin Röggla's *wir schlafen nicht* (2004, We Don't Sleep) expose the normative power that the language and business practices of the consulting industry have developed in neoliberal society.

Apart from the novels discussed in this chapter, topics of work and unemployment in the New Economy also took center stage in dramatic productions. Urs Widmer's play *Top Dogs* (1996) thematizes the loss of status and power that unemployment causes even for those individuals who occupy leading managerial positions.[5] Margareth (Maxi) Obexer's one-act play *F.O.B. – Free on board* (2002) describes the doubts of a talented young woman who tallies up the struggle between the sexes in the professional world before a job interview. Obexer's trilogy of three scenic monologues, *Liberté toujours* (2004, Freedom, Always), presents the economic malaise of three characters that leads to their psychological demise.[6] In Rolf Hochhuth's anti-globalization play *McKinsey*

---

**4** "Man ist … der Vertreter, der Reisende in eigener Sache, und als solcher muss man auch wirklich professionell sein." Von Düffel 2008 (Interview).

**5** *Top Dogs* premiered in 1996 at the Neumarkt Theater in Zurich; *Theater heute* subsequently lauded it as "Play of the Year."

**6** F.O.B – *Free on board* premiered on October 3, 2002 in Tübingen under the directorship of Maxi Obexer herself; the trilogy of monologues *Liberté toujours* premiered on April 4, 2004 at the Stadttheater Bruneck.

*kommt* (2003, McKinsey Comes)[7] the consulting business becomes a cipher of political and economic power, yet the play's poetics remain indebted to the time when industrial production still dominated the work sphere (Deupmann 156). Moritz Rinke's *Café Umberto* (2005)[8] takes place in an unemployment agency and describes the attempts of six different people who all work in creative professions to make sense of their existence at a time when the rules of the market dominate even art and love: "There are no aesthetic parallel universes and private zones of retreat, not even in a dream. The economy is everything,"[9] as fellow playwright John von Düffel noted in his foreword to the paperback edition of *Café Umberto*.

A similar insight led even the German Federal Cultural Foundation (*Kulturstiftung des Bundes*) in 2006 to finance a project on the literary treatment of contemporary working conditions in order to "develop new methods of fostering cultural heritage and tap into the cultural and artistic potential of knowledge required for addressing social issues."[10] Under the editorship of German studies scholar Johannes Ullmaier, the *Kulturstiftung* initiated a project inviting writers to contribute texts detailing the entire spectrum of working conditions in the 21[th] century. While there were no stipulations about research methods or aesthetic forms, authors were encouraged to include some original sound bites and describe that which is supposedly self-evident ("das vermeintlich Selbstverständliche").[11] Suhrkamp published the results in 2007 in book form under the title *Schicht! Arbeitsreportagen für die Endzeit* (Shift's Over! Work Features for the End of Times). The texts span a range from realistic reporting to interviews to avant-garde narratives; from the story of a couple who largely relies on the barter system when renovating a run-down horse farm in Brandenburg (Juli Zeh, "Joe Happy"), to the descriptions of the production of an internet chat peep show (Feridun Zaimoglu, "Peepshow 2"), to the artistic rendering of the workings of Debtors Anonymous in Los Angeles and the lives of individuals in Berlin who have fallen prey to the temptations of consumer society and defaulted on their credit (Kathrin Röggla, "die wiedergänger"). This renewed interest in the sphere of work – one might even call it a renaissance –

---

7 *McKinsey kommt* had its debut at the Brandenburger Theater on February 13, 2004.

8 *Café Umberto* premiered in the fall 2005 at both the Schauspielhaus Düsseldorf and the Thalia Theater Hamburg.

9 "Es gibt keine ästhetischen Parallelwelten und keine Schutzzonen des Privaten, nicht einmal im Traum. Ökonomie ist alles." Von Düffel. "Die Liebe in den Zeiten der Ich-AG. Zu *Café Umberto* von Moritz Rinke." 14.

10 http://www.kulturstiftung-des-bundes.de/cms/en/stiftung/ (July 7, 2010).

11 http://www.kulturstiftung-des-bundes.de/cms/de/programme/arbeit_in_zukunft/archiv/schicht_arbeitsreportagen_fuer_die_endzeit.html (July 7, 2010).

is linked to political, economic, and social factors that in turn are influenced by globalization. Most prose texts discussed in this chapter were written at a time when unemployment in Germany was at an all time high, a noteworthy fact to which I will return.[12] Sociological studies confirm that the importance of work is directly correlated to rising levels of unemployment and growing job insecurity. This has become especially pronounced since 1998 when the German labor market deteriorated considerably (see Borchert and Landherr 210).

## Recent Developments in the German Economy

The economic situation of Germany after unification provides a tangible background for literary texts that are the focus of this chapter. Before turning to the textual analysis, it is necessary to recall some of the objective material shifts the country underwent from 1998–2006 under the Red-Green coalition. During that time, Germany experienced two factors that social scientists commonly regard as signifiers of globalization, namely the spread of neo-liberal policy norms and a retreat from the practices of the Keynesian welfare state and social democracy (Rosamond 657).

To be clear, Germany was not subjected to a true Thatcherite revolution like the deregulated liberal economies of the United States and the United Kingdom in the 1980s. Nevertheless, the famous German Model (*Modell Deutschland*) that relies on balancing the markets and state interventions to link economic success with social justice is seriously under threat (see Hertfelder). Important policy changes influenced by globalization have led to the Americanization of the labor market, which entails deregulation, flexible employment relations, the privatization of social risk, a dominance of the market, and the withdrawal of the state from the social sector. This development entails an escalating commodification of all areas of life and has been met with strong discontent and criticism by the population (Borchert and Landherr 210). While changes to Rhenish capitalism, i.e., the contemporary economic order existing mainly in Western Europe founded on publicly organized social security,[13] already began in the 1980s, the unification process brought these

---

**12** In February 2005 unemployment hit 5.2 million, the highest number since 1933. http://www.guardian.co.uk/world/2005/feb/03/germany.lukeharding.
**13** French economist Michel Albert coined the term in his 1993 book *Capitalism versus Capitalism*. As opposed to the "Neo-American" model instituted by the Thatcher and Reagan administrations, Albert finds that Rhenish capitalism, especially in its German form of a social market economy, is more just and efficient. Among its characteristics are the signif-

changes clearly to the fore. They served as a launching pad for aggressive neoliberal macroeconomic policy (Menz 43). Subsequently Germany experienced a long-term institutional shift and structural changes that put pressure on the system of social capitalism.

A number of aspects play a role here; many political economists agree that the following four are the most significant (Stefan Beck 5). The biggest change concerns the decline of socialism and the ensuing process of unification, which allowed globalizing factors to take hold in the German economy. Large companies in particular were affected by corporate restructuring, which lead to an enormous loss of jobs throughout the 1990s[14] and high unemployment figures.[15] The second facet involves changes to the global production system. While the outsourcing of labor and production to foreign countries where costs are lower started to play a role before the 1990s, it has gained increased significance in the twenty-first century, especially for globally operating companies. Outsourcing in turn has led to a weakening of unions and organized labor groups (Rifkin xxi). The third aspect covers changes in demographic patterns and social values, both of which are influenced by increasing numbers of refugees from the Balkan region following the war in former Yugoslavia and Eastern Europe after the fall of communism.[16] Finally, a leap in the process of European integration also plays an important role. Starting in 1997, the European Union agreed on shared goals for labor market policy, stressing the importance of creating better conditions for entrepreneurship, employability, adaptability, and equal opportunities across what was to become the Euro zone in 2002 (Salomonsson 117). In this context, economic liberalization was painted

---

icance of banks over the stock market, a balance of power between shareholders and management, and a social partnership between unions and employers.

**14** Between 1989 and 1996, almost one third of all jobs in firms with more than 1,000 employees were lost. *Deutsches Institut für Wirtschaftsforschung* (*DIW*) 1998, quoted in Klobes, 70.

**15** From 1991 to 2003, the unemployment rate went up from 7.3% to 11.6%. In the eastern states, the unemployment rate rose from 11.9% in 1991 to 20.1% in 2003. See Siebert's comprehensive analysis, 69–113. In January 2010, the overall unemployment rate had dropped to 8.6%, but was still significantly higher in the new Länder (13.5%). http://www.spiegel.de/flash/flash-12125.html.

**16** Germany accepted the biggest number of refugees of all the European countries during the Balkan wars of the 1990s (350,000), yet barely 80,000 remain today since as an advocate of "temporary protection," Germany expects war refugees to return home as soon as the conflict is over. Three million ethnic Germans returned to Germany between 1988 and 2003. Almost 2.2 million of these arrived from the former territory of the Soviet Union, with Poland (575,000) and Romania (220,000) providing the remaining flows. Source: http://www.migrationinformation.org/Profiles/display.cfm?ID=235 (July 14, 2010).

as "the price to pay for Europe," and the European Commission has acted as a powerful dismantler of state monopolies in railroads, telecommunication, air transportation, and energy distribution (Menz 41).

In light of the recession of the early 1990s, the association of major businesses (*Berufsverband der Deutschen Industrie, BDI*) started a debate about the need to deregulate the labor market, cut taxes and abandon standard wage contracts to secure the future of Germany as an investment and production site. The key assertion was that "inflated wage levels and employer contributions to unemployment compensation schemes [were] putting an intolerable burden on business" and prevented foreign and national investment (Menz 43). In tune with industrial leaders, the head of the Red-Green coalition Gerhard Schröder vowed in 1998 to leave behind the Kohl government's resistance towards social reform and set out to modernize the German economy. The new doctrine "incentives and demands" ("Fördern und Fordern") came increasingly to the fore, and the ensuing policy shifts were geared towards pro-business job creation and modernization. The orientation towards the American and British model is most visible in the 1999 joint paper "The Third Way" that Schröder issued with British Prime Minister Tony Blair. It stressed the need to cut taxes on corporations and high-income earners while capping labor and social protection and forcing welfare recipients to accept jobs offered to them.[17]

Schröder's reviving of the Alliance for Jobs, Education and Competitiveness (*Bündnis für Arbeit, Ausbildung und Wettbewerbsfähigkeit*) in the fall of 1998 was a first move to actively reduce unemployment. The subsequent Hartz proposals under the leadership of Volkswagen personnel manager Peter Hartz were the next step. After its narrow reelection victory, the Red-Green government implemented four different measures that were a central part of the controversial *Agenda 2010*, which aimed to deregulate the labor market and decrease welfare spending, particularly with regard to private health insurance. The so-called Hartz measures (*Hartz-Gesetze*), a set of measures to help the most needy, effectively increased the individual's burden in the job search. In an attempt to cut the number of jobless in half within three years – a goal that failed spectacularly – steps included the implementation of private labor agencies who could temporarily hire unemployed individuals and loan them to third parties (*Hartz I*, effective January 2003); the creation of a tax-exempt status for low-income earners, fostering of entrepreneurism ("Ich AGs") and low-wage employment ("400 Euro Jobs") (*Hartz II*, effective January 2003), and the restructuring of the federal unemployment offices into the federal employment agency (*Hartz III*, effective January 2004). By far the most controversial

---

17 For a comprehensive overview of social policy reforms see Mosebach.

measure was *Hartz IV*, which came into effect in 2005 and merged the reduced unemployment and social assistance (formerly "Arbeitslosengeld" and "Sozialhilfe") into the unemployment benefit II ("Arbeitslosengeld II"), which was subsequently limited to 13 months. Employees who refuse job offers experience benefits cuts under Hartz IV; they might also have to accept jobs that pay up to 30% below standard wage scales.

Following the implementation of the Hartz measures, unions and church groups campaigned against them, organizing numerous demonstrations. Critics pointed out that de-industrialized regions in East Germany effectively could not accommodate most job seekers and that the new levels of support in many cases were below the poverty line.[18] Economists and political scientists continue to question the measures' effectiveness, and many agree that they are "a drastic illustration of choosing US-style workfare policy over traditional Social Democracy and preferring punitive supply side policy to constructive demand side stimulus." (Menz 46) The ongoing political and public debate has brought up larger issues about the viability of social capitalism, social justice, the effects of rising poverty levels (especially among children), and the social and psychological costs of living as a recipient of Hartz IV. The criticism from various sides gained new momentum when the Federal Constitutional Court in Karlsruhe ruled in February 2010 that the standard levels of support under Hartz IV (359 Euros for adults) are indeed unconstitutional and need to be amended by 2011,[19] leading to a heated debate in the newly elected government coalition of CDU and FDP under chancellor Angela Merkel. Interestingly, the neologism "hartzen" – used colloquially as a synonym for either "being unemployed" or "to bum around" – was elected "youth word of the year" in 2009 ("Jugendwort des Jahres").[20] Like other words such as "savings package" ("Sparpaket") for a number of new laws designed to save money, "hartzen" shows how the preoccupation with the economy has captured everyday language and thinking and provides rich metaphors and varied allusions.

The second noteworthy development around the millennium was the creation of the New Economy and the German stock index NEMAX ("Neuer Markt"), modeled after NASDAQ in the U.S., that represents the new technologies such as information, multimedia, biotech, and telecommunications. From the begin-

---

**18** For a detailed discussion of the various reform stages of the Red-Green coalition see Beck and Scherrer.

**19** See "Verfassungsrichter verlangen Hartz-IV-Revision." *Der Spiegel*, February 9, 2010. http://www.spiegel.de/politik/deutschland/0,1518,676708,00.html.

**20** "Hartzen ist Jugendwort des Jahres." *Focus*. December 1, 2009. http://www.focus.de/schule/lernen/lernatlas/rechtschreibung/jugendsprache-hartzen-ist-jugendwort-des-jahres_aid_459101.html.

ning in 1996 to its sudden end in 2001/02, the New Economy spurred hopes of unprecedented growth and was dominated by a discourse of optimism. The digital revolution, so the prophecy went, would unleash extraordinary productivity rates, ideas instead of things would propel the economy forward and the 'knowledge society' would mean less menial and more meaningful work (von Dirke 141). Through the rise of the Internet, the world had become unprecedentedly globalized, and the costs of globalization for underdeveloped countries were just starting to come to the fore. For Western countries, the New Economy meant a "happy" capitalism creating flexible, creative, and lucrative jobs that would hold the specter of unemployment at bay (see Henwood).

This optimistic scenario ultimately only panned out for the US, whereas Germany remained plagued by high unemployment. Despite this, Germans too were encouraged to embrace fewer social services and invest instead in the stock market to provide for their retirement. The privatization of state businesses, such as *Deutsche Post* and *Telekom* and their subsequent stock market notation in the NEMAX lead to a veritable stock buying frenzy, often by people who, encouraged by the buzz created by the media, invested their savings without having the necessary knowledge about the stock market or any prior experience with it. For a few months, it seemed that everyone would make an easy profit and get rich trying. Yet following the terrorist attacks of 09/11 and the subsequent downturn in the worldwide stock exchanges, the NEMAX started falling drastically, from a historic high of 9666 points on March 10, 2000 to just 318 points in October 2002. Due to the historic losses, the German Stock Exchange closed down the NEMAX in June 2003. With the bursting of the dot-com bubble, 200 billion Euros evaporated in only 31 months; hopes were crushed and thousands of jobs lost (Kuhn).

## The Individual in Precarious Times

From a sociological perspective, the broad economic and social changes described above create a problematic situation for the individual who experiences a deep-seated insecurity: "Le précarité est aujoud'hui partout" (uncertainty is everywhere today), as Pierre Bourdieu put it in his argument against neoliberalism (1998, 96). Work certainly is but one factor that contributes to this insecurity; individuality, time/space, and community are others with which sociologists are concerned. Yet due to the systemic underemployment and unemployment in Western societies, the changing work world contributes significantly to the experience of precariousness, by which sociologist Zygmunt Bauman understands the combined experience of *insecurity* (of position, entitlements and livelihood), *uncertainty* (as to their continuation and future stability) and *unsafety* (of one's body and its extensions, namely possessions and communities) (Baumann 2000, 61). The prospect of job loss increasingly puts the individual under pressure and necessitates the reconsideration of old models of work. Sticking to one vocation or remaining with a single company for life is an outdated idea. Flexibility and mobility are two of the key qualities expected in the postmodern work place, as are the commitment to life-long learning and ongoing education. While a better education should enable the individual to fulfill these demands, even a college degree is no longer a guarantee for employment. Lack of job security is simply a reality in modern employment and affects the middle class just as much as the working class. The neologism *precariat* – a category originally coined in French sociology for those working without a safety net and the unemployed, but now adopted into German and English (see Perrin, Bude, Standing) – and the categorization *Generation Praktikum* (generation internship, used for young academics with low incomes and little prospect for a secure future)[21] attest to this development.

Large operating firms of the New Economy that operate globally and mainly deal in technology, finance, and the new service sectors have an enormous influence even on smaller companies because the corporate culture they promote has changed the work environment profoundly. Sociologist Richard Sennett sees the dissolution of traditional institutional forms as the primary reason for this deep transformation. At the center of militarized social capitalism developed under Germany's first chancellor Otto von Bismarck in the late 1800s lay rationalized time that allowed people to conceive of their lives as a narrative, which in turn provided them with a sense of stability. Famously analyzed by Max Weber in his theory of bureaucracy, effective power in this system was shaped like a rationalized pyramid in which each office had a defined function and one was reprimanded for stepping out of line. Despite the rigidity of this "iron cage," individuals gained a sense of agency since each order still needed to be translated and interpreted. These small flexibilities often made up for bad working conditions and low pay. The Weberian pyramid became a structural reality, and the welfare state assumed the same form (Sennett 2006, 33).

Flexible organizations, on the other hand, have dismantled the old institutional structures. The most important factors at play in this restructuring process include a shift of power from the top to the center where the central processing unit sets the tasks, judges results, and expands and shrinks the

---

21 Matthias Stolz coined the term "Generation Praktikum" in his seminal *ZEIT* article.

company as needed (Sennett 2006, 51). Due to outsourcing, intermediate layers of bureaucracy are being erased along with channels of communication. Temporary employees, often in the global South, are hired and fired according to the needs of the task at hand and new technologies provide real-time information of resources and performances, enabling what Michel Foucault described as panoptic surveillance in *Discipline and Punish* (224). Sennett identifies the distanced relationship between those at the center and those working on the periphery as "the geography of globalization" (Sennett 2006, 55). In the office, competition between individual teams promotes a winner-takes-all-mentality, which exacerbates stress and anxieties due to unclear, ill-defined working conditions. Social distance increases, adding to a rise in inequality in the modern economy. The social shortcomings emanating from the described structural changes lead to low institutional loyalty. Employees often do not care about the fate of the company since the company does not seem to care about them. Another deficit concerns a diminishment of informal trust among workers, and a weakening of institutional knowledge since people are often replaced quickly.

Flat hierarchies not only cause changes in power relationships, they also lead to a new cultural ideal of a human being (Sennett 2006, 5). Today's individual needs to be flexible, cooperative, and efficient in order to adapt quickly to new challenges, let go of past experiences and improvise his or her life narrative or even accept that a constant sense of self might no longer be sustainable. The philosopher Byung-Chul Han argues in this context in his book *Müdigkeitsgesellschaft* (2011) that the achievement-oriented society (*Leistungsgesellschaft*) in which we live creates individuals who do not need to be coerced to work but instead pretend to be continually happy and upbeat doing their tasks. The conflicts they experience in the workplace are less about people who were formerly considered adversaries (such as supervisors) and more about their wish to continually exceed expectations. In a reversal of an understanding of globalization that sees people in the Western world primarily as its winners, Sennett contends that globalization articulates "a perception that the sources of human energy are shifting, and that those in the already developed world may be left out as a result" (2006, 90). What speaks to this troubling conclusion is that economic considerations have become a paradigm for social activities. The cipher of entrepreneurship is no longer limited to the professional realm but increasingly describes a general mode of activity, as Sven Opitz has shown in his study on management literature *Gouvernementalität im Postfordismus* (2004). As noted earlier, economic thinking has colonized everyday culture and everyday life (and vice versa) and is encroaching on people's subjectivity (Löfgren and Willim 11). The subject internalizes the coercive mechanisms neoliberal business practices impose upon it, which has repercussions for the construction of subjectivity. The literary analyses will elucidate these developments further.

## A Short History of Work Literature

The working world has always been of interest to writers and artists and the topic has a long tradition in German-language literature.[22] After encountering work already as a literary topos in the Middle Ages (see Gentry), we find the subject in different forms in Weimar Classicism (see Fetscher; Berghahn and Müller), in bourgeois realism, and naturalism (see Hohendahl, Segeberg). Yet compared with other European literatures, such as the works of Charles Dickens in England and Stendhal or Honoré de Balzac in France and due to Germany's "special path" of a relatively late industrialization, the genre truly expanded there only in the second half of the nineteenth century and especially in the early twentieth century. To name just a few examples, Gottfried Keller's novellas, set in the imaginary Swiss town of Seldwyla, introduce the reader to citizens whose cordiality hampers their business spirit, leading to the entrepreneurial failure of many (*Die Leute von Seldwyla*, 1856/1874). Gustav Freytag's novel *Soll und Haben* (1855) is the prototype of the merchant and entrepreneur novel ("Kaufmanns- und Unternehmerroman") that focuses not on the education of the entire person but instead on the achievement-oriented member of bourgeois society (Pott 205). Around the turn of the century, Thomas Mann showed in *Buddenbrooks* (1901) – which, apart from being the most famous entrepreneurial novel in German literature (von Matt 45) can be read as an early form of "management literature" – how the internalized rules of mercantilism shaped the life maxims of Johann Buddenbrook, but are ignored by subsequent generations, accelerating the family's demise (*Verfall*). Taking a journalistic approach, Joseph Roth's accounts in *Briefe aus Deutschland* (1929) described the coal mining industry in the Saarland, and Ernst Jünger's *Der Arbeiter* from 1932 served as a link to the literature of National Socialism, which celebrated work as an elementary, freeing force and elevated it into a value in and of itself (see Eggerstorfer). At the same time, Hans Fallada's novel *Kleiner Mann, was nun?* (1932) illustrated the fate of economically disenfranchised white-collar workers in the volatile Weimar Republic that Siegfried Kracauer had analyzed theoretically two years earlier (*Die Angestellten. Aus dem neusten Deutschland*, 1930). Twenty-five years later, Max Frisch's engi-

---

22 For a historical overview of work literature from the 19th to the 21[th] century, see Kremer 49–76.

neer Walter Faber in *Homo faber* (1957) finally figured as the full-fledged product of the modern achievement-oriented society whose emotional damage leads him into a personal catastrophe of Greek tragic proportions. At the same time, Heinrich Böll's family novel *Billard um halb zehn* (1959) focuses on the moral challenges of life before, during and after World War II by portraying three generations of architects who are actively involved in and become economically successful by contributing to West Germany's rebuilding process (*Wiederaufbau*).

Already with the funding of the Communist Party in 1917 and coinciding with the growing workers movement, interest in social justice entered German literature dealing with the working world (see Emmerich 1974, 11–39). It survived the division into two German literatures in the late 1940s that, while referring to the topic in different ways and influenced by the experiences in a social market economy and socialism respectively, made "work" into a central topos. Authors in the GDR continued to thematize work as the material center of the political system until the latter's demise in 1989, despite the fact that they did so less and less enthusiastically as the flaws of the socialist system became harder to overlook (see Jäger). In the FRG, the conditions under which the proletariat lives and works continued to be important for the literary movement of the Dortmunder *Gruppe 61* and its counterpart *Werkkreis Literatur der Arbeitswelt*, founded in 1970. Most of the authors organized in these groups were concerned with the fate of blue-collar workers and the conditions in industrial production, following the motto "No matter whether you work in the assembly line or sit at a desk, work in the civil service or the private sector, run a household, bring up children or are forcibly unemployed – colleague, write it down."[23] Yet the industrial reportages by authors such as Erika Runge (*Bottroper Protokolle*, 1968), Günter Wallraff (*Industriereportagen*, 1970), and Max von der Grün (*Irrlicht und Feuer*, 1963) revealed the faults and injustices of the capitalist system and debunked the ideology of self-fulfillment through work. They also paid attention to the plight of the "guest workers" from South-Eastern Europe who were still completely marginalized at this point. Since work literature in Germany was always dominated by "the rhetoric of class struggle" (Chilese 294), literature dealing with white collar workers (*Angestelltenliteratur*) of an author like Wilhelm Genazino remained rather an exception.[24]

---

**23** This is the motto of the still existent *Werkkreis Literatur der Arbeitswelt.* http://www.werkkreis-literatur.de/de/aktuelles.
**24** Genazino's *Abschaffel* trilogy consists of the following novels: *Abschaffel* (1977), *Die Vernichtung der Sorgen* (1978), *Falsche Jahre* (1979).

There are at least three reasons for the significant decline in texts dealing with the working world in the 1980s and the early 1990s. First, ideas of self-fullfilment and meaningful participation in the social sphere shifted from the work world to other fields, such as new social and ecological movements (see Roth and Rucht). Second, the *Erlebnisgesellschaft* ("event society"), as theorized by sociologist Gerhard Schulze, linked self-fulfillment closely to specific lifestyles and the experience of "fun," to which the work world seemed to be a hostile counter sphere. Furthermore, the so-called "victory" of capitalism over socialism dampened a critique of the former, as Chilese has suggested (294). My analysis of the rise of new German pop literature in the second chapter confirms that this is true for different genres. However, the lull in interest was only short-lived and the trend reversed itself into a veritable renaissance in the late 1990s, albeit one that was dominated by narratives set in the organizationally and technologically updated service sectors (see Winkels 2002).

## Narratives of Work in the Aughts

In the 1990s, work once again became the center of a social discourse that was motivated and fueled by interdependent events. First of all, the integration and subsequent transformation of the GDR society into a united German state revealed how starkly ideas about the significance of work differed in East and West. While the West German model of a social market economy quickly proved victorious over the possibility of retaining a socialist system in one part of Germany, the development of the globalized work world threw the former equally into question. After the "right to work" that was codified in socialism had come to an abrupt end, now the united German workforce was confronted with rising unemployment and the gradual dismantling of the social state detailed earlier in this chapter. Hand in hand with this development went the formation of a new, achievement-oriented society. Its principles were (and continue to be) most visible in changing conditions that stress individualized forms of work and a heightened personal responsibility of the individual employee. The continuous expansion of the workday that is enforced as "flexible working hours" is a very tangible outcome of this development. The positively coded idea of achievement-orientation was also articulated in the promise of the end of alienating routines and the stressing of individual potential.

A number of established GDR writers who had already thematized work under socialism continued to do so in the 1990s. Apart from Angela Krauß's novel *Sommer auf dem Eis* (1998, A Summer on the Ice), Christoph Hein and

Volker Braun in particular have negotiated the topic of work against the background of the end of the GDR and the ensuing social transformations, Hein for example in his novel *Willenbrock* (2000) and Braun in *Machwerk oder Das Schichtbuch des Flick von Lauchhammer* (2008, A Sorry Effort or The Shift Reports of Flick von Lauchhammer).

Still, I would contend that texts by a younger generation of novelists are most interesting because they signify a new form of *Unternehmer- and Angestelltenroman* that deals with a very different stratum of society from the socially motivated literature of the 1970s and 1980s. Reflecting the post-industrial realities in which we live, such texts mirror Germany's changed economic and social conditions, focusing mostly on the New Economy and its immaterial production, as well as the service industries of advertising and consulting. The characters are, for the most part, the highly educated, flexible, and efficient people Sennett describes as "middle-class workers ... at the epicenter of the global boom in high-tech industries, in financial services, and in the media" (2006, 7).

The bigger context of this development is the end of the so-called entertainment society ("Spaßgesellschaft") that, together with the sociological category of the event society (see Schulze), dominated the late 1990s. The terrorist attacks of September 11, 2001 and a changing political landscape caused a global economic downturn and the forming of an "anti-terror coalition," subsequently leading to the widely contested deployment of the German military in Afghanistan in 2003. Alongside these developments, German cultural criticism detected "a new seriousness" (see Bürger and Leitgeb; Freund, Hielscher and Hettche) in the arts and literature. Factors laid out in the beginning of the chapter, such as the economic insecurity spurred by the bursting of the dot-com bubble and the decline of the New Economy, the fraying of the social net, Hartz IV, and the rise of the new social group of the *precariat* now serve as an inspiration for a younger generation of writers to turn to realistic narrations of the workaday world. They increasingly replace the hedonistic subjective narratives ("Ich-Geschichten") that dominated the second half of the 1990s and are (often misleadingly) labeled as "pop literature," as I have shown in the first two chapters.

## The Aesthetics of the Surface: The Work of (M)Ad Men in Joachim Bessing's *Wir Maschine* (2001) and Rainer Merkel's *Das Jahr der Wunder* (2001)

The world of advertising and marketing is of particular interest to millennial prose production not only in Germany but also in other countries, highlighting the increasing significance this economic sector has gained with the distribution of global brands and technologies. As Naomi Klein argues in her anti-globalization manifesto *No Logo* (2001), branding has been the primary factor for the astronomical growth in the wealth and cultural influence of multi-national corporations over the last twenty-five years. As recently rendered by the American Movie Classics (AMC) network with its successful TV series *Mad Men*, in the 1950s and 1960s advertisers became the "philosopher–kings of commercial culture" (Klein 7). Since then marketing specialists have honed in on the emotional qualities of advertising and sought to utilize mechanisms that conjure people's subconsious desires. Those who shape the stream of products, data, images, and ideas into recognizable brands and communicate them to the global marketplace subsequently have gained tremendous significance.

Although set in the world of 1980s Wall Street investment bankers, Bret Easton Ellis's novel *American Psycho* (1991) is an early and important predecessor of the literary genre that renders the world of advertising and commodities. Ellis introduced the endless listings of brand names and commentaries on popular culture that subsequently became so important for new German pop literature of the late 1990s. The musings of Ellis's infamously sardonic and sadistic anti-hero Patrick Bateman about material possessions, restaurants, women, and pop music made the novel a symbol for the moral implosion of the American dream in the unbridled materialism of the Reagan years, which were, as Doug Henwood argues, the true beginning of the New Economy (8–9).[25] In France, Michel Houllebecq took up the topics of the commoditization of everyday life, human isolation, and violence in his novels *Extension du domaine de la lutte* (1994, *Whatever,* 1998) and *Les particules élémentaires* (1998, *The Elementary Particles,* 2001). At the millennium, Frédéric Beigbeder's novel *99 Francs* (2000, £ *9.99,* 2002)[26], which references its own commodification in the title by referring to its actual purchasing price, reads like a literary counter piece to Klein's *No Logo*. Beigbeder, himself an insider to the world of French advertising, sends his successful copywriter Octave Parango on a narrative rampage to unmask the world of corporate advertising as one that lacks any ethics or sense of aesthetics (see Döbler, Bertschik 2010, 243–245).

Joachim Bessing's evaluation of this sphere is similar to that of his predecessors, showing continuities and thematic threads that underlie the interna-

---

**25** The graphic violence in *American Psycho* led the *Bundesprüfstelle für jugendgefährdende Schriften* to index the novel, which was not freely available in Germany until 2001.
**26** The novel was a bestseller in France and nominated for the short list of the prestigious *Prix Goncourt* in 2001.

tional phenomenon of pop literature. Born in 1971, Bessing achieved a degree of fame in literary circles because of his involvement with the *Popliterarisches Quintett* in 1999. As mentioned in chapter one, Benjamin von Stuckrad-Barre, Christian Kracht, Alexander von Schönburg, and Eckart Nickel had met for a weekend at the Hotel Adlon in Berlin, with the goal "... to solve the riddle. To work out what the basis is .. to fashion an ethical profile of our generation."[27] The five men staged a dialogue about popular culture and conversed for three days about Germany, fashion, trends, politics, and literature. Bessing then published the protocol of their conversation under the title *Tristesse Royale*, which the critics subsequently savaged in 140 reviews, according to Christian Kracht (2000).

*Wir Maschine* (2001, We Machine), Bessing's only novel to date, owes much to Ellis's cult classics *Less Than Zero* (1985) and *American Psycho*, as well as to *Glamorama* (1998), a satire of contemporary celebrity culture that features a group of models-cum-terrorists who strike various cities in the U.S. and Europe with gruesome bomb attacks. Bessing's third-person narrative centers on Gumbo, a former business administration student in hopes of a creative career who now works as an assistant at the advertising agency "Wildcard" in Hamburg. Lengthy ruminations about popular music, the latent homosexuality of various characters and their excessive drug use, recurring fantasies of violence, and the actual terrorist attacks are all a remodeling of Ellis' writing. Yet these aspects, in particular the gratuitous narration of violence, also have become stock elements in a number of other novels of contemporary literature, not only in Germany with texts such as Tim Staffel's *Terrordrom* (1998) but also in other national literatures, indicating that the preoccupation with terror is international and globalized (see Scanlan). Often these texts are functionalized as "tableaux of violence" that, while being narrated realistically, have very little to do with the reality of the Red Army Faction (RAF), the IRA, or Al-Qaida. Nils Werber thus suggests that these novels create a thesaurus of quotable surface elements that can be recombined in different textual configurations, but are void of a historical or political dimension (66).

While *Wir Maschine* certainly has aesthetic shortcomings, visible in its awkward style and use of stereotypical imagery,[28] it is nevertheless interesting for its dystopic evaluation of the (advertising) world. Both Gumbo and his supervisor and one-time lover Barbara are subjected to the constant denigra-

---

**27** "... das Rätsel zu lösen. Eine Art Fundament herauszuarbeiten ... ein Sittenbild unserer Generation zu modellieren." *Tristesse Royale* 11.
**28** Most of the reviews were rather critical of the novel, for example Maus, Varna, and Steinfeld.

tion of "Wildcard" owner Francis Gurt. His company's success is in part due to its exclusivity, as Gurt claims to take only assignments that are "fun" without paying attention to money.[29] In reality, he mostly indulges his cocaine addiction and relies on his employees to produce ideas that he then passes off as his own. Underlying the text is the realization shared by all the characters that they are nothing but cogs operating a machine devoid of meaning – hence the novel's title: "The fear that anyone might say it, that everything is so ridiculous and small. That talented adults sit around all day and chew over the role some laundry detergent might play."[30]

Mirroring the stagnation Gumbo and the other characters experience in their own life, the novel lacks interesting events, focusing instead on daily life and its domination by work. The protagonists' reaction to the meaninglessness they experience is to seek numbness and oblivion through the liberal consumption of various drugs, which in this social stratum are easily procured and socially accepted. Yet their ennui extends beyond professional activities, leading Gumbo to believe that something is fundamentally wrong with society and can only be rectified by drastic action. To escape the vicious circle of the collectivizing of individualism ("Kollektivierung des Individualimus") the motto "to bomb from within" ("von innen bomben" *WM* 116) lets Gumbo spin increasingly out of control. When the novel ends with his boss being blown to smithereens at a snack bar and passersby are hit by pieces of "ground beef, glass shards, and Francis" (*WM* 192), the reader is let to believe that Gumbo had a hand in the attack.

Many features in Bessing's novel confirm the thesis that pop literature archives a globally uniform (brand) knowledge, as Julia Bertschik has suggested in her 2010 article. Apart from the liberal consumption of drugs that is one of the most common tropes of said literature, *Wir Maschine* invokes many global brand names. One obvious example is the work of Gumbo and Barbara who are conceptualizing the catalogues for the winter collection of Jil Sander, a fashion company formerly German that is now owned by a globally operated investment firm based in London. Brands also possess a great significance for Gumbo's self-identity. His wish to belong and fit in with his colleagues makes him live above his means; he buys Eames chairs and designer dress shirts at Helmut Lang, although he knows that he will not be able to pay off either any time soon (*WM*, 110–12). The novel also illustrates how global advertising and

---

29 Bessing. *Wir Maschine*. 45. Henceforth quoted as *WM* plus page number.
30 "Die Angst, daß es einer ausspricht, daß alles so lächerlich ist und so klein. Daß begabte und erwachsene Menschen den ganzen Tag herumsitzen und brüten, welche Rolle ein Waschmittel spielen könnte." *WM* 22.

marketing strategies have standardized ideas about human beauty to the point that attaining an abstract ideal is a prerequisite for feeling attractive. With regards to the possibility of rising through the ranks and achieving a prime professional and social position, Hamburg and Los Angeles are principally interchangeable in Gumbo's mind as long as one displays the right attitude, quoting the famous Nike slogan: "Do it. Just do it. Get going. Start." (*WM* 41)

At the same time, the novel is quite specific with regards to its locality. Already on the first page the plot is situated in Hamburg, which is concretized through the naming of specific streets and existing local restaurants and bars (for example *WM* 69). In conversation Francis and Barbara gossip about real people such as Hubert Burda, Ulla Kock am Brink and Marcus Peichl, all of whom are part of the German media industry (*WM* 49). Along the same lines, the text is interspersed with historical references (for example about the Red Army Faction and the events of the German autumn in 1977, *WM* 40), as well as local and national idiosyncracies and clichés (for example about Hamburg women *WM* 40–41, or food habits in northern and southern Germany, *WM* 25). What the novel thus illustrates is an exchange between a global and a local knowledge that is typical of international pop literature that often locates the local in the global and vice versa (Bertschik 2010, 249), making Bessing's text another example of a glocalized literature.

Like *Wir Maschine*, Rainer Merkel's[31] *Das Jahr der Wunder* (2001, The Year of Miracles) was published just before it became clear that the New Economy in Germany had failed. The novel brings up a number of topics that are prominent in all of the texts interpreted in this chapter. Surprisingly it has not yet been the subject of much scholarly attention. In contrast to Bessing's text, Merkel's novel, for which he received the *Förderpreis* of the Jürgen Ponto Foundation in 2001, is much more introspective in its judgment of the marketing world.[32] Through the eyes of the main character and narrator Christian Schlier, the text conveys the optimism and fascination felt in the early years of the digital revolution and the New Economy. Yet Merkel's novel also illustrates the problematic effects the new work order means for the individual. A practicing psychologist, the author offers a more nuanced picture than Bessing, by focus-

---

**31** Rainer Merkel was born in 1964 in Cologne. He studied psychology and art history and continues to work as a freelance psychologist, although his primary occupation is writing. He has published three other novels since *Das Jahr der Wunder*, of which the last one *Lichtjahre entfernt* (2009) was nominated for the shortlist of the German Book Prize. Merkel has won various other literary prizes and was a fellow at the Villa Aurora in Los Angeles in 2003.
**32** Consequently, the reviews of the novel were overall positive. See Auffermann, Spreckelsen, and Overath.

ing on the emotional and psychological state of his main character who is a perceptive and astute observer of his surroundings. All the events are refracted through the prism of Christian's perception, and he interprets everything in direct relation to himself, making him a narcissistic and biased narrator. The text suggests, however, that his job exacerbates his narcissism. In fact, narcissism might just be the precondition for doing the job well.

The novel is set in late 1990s Berlin and deals with the operating processes in a marketing agency. After having just failed his *Physikum*, the preliminary examination for medical school, twenty-something year-old Christian decides to leave behind his life as a student and part-time taxi driver. He interviews with a multimedia agency with the mysterious name "GFPD" where his best friend Titus Mögenburg holds a leading position.[33] Without being asked about his education or work experience and without negotiating a contract (*JdW*, 14), Christian is hired on the spot as a "Konzepter" to create a communications strategy for a rather unexciting building and loan association (*Bausparkasse*). The following "annus mirabilis"[34] turns out to be a rather stressful year for him, partly because he devotes himself entirely to learning the jargon and modus of operation of the agency by working all the time. In his attempt to fit in at all costs, he neglects both his health and girlfriend Sonja and limits his social interactions exclusively to colleagues at the agency.

Erhard Schütz has shown how in fictional texts "work" is difficult to render since it is neutralized and disappears in the products it creates (17). I assert that this is especially true for the world of advertising, where end results mostly come in the form of immaterial ideas. In Merkel's and many other millennial prose texts, the working world is represented only indirectly, foregrounding the aesthetic dimensions of the topic over the ideological inflections earlier work literature might have highlighted. What is at stake here is how social relations and power structures are reconstituted through language, showing how linguistic practices barely mask a general inhumanity behind the phraseological facades of a dynamic neoliberalism. Furthermore, the texts process the question of identity construction through the professional activities of the characters, as Kremer points out (55).

---

**33** Merkel. *Das Jahr der Wunder*. Henceforth quoted in the text as *JdW* plus page number.
**34** The title alludes to the religious underpinning of the novel. According to the Oxford English Dictionary, the phrase "Annus Mirabilis" goes back to a poem by Englishman John Dryden about the events of 1666. The translation as "wonderful year" or "year of miracles" contradicts that it was filled with calamities for England (including the Great Plague and the Great Fire of London). Dryden, however, chose to interpret the absence of even greater disaster as a miraculous intervention by God.

Consequently, while Christian Schlier's attempt to develop a "concept" is all consuming and challenges him greatly, it remains obscure to the reader. Cryptic clues strewn throughout the novel, such as the advertisers' idea to reference Douglas Adams's cult classic *Hitchhiker's Guide to the Galaxy* from 1979 (*JdW*, 13, 231) and the ongoing revisions of the concept up to the day of presentation obfuscate the objective of the project. Because it remains insubstantial, the ability to sell it to the client hinges largely on the personality and charm of the manager in charge:

> Titus exudes a great confidence. With his felt marker ... he builds a complicated mechanical structure with tentacles, light barriers, and sensory instruments. The drawings make up a confusing felt marker painting... I don't understand myself what he's getting at. I have the feeling that he doesn't understand my exposé but he conveys it in such a unique way that in the end, I get the feeling that it really couldn't be any other way.[35]

The opaqueness of work as it is presented in *Das Jahr der Wunder* is a prominent leitmotif in most of the prose texts dealing with work. Although work is the central topic, its procedures and development remain largely hidden from the reader's view, while the characters' emotions and psychological reactions take center stage. In Merkel, passages like the one above convey the imaginary quality of the multimedia agency's projects and provide a relevant example for Zygmunt Bauman's statement that profits in today's world often depend on "symbol manipulators, people who invent the ideas and the ways to make them desirable and marketable" (Bauman 2000, 152). In an ironic misappropriation of the ideas that Karl Marx developed in *Das Kapital* (1867, *Capital*) about the fetishized character of commodities, advertising also seeks to create an interpretational or aesthetic surplus ("Mehr-Wert"[36]) that is communicated to the client and the public. The creative energy invested often stands in sharp contrast to the relative insignificance of the products, and even the team can-

---

**35** "Titus strahlt ein großes Vertrauen aus. Mit seinem Filzstift bildet er ... ein kompliziertes mechanisches Gebilde mit Greifarmen, Lichtschranken und Tastinstrumenten. Die Zeichnungen bilden ein verwirrendes Filzstiftgemälde... Ich verstehe selbst nicht, worauf er hinauswill. Ich habe das Gefühl, dass er mein Exposé nicht versteht, es aber auf so unnachahmliche Weise vermittelt, dass ich am Ende selbst das Gefühl habe, es könne gar nicht anders sein." *JdW* 88–89.
**36** This is how Grey, Germany's second largest marketing group, defines its corporate philosophy: "Wir kreieren den Mehr-Wert. Mit überraschenden Ideen und eindrucksvollen Ergebnissen. Für Marken. Für Kunden. Für Mitarbeiter. Wir sind das Energiefeld für inspirierende, effektive Kommunikation" (We are the ones who create the surplus. With surprising ideas and impressive results. For brands. For clients. For employees. We are the field of energy for inspiring and effective communication). http://www.grey.de.

not always be counted on to understand the imaginative vision behind the advertising concept.

Christian's occupation makes him a part of the "creative class" that economist Richard Florida has identified as a sign for the emergence of a new society and the most important warrant for economic prosperity.[37] The significance of this social group should not be underestimated in Germany either, where the number of people working in the cultural and media sectors has risen by 320% between 1995 and 2003, according to German bloggers Sascha Lobo and Holm Friebe (32). They claim that this new *digital bohème* has developed an optimistic take on the dwindling of secure employment by opting instead for independent careers that rely on the networks and collectives of the 'digital natives' (see Palfrey and Gasser). Contemporary texts reflect this social development in the choice of their characters and occupations. Protagonists might be long-term students like the narrator in Jörg Uwe Sauer's *Uniklinik* (2001), (unemployed) academics like the protagonists in Christoph Peter's *Stadt Land Fluß* (2000) and Steffen Mensching's *Lustigs Flucht* (2005), graphic designers such as Isabelle in Katharina Hacker's *Die Habenichtse* (2006, The Have-Nots, 2008) or IT (information technology) specialists such as Darius Kopp in Terézia Mora's *Der einzige Mann auf dem Kontinent* (2009, The Lone Man on the Continent). In this particular social stratum opportunities to work are actually plentiful, which qualifies my earlier statements about the dire scarcity of work. However, the overall labor market and the difficulty of finding a permanent position have led to an uncoupling of work and pay. The former loses its function as a gainful occupation although it remains the decisive marker for social recognition (Bertschik 2007, 70). Precarious circumstances lead especially interns to forgo a salary voluntarily in order to attain a permanent position later, as the discussion of the internship generation (*Generation Praktikum*) in the German media has shown (Stolz).

Merkel's hero Christian Schlier is a case in point. In his interview, he is actually the one who avoids talking about a salary, being well aware that his friend Titus had worked at the agency for half a year without being paid and even slept nights under his desk (*JdW* 15), and accepting this as a possibility for himself also. Later, salary negotiations with Wosch turn into an intricate game, in which Christian needs to convince his supervisor that he actually *deserves* a salary since the work is intrinsically meaningful and entertaining,

---

37 Many of Florida's conclusions are similar to Sennett's and Bauman's but they lack the critical appraisal of the sociologists. Florida sees the more precarious employment situations of the creative class largely as positive because they allow the individual to develop independence and agency.

"'I don't even know why I am giving you money at all', he asks, for example ... 'actually *you* should pay me.'"[38] The nonchalance with which negotiations are executed feeds into the assumption that in creative professions, personal fulfillment trumps a salary. The ongoing negotiations between Wosch and Christian that form a recurring narrative thread (*JdW* 58–59, 64, 185) as well as Christian's obsessive reflection of the right negotiation tactic debunk this myth. Just like in traditional employment contracts, money still signifies the worth of someone's work; in Christian's case, that is six thousand Deutschmarks per month, a handsome salary for an entrant.

The behavior of Merkel's protagonists identifies them as the type of flexible individuals who, according to Sennett, are brought about by the logic of late capitalism. The employees of GFPD become one with their professional activity and exploit themselves happily in the service of the agency. A fourteen-hour workday on a Sunday resembles an initiation rite that holds an almost mythical quality for Christian (*JdW* 120); a free day seems like a burden since he has lost the ability to relax and rest. It is not the managers that require that much work. Instead the group dynamics exert the pressure, affirming Bauman's argument that in modern organizations there is little need for panoptic control and surveillance. Out of fear of becoming redundant, employees want to appear enthusiastic about work at all times. The specter of insecurity makes them control and manage themselves (Bauman 2002, 35).

The text is laced with religious imagery and motifs that highlight the mythical quality the employees attribute to the agency and their work. Most obviously, it is visible in the novel's title and the aptonym of the main protagonist Christian and it extends to the biblical name Titus who brings his friend into the fold.[39] On his first visit the agency seems like a gothic cathedral to Christian (*JdW* 18–19); the architecture corresponds to the founders' understanding as prophets of new economic and social structures. The employees like to think of GFPD as a spiritual community, as signified in the reaction to one of the programmers who states "'We are not a sect'... We are laughing at him a little bit."[40] In this regard Merkel's text appears as a literary manifestation of Max Weber's analysis of modern capitalism as a transformed application of the protestant tradition in *Die protestantische Ethik und der Geist des Kapitalismus* (1904; *The Protestant Ethic and the Spirit of Capitalism*).

---

**38** "'Ich weiß gar nicht, warum ich dir überhaupt Geld gebe', fragt er zum Beispiel ... 'eigentlich müsstest *du* mir Geld geben.'" *JdW* 59.
**39** In the New Testatment, Titus is mentioned in several of the Pauline epistles as his companion; he is also said to have organized the church in Crete as a missionary.
**40** "'Wir sind doch keine Sekte' ... Wir lachen ihn ein bisschen aus ..." *JdW* 155.

To Christian the agency feels like a community in which everybody is free to exercise his creative inspirations and voice his opinions independently of rank; they are like a family according to Grassi, one of Christian's supervisors (*JdW* 115). The managers of GFPD cement this familial impression and its flat hierarchy by encouraging a blurring of professional and private time. The employees hold meetings at their apartments, spend time together at the bar after work, and go swimming together to recharge, while still talking about their projects. Grassi wants Christian to be "happy" and feel "at home" at the agency and encourages him to express how he feels (*JdW* 115–16), echoing Bauman's evaluation of 'liquid modernity' as a time in which "leadership has been replaced by the spectacle, and surveillance by seduction." (Bauman 2000, 155) The architecture and spatial layout of the agency also support the illusionary transparency that a flat hierarchy seems to entail. Open floor plans with office spaces divided by frosted glass enable an open door policy and the flow of information. The agency's seclusion from the outside world, marked by "narrow, embrasure-like windows" (*JdW* 7) and "steel doors" that seem to be mock entrances leading into cul-de-sac (*JdW* 9) heighten the impression of a nuclear unit to which the outside world has only limited access.

But just like any family unit possesses a particular structure and implicit hierarchy, so does the agency. While Christian does not understand in the beginning "who has which function, who is in charge and who decides what when" (*JdW* 68), he soon internalizes the subtle pecking order and demarcating lines between the creative department at the top (directors and copywriters) art directors and "Konzepter" like Christian in the middle, and production (graphic designers, programmers) at the bottom. He starts to exert pressure on those underneath him, such as graphic designer Tatjana (*JdW* 152), attempts to outplay possible competitors and to flatter his superiors, for example Gudula, the agency's 26-year-old creative director. The narrative reveals the intense pressures Sennett identifies as a side effect of teamwork, which leads Christian to bad-mouth even his best friend Titus to whom he owes his chance in the first place (*JdW* 238–41).

The close ties teamwork brings about at the agency also have positive sides. Organizations with reduced bureaucratic structures and flat hierarchies produce a sense of independence that translates into an empowerment of the individual. Social control changes its form from discipline to "therapy" and new forms of organization tie people together informally and might reduce feelings of insecurity, as researchers less pessimistic than Bauman have suggested (Poder 141). Along the lines of this sociological argument critics find that Christian perceives and analyzes his surroundings with a sense of wonder and remains strangely dégagé (Knipphals). According to Viviana Chilese, his strong uncritical identification with the agency also indicates ambivalence on Merkel's part (297). That the author himself also worked in a Berlin multimedia agency and was part of something that for him had revolutionary potential (see Chilese) might also be a reason why the novel does not culminate in terrorist mayhem like Bessing's *Wir Maschine* or Ellis' *Glamorama*.

Nevertheless, there is a noticeable critical undercurrent in Merkel's text. Both the images of the prison and the agency conjure notions of power, knowledge, and control that Foucault analyzed in his works, especially his ideas about the disciplining of bodies in *The History of Sexuality* (1976). *Discipline and Punish: The Birth of the Prison* (1975) is even prominently mentioned in the novel as one of Grassi's favorite books. Yet the supervisor explicitly advises a curious Christian against reading it, as if he fears that this might spark an unwelcome epiphany: "... But you should rather not buy it. We need you here. *With us*" (*JdW* 67). On a different occasion, Christian uses the book as a conversation opener to make the acquaintance of a woman, but reveals in the process that he believes the book to be a novel and has no idea of its content (*JdW* 124–25). The mention of Foucault is the most obvious hint to the hidden forms of coercion that the agency exerts over its employees. Those individuals do not question the web of power and dependencies in which they find themselves, nourishing instead the notion of being in control. What betrays this idea, however, is Christian's relationship to his body. When he is at the lake with Gudula, his teammate and superior, she asks him to dive in headfirst. Despite not being an experienced swimmer, he overcomes his uneasiness but badly bruises his abdomen in the process.

> And then I imagine how I dove in. It really is a nice feeling. How I lean forward and enter into a conversation with my body, as if I had to convince it of something. I also think: it is very simple, I just need to give my body a command.
> My body says: "Don't believe that I can stand pain."
> I say: "Don't think I'll take anything from you."
> My feet cling to the wooden boards.
> My body says: "*I am not diving in,*" or it says "I am not diving in just like that." ...
> My body says something, I say something. ... I make an agreement, I agree to a pact with my body. ...
> "You were great," she says. "It was a gigantic leap."
> "Was it a header?" I ask while I remember the stabbing pain in my chest and the feeling that my whole body was ripped into two.[41]

---

41 "Und dann stelle ich mir vor, wie ich gesprungen bin. Es ist eigentlich ein schönes Gefühl. Wie ich mich vorbeuge und mit meinem Körper in Zwiesprache trete, so als müsste ich ihn zu irgendwas überreden. Ich denke noch: Es ist ganz einfach, ich muss meinem Körper nur einen Befehl geben. Mein Körper sagt: 'Glaub nicht, dass ich Schmerzen aushalten kann.' Ich sage: 'Denk nicht, dass ich mir alles gefallen lasse.' Meine Füße krallen sich an den Holzbrettern fest. Mein Körper sagt: '*Ich springe nicht*', oder er sagt 'Ich springe

Christian is deeply at odds with his own body. In his first year at the agency he deprives himself of sleep, does not eat properly and is exposed to constant stress. In order to become part of a successful team he overlooks the signs of burnout his body sends him and forces himself to function instead. Towards the end of his *Jahr der Wunder* he starts a running regimen that, given winter in Berlin, seems like an enormous challenge: "I can already see it, the image of a pitch-dark night and how I have to struggle with closed eyes against the icy wind." (*JdW* 281) Considering recent developments at the agency, we should view Christian's new routine as the metaphorical race to stay in the game. An American company has just bought out GFPD, leaving the employees in doubt about the future. While Titus is promoted, Mohlberger is forced into early semi-retirement and Wosch leaves the agency. Christian, whose work on the *Spar-kasse* project is finished, cannot be sure that he will be part of the new company. Since the disciplining of his own body worked before as a strategy, he begins his gruesome training program ("martialische[s] Training," *JdW* 279) following the belief that a trained body is the precondition for a functioning employee. Because Christian has no control over his professional fate, being able to control his own body reassures. Furthermore, the body is the concretization of the economization of the social reality (Ablass 164) that both Sennett and Bauman diagnose. Foucault's analysis of the relationship between power and the body comes to mind that illustrates the economization of the social sphere manifesting in the body:

> In fact nothing is more material, physical, corporal than the exercise of power. What mode of investment of the body is necessary and adequate for the functioning of a capitalist society like ours? (Foucault 1980, 57–58)

The production of over-disciplined bodies through the process of capitalist normatization is also an important topic in the second sphere of work that is under scrutiny in millennial literary texts, namely the consulting business. The profession holds a particular interest for both prose authors and playwrights as a narrative object, which is due to the fact that it illustrates well how detachment plays out in the reality of the workplace. As explicated earlier in this chapter with the help of Richard Sennett's work, social distance increases and adds to the inequalities that are inherent to modern bureaucracies. Consultants

---

nicht einfach so.' … Mein Körper sagt etwas, ich sage etwas. … Ich treffe eine Vereinbarung, schließe mit meinem Körper einen Pakt. … 'Du warst großartig', sagt sie. 'Es war ein gigantischer Sprung.' 'War es ein Kopfsprung?', frage ich, während ich mich an den stechenden Schmerz im Brustraum erinnere, das Gefühl, mein ganzer Körper würde entzweigerissen." *JdW* 268, 270.

reorganize companies according to the rules of efficiency, which generally coincides with lay-offs and the abolition of entire departments. They do not, however, take responsibility for implementing these changes. Also, they often have little understanding of creative processes and their inherent value. Hence consulting activities carried out by big companies effectively divorce command from accountability and thus reveal a fundamental shifting of bureaucratic ground (Sennett 2006, 55–57).

Furthermore, globally active companies such as McKinsey & Co. and BCG (Boston Consulting Group) hold an important place in the social imagination of Germany and have become an increasingly important reference point for the individual. Author Kathrin Röggla, whose novel *wir schlafen nicht* (2004) is set in the consulting business and will be analyzed later in this chapter, claims that it plays an enormously important societal role: "We base our values and norms [on management consulting], and it straps us into a corset of neoliberal values. The Federal government conducts its politics in exactly the same way: suddenly the unemployed are loafers, while you yourself become Me, Incorporated."[42] Röggla suggests that our fascination with consultants generates a social phantasm expressing the ideological premise of neoliberalism, namely that social change is only possible through and in the economic field. John von Düffel echoes this sentiment almost verbatim when he expresses his belief that consultants determine the mechanisms by which our world operates and hold a monopoly on the current ideology that prescribes how people are supposed to function.[43]

The significance authors and their literary texts assign to the consulting business is interesting because it points to the different social histories of Germany and the United States. Germans in general seem much more critical about the practices of these firms, which consequently leads to more discussions in the public sphere than in the U.S., as is especially obvious in the *Feuilleton*. One possible explanation is the widespread belief in social welfare and equality that has more currency with Germans, despite the fact that in a globalized economy, neoliberal economic practices rule their markets as well. Yet Germany's social market economy – characterized by the significance banks have over the stock market, a balance of power between shareholders

---

**42** "Wir richten unsere Werte und Normen nach [der Unternehmensberatung], und sie spannt uns in ein neoliberales Wertekorsett ein. Genauso macht die Bundesregierung Politik: Auf einmal sind Arbeitslose Faulenzer, und man selbst ist eine Ich-AG." In Tollmann.

**43** "Ich hatte mich für meinen Roman *Ego* viel mit Unternehmensberatern beschäftigt, die ja im Prinzip heute die Programmierungshoheit für unsere Welt haben. … Das Interessante ist, das [die Unternehmensberatung] gegenwärtig eine Art Ideologie-Monopol innehat. Dass von ihr die Programme formuliert werden, nach denen die Menschen ticken." In Tabert 255.

and management, and a social partnership between unions and employers – is more just and efficient than the "Neo-American" model instituted by the Margaret Thatcher and Ronald Reagan in the UK and U.S. respectively (see Albert). This is mirrored not just in the public but also the literary discourse of the country, as the following readings show.


## Economized Bodies: John von Düffel's *EGO* (2001)

The novel *EGO* (2001) by John von Düffel[44] illustrates how these cross-social issues influence notions of subjectivity. At the core of Düffel's dramatic and prose works are often social problems, such as globalization, terror, and power that necessitate grappling with the question how to aesthetically render these complex topics, which due to their abstractness are detached from the individual. In a discussion about his play *Elite I.1* (2002), which he developed after finishing *EGO*, Düffel explains that many of our contemporary conflicts are diverted into the individual's own perception and processed in a radically subjective manner:

> The war is what one battles within. ... These are inner conflicts, even though the theater is an objective medium, a panoramic medium ("Medium der Totalen") ... The inner monologue really is not a performance form ("Spielform"), maybe it even is the negation of theater. ... But what is interesting is that *Elite I.1.* is closest to my novels, especially *Ego*, which is also an extreme inner monologue.[45]

The mention of inner monologue and what we might call monadic subjectivity are two important aspects of the novel. Told over the course of three days from the perspective and in the voice of Philipp, a "turbo egoist trapped in wellness, control, and career delusions" (Maus), *EGO* narrates Philipp's obsession with

---

44 Von Düffel was born in 1966 in Göttingen. He truly is a multi-talent who studied economics and philosophy and completed a doctorate in the latter subject in 1989. Since 2001 he has worked at various German theaters as a dramaturg, among them the *Thalia Theater* Hamburg and the *Deutsches Theater* in Berlin. Von Düffel is also one of the most prolific German playwrights, whose plays are staged all over Germany; he also writes radio plays and scripts (for example, for Max Färberböck's film *September*, 2003), essays, and has published seven novels since 1998 besides *EGO*. Information taken from Düffel's web site: http://johnvondueffel.de/John/Start.html.
45 "Der Konflikt, der Krieg, ist der, den ich mit mir selbst kämpfe. ... Es handelt sich um innere Konflikte, obgleich das Theater ein Medium des Objektiven, der Totalen ist. ... Der innere Monolog ist an sich keine Spielform, vielleicht sogar die Verneinung von Theater. ... Interessant ist, dass *Elite I.1.* meinen Romanen am nächsten ist, besonders *Ego*, auch ein extremer innerer Monolog." Von Düffel/Schößler 49.

his body and fitness, as well as his attempts to climb the corporate ladder of Stickroth & Partner, the consulting firm for which he works. Interestingly, Philipp is another clone of Bret Easton Ellis's Patrick Bateman in *American Psycho* (1991). The two characters resemble one another because of their obsession with the body and the ways other people react to them, their misogynist attitudes and a tendency towards sadistic behavior. What connects the two novels aesthetically is the stylistic device of the inner monologue, through which the male characters narrate realistic, detailed descriptions of the surrounding world while remaining entirely on the surface of things. By using *American Psycho* as intertext, Düffel gestures towards the beginning of hyper-capitalism and neoliberalism during the Reagan years and suggests that on an interpersonal level, things might not have changed all that much.

As we have already seen in *Das Jahr der Wunder*, contemporary literature shows a sensibility for the intertwining of economic and bodily motives, and Düffel's narrative is another distinctive example of this trend. In *EGO* the main character's professional and fitness goals are completely enmeshed. Taking the Roman poet Juvenal's *mens sana in corpore sano* to a different, satirically elevated meaning, Philipp believes that achieving a perfectly sculpted body with a completely flat navel ("Nabeltiefe null") is directly related to his professional success and career advancement: "Anyone who wants to be taken seriously these days must absolutely be an athlete, whether he works in the computer sector or as branch manager in a supermarket. To be an athlete is dogma."[46] Consequently he invests an enormous amount of time, effort, and money into his fitness training and tirelessly analyzes the effect his sculpted physique might have on the people with whom he interacts. He positions himself, both literally and figuratively, in the best possible light to impress his bosses Stickroth and Sprick, his office adversary Claaßen, his fiancé Isabell, his attractive secretary Viola, as well as random people he meets in the outside world, i.e. at the gym. Philipp's appearance always has the character of a performance and his body is the advertising canvas for favorable self-presentation:

> Meanwhile I am searching for the best possible angle against the backlight and remain for a moment in a profile position to duly accentuate my torso. Then I am standing with my back to her, put my hands in my pockets and play very slowly with my muscles. My white shirt should almost look transparent in this light, my upper body a dark silhouette. First I pump up my arms and then hold the tension in the shoulder muscles. If she looks

---

**46** "Jeder, der heute ernstgenommen werden will, muß absolut Athlet sein, ob er nun in der Computerbranche arbeitet oder als Filialleiter in einem Supermarkt. Athletsein ist Dogma." John von Düffel. *EGO* 121.

up from her notes now, she should see my back like a V-shaped silhouette against a light background. I am listening to her voice to see when she will lock on with her eyes.[47]

His obsession with his body ultimately reveals Philipp as a very insecure person. This paradoxicially makes him an ideal consultant, according to research Düffel did about McKinsey & Co., the global management-consulting firm. One of the founder's principles concerns employees' need to be "performance-oriented and insecure." This seems counterintuitive to what we expect of consultants, but Düffel explains further: "Someone who is insecure has more ambition to create himself, to literally work out his self-assurance. People who are ego dependent ("Ego-süchtig") ... are willing to do anything."[48] To return to the novel, Philipp, then, appears as a mixture of the mythological figures of Narcissus and a "reversed" Pygmalion whose aim it is to make his own living, moving body into a sculpture. This leads one critic to call the novel an "artist's tale" (Marx 102).

On both a thematic and formal level, Düffel makes extensive use of repetitious structures (see Stricker 138). For example, on the three days narrated in the novel, the beginnings of the respective three chapters vary little. First, this illustrates Philipp's obsessive worrying about the state of his body, which he tries to remedy by performing an especially challenging morning training, and reveals his intellectual limitations. In fact, partly due to his repetitive speech and endless circling of the same topics, the reader is reminded of the clichéd image of a 'workout automaton' that Arnold Schwarzenegger popularized through his movies. Yet the text's repetitious nature and the use of hyperbole also make it a "wellness satire," as critic Stephan Maus calls it, heightening the comedic effect.

---

**47** "Unterdessen suche ich den günstigsten Winkel zum Gegenlicht und verharre einen Augenblick im Profil, um meinen Brustkasten gebührend hervorzuheben. Dann stelle ich mich mit dem Rücken zu ihr, stecke die Hände in die Hosentaschen und lasse sehr langsam die Muskeln spielen. Mein weißes Hemd müßte bei diesen Lichtverhältnissen beinahe transparent sein, mein Oberkörper eine dunkle Silhoutte. Ich pumpe zunächst die Arme auf und halte dann die Spannung in der Schultermuskulatur. Wenn sie von ihren Notizen aufschaut, müßte sie jetzt meinen Rücken sehen wie einen V-förmigen Scherenschnitt auf hellem Grund. Ich lausche ihrer Stimme, um herauszuhören, wann sie mit den Augen andockt." *EGO* 20.

**48** "Die Menschen, die für mich arbeiten – soll McKinsey gesagt haben –, müssen erstens leistungsbewusst und zweitens unsicher sein. Ich fand das erstaunlich und dachte zuerst, es müsse 'selbstsicher' heißen. Aber im Zuge des Romans merkte ich, dass 'unsicher' stimmt. Denn jemand, der ein Gefühl für sich selbst hat ... ist nicht bereit, bestimmte Leistungsgrenzen zu überschreiten. ... Dagegen hat jemand, der unsicher ist, stärker den Ehrgeiz, sich selbst neu zu erschaffen, sich sein Selbstbewusstsein buchstäblich zu erarbeiten." In Tabert 255.

Although the protagonist's ambition and the prospect of becoming the firm's junior partner motivate constant plotting and elaborate maneuvers to outsmart Claaßen and endear himself to his boss, Philipp spends little time actually working because he consistently puts his elaborate training schedule, sauna visits, and nutritional needs first. Even when he is in the office, he constantly works out, using his desk to do push-ups while distractedly talking on the phone (25) or flexing one of his various other muscles. *EGO* describes a working world where gainful employment is redefined as working on the body,[49] which corresponds to the theoretical insight that neoliberal practices have made the body into a performative instrument meant to serve as a flawlessly operating social resource. At the same time the body itself becomes a "Me stock" ("Ich-Aktie," Maus), an enterprise that needs constant planning, investment, and calculation (Ablass 171).

In order to survive and triumph in the work place, Philipp has to internalize the rules of the economic market place and relentlessly strive to improve his body and athletic performance, pushing himself beyond psychological weakness, sore muscles, motivational problems, and the desire to eat unhealthy foods and consume alcohol. He needs to control his body at all costs and consequently ignores the somatic dysfunctions signaling its fragility. Philipp's will triumphs over his physical being, in order to worship and uphold the "religion of the body" presented to us every day in advertising and other media; physical matter provides but the raw material to model oneself according to one's own desires and create a perfect form.[50] The protagonist thus embodies the effect of the body's occupation by power that Foucault describes: "Mastery and awareness of one's own body can be acquired only through the effect of an investment of power in the body: gymnastics, exercises, muscle-building, nudism, glorification of the body beautiful. ... Power, after investing itself in the body, finds itself exposed to a counter-attack in the same body." (Foucault 1980, 56)

The logic of neoliberalism determines not only the character's relationship to his own body but also rules his personal life. His engagement to the beautiful, successful, and athletic consultant Isabell is based on competitiveness and manipulation. Both need each other to achieve their goals; they depend on their partner's physical attractiveness to valorize their own ego and social

---

**49** "Erwerbsarbeit wird zur Arbeit am Körper." Kremer 100.

**50** In his essay "Auslaufmodell Ich" (2002) Düffel analyzes the pressures of modern men to live up to the standards of physical attractiveness promoted by the media. Philipp is the living example by perceiving his own body as something that needs to be whipped into shape at all costs.

standing. When Isabell does not give up her plan to have a child despite Philip's resistance, he agrees to it in a strategic move meant to sidetrack her career and surpass her on the corporate ladder, only to find out that an already pregnant Isabell is ahead of him by becoming the successor of one of the firm's two founders. Yet it is not just the female body that becomes the biopolitical playing field[51] in the corporate rat race. Philipp will have to use his own body to sexually "service" and repay his boss's wife, who was instrumental in his promotion.

With the relationship of Philipp and Isabell, the text demonstrates how economic principles influence and shape all interpersonal relationships, even those that are traditionally based on love, emotions, and mutual respect. Düffel furthermore comments on the dissolution of traditional gender roles and reveals that callous egotism is not relegated exclusively to the male sphere traditionally linked to economics. Both female and male bodies become streamlined in confrontation with neoliberalist business practices and are integrated into the circuits of the capitalist machinery.[52] Through the amalgamation of economic principles and the body, the subject is no longer created through discipline and punishment, but is the result of an optimization process. The real subject now is the economy itself.[53]

## The Readability of the World in Ghostly Times: Kathrin Röggla's *wir schlafen nicht* (2004)

Although Kathrin Röggla, born in 1971 in Salzburg, nominally belongs to the *Generation Golf*, her texts differ fundamentally from those of her contemporar-

---

**51** Ablass calls the body a "biopolitischer Spielball im Karrierewettlauf," 174.

**52** This is also visible in Ernst-Wilhelm Händler's *Wenn wir sterben* (2002). At the center of the novel are three former girl friends, Charlotte, Stine, and Bär and their attempts to overtake each other in a business venture, which leads to their eventual downfall. The novel is distinctly not plot-driven but an orchestra of voices and different narrative perspectives that was well received by critics. My main reason for not including a detailed reading of the text in this chapter is that Händler was born in 1953 and thus is not part of the *Generation Golf*. *Wenn wir sterben*, as well as Händler's other works, has also received much critical attention already. See Hagestedt and Unseld.

**53** In *Wenn wir sterben*, the character Charlotte thinks of her factory as a son that has just "come into this world" and that she prefers over her real daughter Ethel: "Die Fabrik brauchte keinen Hüter. Dennoch war Charlotte die Hüterin der Fabrik. Sollte sie begründen, warum sie das war, wollte sie nicht sagen, weil sie als einzige die Fabrik verstanden hatte. Auch Bär und Stine hatten die Fabrik verstanden. Sie drückten nur alles anders aus, aber auch sie wußten, wie Charlotte, daß die Fabrik ein Wesen war, das fühlte und dachte." 34.

ies. True, her artistic projects are radically focused on the present, in other words on the issue of aesthetic representations of the Here and Now, something that applies to many younger authors. However, Röggla goes far beyond realistic representation and authenticity of the everyday (*authentische Alltäglichkeit*) analyzed in chapter two and rejects chronological narrative strands and identifiable characters. Her consistent use of lower-case letters, combined with a writing style that works with a rhythmic structure, repetition and ellipses and is dominated by the subjunctive mood used to convey reported speech, prevents the straightforward consumption of the texts whose meaning often only unfolds after multiple readings.

With this approach, Röggla is consciously following the traditional impulse toward linguistic criticism seen in historical avant-garde movements, such as the *Wiener Gruppe* and experimental forms of pop literature in the 1960s and 1970s.[54] Furthermore, she is strongly influenced by poststructuralist theories; in particular, the discourse theories of Judith Butler and Michel Foucault have left clear traces in her work. In her more recent texts, Foucault's concept of governmentality serves as a canvas upon which Röggla sketches out strategies for dealing with societal situations shaped by neoliberal thinking and the internalization of authority. In terms of content, the central issue here is what it means to live in a globalized, post-national community regulated by neoliberalism, and how to go about describing the construction of identities and subjects within social systems (see Foucault 2004).

Poetologically speaking, Röggla takes up the discourse-theory approach according to which language constitutes people as subjects and political beings and attempts to translate it into an aesthetic form, highlighting the linguistic power structures that frame both social space and the individual. However, Röggla is not attempting to implement Foucault's theory directly, to obliterate the boundary between theory and practice in literature, or – as in Thomas Meinecke's novels *Tomboy* (1998) and *Musik* (2004) – to develop behavioral "guidelines" for the protagonists. Instead, she undertakes a form of aesthetic appropriation that demonstrates the forms subjectivity takes, the coercive mechanisms that arise through the self-regulation of the neoliberally administered subject, and the price paid by the individual as a result of transferring social organizational structures into the subject itself. In so doing, she refers

---

**54** The consistent use of small letters is the most obvious link to the *Wiener Gruppe* and enables the reader, according to Röggla, to see language as a medium molded by mass media and pervaded by power structures. See Kasaty 262. The skepticism regarding language and its limits connotes Röggla with Elfriede Jelinek's early works *wir sind lockvögel, baby!* (1970) and *Michael* (1979), where the aesthetics of pop, theorems of Marxism, feminism, and postmodern thought intersect, similarly to Röggla's writing.

to a study by Sven Opitz (2004) who through an analysis of management literature details how the postfordist business regulates itself through governmental
structures, thereby creating subjectivity. For example, Opitz shows that the
cipher of entrepreneurship is not limited to the professional realm anymore
but increasingly describes a general mode of operation. The individual is given
more responsibility, which leads to an identification with the corporation and
a higher degree of productivity.

Röggla's aesthetic translation of poststructuralist thought reveals its politically productive moments, because her novels and plays take up the questions
that arise from this field and apply them to certain life practices and problems.
The spectrum ranges from representing peripheral everyday lives beyond the
hyped center of the New Berlin in *irres wetter* (2000), to dealing with structures
of fear, such as aviophobia in the play *junk space* (2004), to addressing the
issue of debt-counseling mechanisms in the play *draußen tobt die dunkelziffer*
(2005,) and in the prose piece *die wiedergänger* (2005). Röggla describes the
vanishing point of this artistic project as an attempt to develop "a type of
counter-charm, a type of counter-ghost to the ghostliness of the world that
surrounds us."[55]

Röggla's engagement with theoretical questions goes hand in hand with
the fundamental motivation for her own work, which can be identified as a
striving toward social justice (see Behrendt). Accordingly, her subjects are
taken from contemporary reality, and her material comes from experiences that
are collected in interviews and protocols from the working world. Through this
mixture of documentary and fictional sources, Röggla is consciously updating
certain positions held by Alexander Kluge, who in the mid 1970s had identified
the will to protest, in other words the anti-realistic moment, as a motif of
realistic behavior.[56] In this way, Röggla – clearly following also in Adorno's
footsteps – subscribes to the idea of continuing and renewing a project of
enlightenment, in which political thinking and social commitment are central.
While literature cannot be political per se, for Röggla it can have political
effects and thematize political issues:

> in any case it seems impossible to me to imagine the literary aesthetic field minus its
> tension with the political [...] [texts] are communications, so they are also inherently
> inscribed with a social relationship – and this social element is not disinterested. [...] the

---

55 "... eine art gegenzauber, eine art gegenspuk zu jener spukhaftigkeit der uns
umgebenden welt." Röggla 2006.
56 „Das Motiv für Realismus ist nie Bestätigung der Wirklichkeit, sondern Protest." Kluge
128.

goal cannot be to defuse this tension between aesthetics and politics, but instead to make it clearly focused and visible.[57]

One can further investigate "the aesthetic back alleys through the political" ("schleichwege des ästhethischen durch das politische," Röggla 2004) by analyzing the novel *wir schlafen nicht*. Surprisingly, despite her positive reception by literary critics, Röggla's texts have until now gone almost unanalyzed in Anglo-American German studies, a lacuna that is all the more surprising because Röggla has been extremely prolific.[58] Interestingly, she often works with the same material in various genres and media, as demonstrated by the simultaneous production of *wir schlafen nicht* as a novel, a stage play and a radio play.[59]

The process of switching from one genre or medium to another is virtually programmatic for Röggla's work. The multimediality expressed through this hybridization takes us to the core of her material concept. Röggla sees herself as an "architect" of her texts, one who does not hold a sovereign authorial position but instead often functions as a "translating organ" ("Übersetzungsorgan," Kaiser and Böhnke). She identifies the availability of many-faceted, disparate pieces of information about the world as the decisive starting point for her writing, which then manifests itself as various "small media-based classifications" ("mediale kleinanordnungen") such as interviews, photos, readings, transcripts, etc. These make their way into the literary prose or the stage play, so that each text always bears the traces of various media. In Röggla's view, the process of finding an aesthetic form that best complements the material, rewriting a book five to ten times in the process and moving again and again through a "textual space" ("textraum") is what most closely corresponds to the

---

**57** "das literarisch-ästhetische ohne seine spannung zum politischen zu denken, scheint mir jedenfalls unmöglich. … [texte] sind kommunikationen, also ist ihnen auch ein soziales verhältnis eingeschrieben – und dieses soziale ist nicht interesselos. … es kann nicht darum gehen, diese spannung zwischen ästhetik und politik zu entschärfen, sondern [sie] im gegensatz scharf und sichtbar zu machen."
Röggla 2004.
**58** Apart from five prose works of which only two are labeled as "novels" – namely *abrauschen* (1997) and *wir schlafen nicht* (2004) – Röggla has written dramatic texts that are regularly staged in Germany, Austria, and Switzerland, as well as other prose texts and essays. She also works in broadcasting and has produced eighteen radio plays and features since 1999. See http://www.kathrin-roeggla.de/aether/.
**59** The novel *wir schlafen nicht* (S. Fischer) was published in March 2004; the premiere of the play took place on April 7, 2004 at the Schauspielhaus Düsseldorf (Director: Burkhard Kosminski); Bayrischer Rundfunk broadcast the radio play on February 16, 2004 (Director: Barbara Schäfer).

real circumstances of a media-saturated world (Kasaty 273, 283). It also quickly leads to a dead end for any reader following the traditional rules of textual hermeneutics. This is not only true for Röggla, but also other contemporary texts that consciously showcase their intermediality. I am thinking of Thomas Meinecke who in his novels samples poststructuralist gender theories with pop discourse, or Rainald Goetz's books *Abfall für alle* (1999) and *Klage* (2008) that consist of material first published in online blogs.

*wir schlafen nicht* deals with the stress of everyday work in the field of management consulting, and the social and psychological dislocations that employees experience as a result of work routines and company ideologies. As already mentioned with regard to John von Düffel's *EGO*, Röggla sees globally active consulting companies as an important point of social identification. The novel unmasks the belief that the economic field can bring about social change on various levels. In its content, it does so by representing "flexible" employees who are transformed by the demands of the neoliberal working world into ghosts alienated from themselves, perhaps even zombies. On a formal level, forms of unrealistic speech reinforce the impression of a "ghost novel" ("gespensterroman"), as Roeggla has repeatedly called her own book. In consequence, the desire to achieve a professional existence in which one can be identical with oneself is revealed as a fiction of authenticity.

The novel is a highly structured hybrid of fictive and documentary elements. The narration – it is difficult to identify a plot – is based on Röggla's research in the consulting sector. From 2000 to 2003, she conducted extensive interviews with employees in the New Economy, as well as various management-consulting firms. In her interviews, Röggla uses a journalistic technique that she describes as "hysterical affirmation " ("hysterische Affirmation") and which she credits to author Hubert Fichte: Questions are used to drive the conversation partner more and more deeply into his own rhetoric, in order to arrive at an essence that highlights the cracks and contradictions in the discourse.[60] The characters' "business jargon" ("bwler-deutsch")[61] thus reveals the way in which the sector downgrades people to material, and it indicates the power structures in which they are trapped:

> "we just defined who our 'a' people are. i mean, we did a simple ranking. the 'a' people, they're our top performers, those are the ones – we want to keep them no matter what, the really strong performers, the ones who really know a lot and who've been here a long

---

60 "Zuerst erzählt dir jeder einmal, wie toll es ist, wie spannend es ist und was man alles machen kann. Und selbst wenn du sie bestärkst, kommt dann irgendwann recht schnell der Kipppunkt, an dem das alles abstürzt." Röggla in Kaiser and Böhnke.
61 *wir schlafen nicht* 219. Henceforth quoted as *WSN* plus page number.

time. that's the core of the company. if they go away, you can close up shop. then there are some where we say, they're good too, but everything won't fall apart if they leave. ... and then there are the 'c' people. ... they can read and write, maybe they've studied economics, but that's it. and then you have to say, we can't do anything with these people anymore." (the partner, *WSN* 84–85)[62]

In this way, the novel illustrates Judith Butler's theory that linguistic utterances not only reflect social power structures, but also, again and again, performatively reconstitute the power structures exercised through language.[63] This becomes particularly clear in the consulting milieu, since the rhetoric here is constantly subject to strategic language about efficiency and maximizing performance.

Röggla used the attitudes and characteristics revealed in the protocols to develop six fictional characters, whose names, ages and professional titles are identified on the first page of the novel. Over the course of the book's thirty-two chapters, these people – three men and three women on various rungs of the corporate ladder – speak with a female interviewer (possibly a journalist) at a trade fair about their day-to-day work. The questions, however, are omitted, and we learn nothing about the narrator, who acts as a type of ghostly translating organ. The narrator simply reports what the employees share about their experiences leading a "yuppie-high-flyer-life" ("yuppie-high-flyer-leben") – how they deal with the omnipresent stress and the resulting lack of sleep, or with the fact that they hardly have any time for a personal life, or with knowing that their work primarily leads to layoffs and ruins careers:

"so you boiled things down for yourself, something like this: there was really no such thing as the family man with three children who ended up without an income and couldn't put food on the table. or at least that was relatively rare. ... no, usually people left not so much for moral reasons, more because they were just sick of the lifestyle: all of those power naps, quick meals and that sort of thing. And all that hotel sleeping, business-class flying and first-class living. At some point you just couldn't take any more

---

62 "'wir haben eben definiert, welche unsere a-personen sind. also wir haben ein einfaches ranking gemacht. die a-personen, das sind unsere top-performer, das sind die, die wollen wir auf jeden fall halten, die ganz starken leistungsträger, die, die unheimlich viel wissen und lang dabei sind. das ist eben der kern des unternehmens. wenn die weggehen, kann man zusperren. dann gibt es welche, da sagen wir, die sind auch gut, aber wenn die gehen, bricht nicht alles zusammen. ... und dann gibt es die c-personen. ... die gerade lesen und schreiben können, die vielleicht wirtschaft studiert haben, aber sonst gar nichts. und da muß man sagen: mit diesen leuten können wir nichts mehr anfangen' (der partner)." *WSN* 84–85.

63 "What does it mean for a word not only to name but also in some sense to perform and, in particular, to perform what it names?" Butler 43.

of it. … but there was also that logic of constant growth, which at some point you even turned against yourself." (the senior associate)[64]

As this passage and the subjunctive that dominates the novel make clear, Röggla is not attempting to create an authentic oral transcript. The language is a hybrid mixture of hypotactic sentences, dialogic fragments, Anglicisms and repetitions that takes on increasingly hysterical, hyperbolic traits toward the end of the novel. The artificiality of this structured, rhythmic language, together with the use of reported speech, creates distance and prevents the reader from identifying with the figures or their lives. In this way, the text undermines the longing for a new realism with which the viewer or reader can attempt to counteract an increasingly mediated and regulated world – currently, popular media formats like reality shows and documentary soaps satisfy this need (Röggla 2005, 2). However, any form of media framework is ultimately a staging process, since media only creates the appearance of authenticity in its representation of reality, and cannot ever truly be authentic. Thus Röggla's linguistic form is an updated version of the Brechtian alienation effect (*V-Effekt*). In keeping with the dictum of Brecht's *A Little Organum for the Theater* (1948), according to which the material must distance the audience in order to allow critical reflection, the linguistic form in Röggla's work undercuts any possible authenticity fantasies on the part of the reader. This is also true for her dramatic texts, which follow epic-didactic principles as well.

The end of the novel plays a decisive role in this. In the last three chapters, the figures talk their way into an increasingly irritated, claustrophobic "trade-show tantrum" ("Messekoller," Kormann 237). The story builds up to an eerie, catastrophic scenario, in view of which the narrative tempo paradoxically grows slower and slower. Under the pressures of their day-to-day work, the figures are transformed into ghosts, or rather the living dead for whom, as outlined in Chapter 25 ("shock"), there can be no way out of the exhibition hall: "how long one had already been deceased, that was the real question after all" (the partner, 203); "he believed he had been deceased for some time" (the senior associate, 203) *"the key account manager: no, resurrection, that*

---

64 "so koche man die dinge für sich runter, so unter dem motto: der dreifache familienvater, der dann ohne lohn und brot dastehe, den gebe es ja doch eher nicht. oder zumindest relativ selten. … nein, meist gingen die leute dann weniger aus moralischen gründen, sondern weil der life-style sie total ankotze: all das short-sleeping, quick-eating und diese ganzen nummern. Und das hotelgeschlafe, das business-class-gefliege, das first-class gewohne. Irgendwann könne man das alles nicht mehr sehen. … aber auch diese ewige wachstumslogik, die man irgendwann gegen sich selbst anwende. (der senior associate)." *WSN* 37–38.

was what they had been talking about all along" (204); the senior associate talks about the feeling of "walking through a constant catastrophe, feeling constantly at war" ("durch eine permanente katastrophe zu gehen, einen permanenten kriegszustand wahrzunehmen," 215). There are indications of the dismissal of a firm partner and his possible suicide, under the influence of which time begins to stretch out. Here Röggla's narrative technique becomes filmic and acoustic; her focus on details that are insignificant in and of themselves – the constantly working answering machine, a fly, the smell of the synthetic carpet, the sounds of the office furniture – evoke a time-lapse camera journey underscored by the corresponding soundtrack.

In the 31[th] chapter ("strike"), the interviewees finally rebel against the interviewer's constant questioning. She in turn undertakes a "reanimation" of her own identity. However, the ending remains uncertain, for even the narrator is subject to the risk that "the ghost inside one might continue to grow" ("dass das gespenst in einem immer mehr zunimmt," *WSN* 197). Thus the novel is not attempting to pit two competing positions against one another. Instead, it illustrates the negative energy of society as a whole that is created by the neoliberal working world. Increasingly, this leads to shapeless non-selves and a ghosting of society, and *wir schlafen nicht* suggests that this "Vergespensterung" is indeed almost a requirement for economic success. As such, Röggla's works clearly demonstrate their valency as a "fait social" by being situated in the contemporary world and by questioning governmental structures, yet they also transcend this through her concentration on the aesthetic form.

# 4 Forms of Social Realism: Unemployment in Contemporary Narratives

As of May 2011, Germany had the lowest unemployment rate since 1992 and experienced growth rates of 2,2% in 2010 and 2.6% in the first quarter of 2011, respectively. This was the biggest economic growth since unification, which led the British paper *The Economist* in February 2011 to proclaim a "new German *Wirtschaftswunder*."[1] Yet since the 1970s, with the oil crises and a change in monetary policy toward an anti-inflationary course, Germany was unable to permanently reduce its unemployment rate. Deindustrialization resulted in substantial job losses across Europe and has since contributed to persistently high levels of unemployment in many industrial cities and regions.[2] This is equally true for Germany. While unification did add structural problems in eastern Germany, contrary to popular belief it was not the root cause for the vanishing of work (Siebert 69), which, as researchers predicted as early as in the 1980s, would lead to groundbreaking systematic change. Decentralized and more flexible forms of labor were invented as countermeasures to the threat of mass unemployment (cf. Ulrich Beck 1986, 220–247). Twenty years later, the rise of the global economy has only increased the pressure and complicated the picture since cheap labor facilitated by a global stream of labor migrants is now being imported from all over the world, especially into the European Union and the United States. Concurrent with this development, companies export their manufacturing into countries where labor costs are much lower.

Unemployment in Germany continued to increase over the 1990s and into the new millennium. In February 2005, the figures rose to 12.6 percent, with 5.2 million people out of work, which was the highest number since World War Two (Dougherty). While the picture is obviously complicated since economies are multi-faceted systems influenced by many different factors, economists and political scientists agree that the reasons for Germany's "high and sticky unemployment" (Siebert 69) are largely due to structural causes such as its high wage costs and a lack of wage differentiation. This could only be remedied by higher institutional flexibility and reforms (Berthold and Fehn).

It is true that due to its practice of promoting *Kurzarbeit* instead of eliminating jobs and its strong export sector, Germany fared much better than other

---

1 "Angela in Wunderland: What Germany's Got Right, and What It Hasn't." February 3, 2011 (http://www.economist.com/node/18070170). Cf. also Kulish.
2 For a comprehensive historical overview of European employment and unemployment, see Ostergren and Le Bossé, 335–371.

European countries in the economic downturn at the end of the first millennial decade. Nevertheless, unemployment remains overall a virulent social problem in Germany, which has been exacerbated by the latest global financial crisis (Borchert and Landherr 214).[3] Since the mid 1990s jobs with fixed-term contracts have drastically increased, indicating that there are now two separate job markets in Germany: One with employees in standard employment liaisons that remain the basis of *Modell Deutschland*, and another one that is more flexible and varied, but also provides considerably less security.[4] Especially for the traditionally risk-averse Germans that still look to the government for regulation, these paradigmatic changes have been difficult to negotiate.

The backdrop to the prose texts analyzed in this part of this chapter is the "death of the working society," as playwright Moritz Rinke called it in conversation about his 2005 play *Café Umberto* (Wille 69), i.e., deep structural changes that work, employment, and our attitudes about them have undergone over the last decades. Whereas in the 1970s the industrial sector was the decisive segment, since the 1980s we have witnessed the rising significance of the service sector.[5] The first result of the structural changes is the need for the individual living in precarious times to subscribe to the principles of life-long learning, flexibility, and adaptability, as analyzed earlier. The second outcome concerns the diminishment of traditional full-time employment and a rise in "precarious" work arrangements such as job-creation measures, temporary employment, "one euro jobs" etc. Many people are forced to work two jobs because wages are too low to support them otherwise, and the ratio of full-time employment to part-time or precarious work conditions is now 2:1.[6] As countless studies show, neoliberal economic policies lead to the systematic reduction of work and consequently also to ever-rising unemployment numbers in Western societies.

While firmly rooted in the social landscape of contemporary Germany, the novels subsequently analyzed address, at least indirectly, many of the ques-

---

3 For a challenge of the notion of the current German "job miracle," cf. Ralph Jeremias.

4 In 2009, less than two-thirds of all jobholders in Germany still had an open-ended job that was subject to social insurance contributions. From 1996 to 2008 the number sank by 7% to 22.9 million. In 2011, about 20% of the work force of big corporations is in flexible, short-term contracts. Dettmer et al. 85, 88.

5 In 2003, 66.4% of all employees worked in the service industries versus 31.1% in industrial production. Stahl 86.

6 According to the *Statistisches Bundesamt*, in 2010 the number of peope in atypical employment reached 7.84 million and increased by 243.000 compared with 2009. http://www.destatis.de/jetspeed/portal/cms/Sites/destatis/Internet/EN/Navigation/Statistics/Arbeitsmarkt/Arbeitsmarkt.psml (July 27, 2011).

tions that have also been discussed theoretically in the nuanced research on the consequences of not being part of the labor market. Medical studies show a clear correlation between rising unemployment and mental problems (Vinokur and Schul), as well as between levels of unemployment and higher psychotic morbidity (Goldman-Mellor et al.). This is on par with the mainstream psychological and sociological tradition that has argued since the 1970s that unemployment is a major psychological stressor, with monetary problems being only of secondary importance. This approach is often labeled as the deprivation theory: It posits that unemployment damages mental well being because it deprives people of the latent functions that employment provides, such as a clear time structure, purposefulness, social participation, contacts and regular shared experiences outside the family, and information about their personal identity (Ervasti and Venetoklis 120). However, sociological studies based on the theories of structural unemployment and job searches in recent years have developed and advanced the incentive theory, arguing that an individual's ability to get a job is to a large extent determined by his/her job-seeking behavior and motivation (ibid. 122).

Given the changing nature of the working world and the topic's persistent currency in the German public sphere, it is not surprising that a number of literary texts in the aughts focus on the experience of unemployment. Contrary to the narratives discussed in chapter three that shed light on individuals employed in the New Economy, the texts analyzed here entail realistic narrations of the processes of work, which requires a qualification of my earlier statement that work itself is rarely thematized in literary texts. Here, work indeed figures prominently, and the noted difference might be due to the novels' focus on the so-called "old economy," either in the material production of goods or administrative and supply services. Furthermore, the material aspects of being out of work, such as lack of money, depression, or loss of self worth are narrated also. Both Jakob Hein's *Herr Jensen steigt aus* (2006, Herr Jensen Calls it Quits) and Annette Pehnt's *Mobbing* (2007, Harassment) address how economic realities influence constructions of self, human relationship, and the individual's relation to the surrounding social and material world. The need to streamline the self and the body that I discussed with regards to *Das Jahr der Wunder, Wir Maschine, EGO,* and *wir schlafen nicht* is also present here, as is the uneasiness vis-à-vis globalizing factors. Joachim Zelter's *Die Schule der Arbeitslosen* (2006, The School of the Unemployed) on the other hand, is a blistering satire criticizing the ways in which neoliberal societies deal with being out of work and the unemployed.

## Sentenced to Idleness: Annette Pehnt's *Mobbing* (2007) and Jakob Hein's *Herr Jensen steigt aus* (2006)

Annette Pehnt's fourth novel *Mobbing* (Harassment), released in 2007, is set against the backdrop of the changed landscape of work and the high unemployment numbers Germany experienced in the aughts. An unnamed female narrator and stay-at-home mother of two relates the story of her husband's exposure to mounting harassment in the work place and the subsequent unraveling of a marriage and personal happiness under the strain of unemployment. The narrative focuses on the psychological and emotional toll that being laid off and an ensuing lawsuit take on the family and the threat that this implies for their middle-class existence.

Annette Pehnt, born in 1967 in Cologne, lives as a freelance author in Freiburg. After studying English and Germanistik in Cologne, Galway, Berkeley, and Freiburg she received her doctorate from the University of Freiburg in 1997. Apart from *Mobbing*, she has published four other novels: *Ich muss los* (2001, I Have to Go), *Insel 34* (2003, Island 34), *Haus der Schildkröten* (2006, House of Turtles), *Hier kommt Michelle. Ein Campusroman* (2011, Here Comes Michelle. A Campus Novel) and a collection of prose stories, *Man kann sich auch wortlos aneinander gewöhnen das muss gar nicht lange dauern* (2010, One can get used to one another without words it does not need to take very long).

*Mobbing* begins with Joachim (Jo) Rühler's termination from his current job as an administrator in city government. Married with two small children in a medium size German town, his job as a public official has qualities that Germans, many of whom are traditionally risk-averse, think of as highly desirable: it is secure and enables a comfortable, bourgeois lifestyle that includes home ownership, season tickets to the symphony, and regular vacations. This content life starts to unravel when the new female head official in his department begins to harass Jo, taking away work projects and excluding him from office communications. Her behavior and that of his immediate colleagues are captured in the novel's anglicized noun "mobbing," which Germans use to describe bullying in the work place. Jo resists his unfair treatment in a manner reminiscent of Heinrich von Kleist's character Michael Kohlhaas, a fact that greatly incenses Jo's wife: "You think there is but one thing, to fight or to die, fighting or staying still, fighting or bending over. Yes, said Jo. Everything else is a cop-out."[7]

---

7 "Du glaubst, es gibt nur das eine oder das andere, kämpfen oder sterben, kämpfen oder stillhalten, kämpfen oder sich verbiegen. Ja, sagte Jo. Alles andere sind Ausreden." Pehnt. *Mobbing* 59. Henceforth quoted as *M*, plus page number.

As sociologist Poul Poder has pointed out in a study on interpersonal relationships in work life, managers perform a gate-keeping function connected to generating confidence since they control resources. The supervisor's sidelining of Jo and her refusal to communicate her reasoning thus effectively undermine his agency, which, according to Poder, is based on power resources such as knowledge, authority and money, but also on confidence (145). The stress Jo experiences in the battle with his supervisor leads to psychosomatic ailments that manifest themselves in a debilitating vertigo, causing him to miss more and more work. When he is eventually fired for a financial misappropriation he did not commit, he sues the city government in labor court and gets his old job back. But his triumph is short lived when his boss retaliates by relocating him to a service container where he works by himself without a telephone, computer, and access to a bathroom or air-conditioning. His new task is to translate protocols from the French despite not knowing the language, only for his boss to throw them away at the end of each workweek, at least "according to Jo" (*M* 126). His second trial in labor court in order to fight his demotion will most likely end in the family's financial ruin as well as finalize his wife's emotional withdrawal, both of which are palpable throughout. The text's open ending suggests as much: "Our account, said Jo, looks rather empty. But, he said, I am glad nevertheless. At that moment I gave up." (*M* 165–166)[8]

What makes *Mobbing* particularly interesting is the narrative perspective. The reader learns about Jo's ongoing humiliation and the escalating harassment measures exclusively through the sober narration of his wife, who recalls the story of her husband's professional downfall over the course of a single Valentine's Day. Thus Pehnt's novel thematizes the topic of unemployment only indirectly through the couple's deteriorating relationship and negative repercussions for the entire family. Jo is constantly tired, spends a lot of time in bed, and communicates less and less about his situation at work, leaving the narrator worried about his mental and physical well-being. The burden of household chores and child rearing falls increasingly on her since she can never be sure whether he will feel well enough to take care of the children.

Jo tells his wife few details about the behavior of his colleagues and the mechanisms at play in his work environment, leading Viviana Chilese to suggest that the new mores established in the workplace cause Jo's language to disappear, which infects all aspects of his life (300). Pehnt's use of this narrative strategy aligns the female protagonist and the reader; neither one can know what is really true, and an understanding of Jo's problems remains frag-

---

8 "Unser Konto, sagte Jo, sieht ziemlich leer aus. Trotzdem, sagte er, bin ich froh. In diesem Moment gab ich auf." *M* 165–166.

mented and confusing. This leads both his wife and the reader to question whether her husband really is as much of a victim as he makes himself out to be; as readers, we are also left to wonder whether the wife knows enough and is fair enough to tell Jo's story.

The narrator's account of the escalating events at Jo's work place is interspersed with descriptions of her daily routines as a stay-at-home mother, confirming that the distance between work place and home sphere has effectively collapsed. Alongside Jo's speechlessness, patterns of thinking and acting are transferred from the professional to the private sphere and infiltrate it. Through the man's battle and his psychosomatic vertigo, the effects of the war at work are now also carried into the private realm of his family's house, affecting even the small children.

One important dimension of the narrator's thought process is how the impending unemployment leads to looming financial strains and concerns about the future of the children (*M* 83), which is in line with studies that show how lack of money due to unemployment leads to feelings of shame and degradation, as a result of the perception of the views of others (Ervasti and Venetoklis 121). Many of these feelings are directly linked to the narrator's anxiety about maintaining the family's established lifestyle and expecting a loss of social status. The symbol of these misgivings throughout the novel becomes the espresso machine, by linking the office and the home through its great significance in both spaces. At work, the espresso machine is where folks gather, strengthen social bonds and informally exchange information, activities from which Jo becomes increasingly cut off.[9] At home, the material object is a measure for economic success, as the narrator's comparison with the neighbors makes clear, "our espresso machine is smaller, but Jo uses it every morning, every morning we get up like everyone else, we belong again" (*M* 144).[10]

The security of Jo's job in city government had enabled the narrator to stop working as a freelance translator after the birth of her first daughter when she had realized that her attention was constantly divided. After Jo has been laid off, she thinks about contacting her old employer again, yet she never executes her plan. Although the text suggests that her exhaustion keeps her from even

---

**9** In the context of Jo's work place, the espresso machine becomes "Dingsymbol der Verfehlung: der puren Heuchei einer kooperativen Arbeitsweise, in der Privates, Berufliches und Öffentliches zwanglos miteinander zu verquicken wären" (… a material symbol of lapses in judgement: the pure hypocrisy of working as a cooperative that would amalgamate private, professional, and public issues). Winkels 2007.

**10** "… unsere Espressomaschine ist kleiner, aber Jo bedient sie jeden Morgen, jeden Morgen stehen wir auf wie alle, wir gehören wieder dazu." *M* 144.

trying, it also becomes evident that her wish to be taken care of by her husband is the bigger impediment. She enjoys their solidly middle-class life style and has come to expect it, an attitude widely prevalent in Germany (and Europe), in which regular vacations and leisure are considered a basic human right that at the same time define social status (Ostergren and Le Bossé 387). Furthermore, the novel comments on and critiques the traditional model of the bourgeois family of a working father and stay-at-home mother. The house and the familial space seem like a prison for the well-educated female character that she can leave for personal time only when she negotiates with Jo, to go to the gym, for instance. Pehnt illustrates the woman's internal tension, in which resentment and expectations of her husband form an explosive mélange (*M* 47–48, 50, 73). The female character has not learned how to try a different model because she has not needed to until now; the crisis introduces doubts about the choices she and Jo have made (Hoch and Pehnt).

Pehnt's novel successfully conveys how impending unemployment leads to massive personal insecurities and worries about the loss of social status. The choice of Jo's profession lends the text an even more critical touch, precisely because it is part of the "old economy." Even in this established sector that at least in Germany is relatively safe from the volatility of the labor market, the specter of worklessness hovers over every decision. Throughout the novel the country's high unemployment numbers of five million become an argument for both Jo's wife and his colleagues to get him to cease his battle (*M* 35). This leads to the depressing conclusion that in precarious times, financial security must trump job satisfaction and receiving justice. Yet Jo is also well aware that as someone over forty he falls into the category of hard to place employees ("schwer vermittelbar"), which his unsuccessful job search confirms (*M* 81–82).

The novel ends before Jo enters into his second trial in labor court, which would possibly be followed by one of the infamous occupational re-training programs so ubiquitous in Germany since unification. The absurdity of these measures is vividly illustrated in Jakob Hein's *Herr Jensen steigt aus* (2006, Herr Jensen Calls it Quits), a short "Hartz IV novel" (Streisand) that has not received much critical attention. Its author Jakob Hein was born in 1971 in Leipzig and grew up in East Berlin as the son of writer Christoph Hein. He studied medicine in Berlin, Stockholm, and Boston and was a practicing psychiatrist at the Charité Hospital in Berlin until 2011, while concurrently working as a freelance author. He has published a number of prose texts and novels, among them *Mein erstes T-Shirt* (2001), *Formen menschlichen Zusammenlebens* (2003, Forms of Human Cohabitaton), and most recently *Liebe ist ein hormonell bedingter Zustand* (2009, Love Is A Condition Caused By Hormones). Hein has been a member of *Reformbühne Heim & Welt* since 1998, a literary performance cooperation of various authors that meets regularly at Berlin's *Kaffee Burger* for public readings and poetry slams.

In *Herr Jensen steigt aus*, the title character is one in a long line of literary eccentrics from Don Quijote to Gregor Samsa to Oblomov (Cosentino), an outsider without much contact to his family or any real friends, who is as quiet and introverted as he is friendly and does not mind his outsider status too much. His missing first and run-of-the-mill last name mark him as an everyman, and I therefore argue that it positions him in close proximity to Bertolt Brecht's character Herr Keuner. Brecht conceived of his *Geschichten vom Herrn Keuner*, written from 1930 onward over three decades, as a model for casuistic philosophizing that links up with the didactic narrative forms of Johan Peter Hebel's *Kalendergeschichten* in the 19th century. The Keuner stories oscillate structurally between parable, anecdote, aphorism, and proposition (Riedel) and rely on an attentive, pensive reader who might find a general truth in Keuner's musings. Herr Jensen shows a similar aptitude for realizations that on the surface seem deceivingly simple while revealing a deeper critical insight into our contemporary world. The association to Brecht's writing is furthermore underlined by the simple, paratactic style and brevity of the novel, which make it read like a Brechtian didactic play ("Lehrstück"). Jensen indeed has much to teach the reader, because the experience of losing his job leads to an "ominous 'metamorphosis'" (Cosentino) of the central character whose life is exemplary of many individuals living in neoliberal times (L. Hermann).

The novel leaves no doubt that Jensen lacks natural talent and ambition, which is part of the reason why he does not take over the family business. Yet it also becomes clear that this prospect was thwarted due to the situation globalization has created for Germany's independent businesses:

> The company *Jensen Hydraulics* had a good name in the market. But the competition from Asia had become oppressive over the years. *Jensen Hydraulics* could not underbid their prices. The old Jensen was too good a businessman to even think about handing the company over to his son. He closed *Jensen Hydraulics* when it became unprofitable.[11]

After dropping out of university Jensen junior returns to a job at the post office, where he had already worked as a student in *Gymnasium*. His quiet and con-

---

11 "Die Firma *Jensen Hydraulik* hatte einen Namen auf dem Markt. Aber die Konkurrenz aus Asien war im Lauf der Jahre erdrückend geworden. Ihre Preise konnte *Jensen Hydraulik* nicht unterbieten. Der alte Jensen war ein zu guter Geschäftsmann, um auch nur daran zu denken, seinem Sohn die Firma zu übergeben. Er schloß *Jensen Hyrdraulik*, als sie anfing, unrentabel zu werden." Hein. *Herr Jensen steigt aus* 10. Quoted henceforth as *HJ* plus page number.

tent life, in which the monotonous work schedule provides a sense of structure and security and paradoxically gives Jensen freedom (Rüdenauer), changes dramatically after he gets laid off from his job "due to our new program to circumvent operational layoffs" (*HJ* 25). Since he is not a regular employee, he is ineligible for the social plan that would have prevented his layoff, despite the fact that he has worked full-time at the post office for the past ten years; this is a logic Jensen simply cannot understand in its absurdity. The realization that it will be almost impossible for him to find another position because he did not complete any formal education or training program (*HJ* 106), as well as the requirements imposed by the employment office of regular visits with his case worker and re-training measures rattle him deeply:

> "You know," said Mr. Jensen, "I would rather like to become a mail carrier again. I don't want to do anything else, especially not a training program. I'd rather wait until something opens up at the post office again."

> "Listen to me," said the caseworker in a now distinctly irritated tone. "You cannot document any effort and have been unemployed for too long. If you decline now we will cut your benefits. Do you understand what I mean: you *have* to attend a training program."

> "'I see. I *have* to attend a training program', said a dumbfounded Mr. Jensen. He had never thought so much pressure would be put on him in his unemployed state. For years he had paid his dues and had always assumed that his benefits were righteously his. Unemployment was something so terrible that nobody could believe he was voluntarily unemployed. It was like a severe disease that afflicted many who now needed help. That he was supposed to be shooed around for his money left Mr. Jensen very dissatisfied."[12]

Subsequently the caseworker assigns Jensen to a six-week training program called "Fit for Gastro," whose sole purpose is to secure the continuation of his unemployment benefits: "There was nothing to learn, thus there were no notes

---

12 "'Ach, wissen Sie', sagte Herr Jensen. 'Ich will eigentlich am liebsten wieder Postbote werden. Etwas anderes will ich nicht machen, schon gar keine Qualifikationsmaßnahme. Da warte ich lieber, bis auf der Post wieder was frei wird.' 'Hören Sie mir zu', sagte die Sachbearbeiterin in einem jetzt merklich gereizten Tonfall. 'Sie können keine Bemühungen nachweisen und sind schon zu lange arbeitslos. Wenn Sie jetzt ablehnen, kürzen wir Ihre Bezüge. Verstehen Sie, was ich meine: Sie *müssen* in eine Qualifikationsmaßnahme.' 'Ach so. Ich *muß* in eine Qualifikationsmaßnahme', sagte Herr Jensen verdutzt. Er hätte nie gedacht, in seiner Arbeitslosigkeit so bedrängt zu werden. Jahrelang hatte er eingezahlt und war davon ausgegangen, daß ihm seine Bezüge rechtmäßig zustanden. Arbeitslosigkeit galt als etwas so Schreckliches, daß niemand annehmen konnte, daß er freiwillig arbeitslos war. Es war wie eine schwere Erkrankung, von der viele betroffen waren und die jetzt Hilfe brauchten. Daß er für sein Geld herumgescheucht werden sollte, stimmte Herrn Jensen sehr unzufrieden." *HJ* 53.

to be taken ... All pocketed their attestations carefully, after all, receiving this piece of paper was the sole meaning of the past weeks." (*HJ* 63, 67) The sequencing of the novel suggests that the "training program" he had to attend accelerates Jensen's descent into a full-blown psychosis. He begins to isolate himself completely, stops reading the paper, throws his television and VCR out the window, and removes his mailbox in order not to receive any more mail from the unemployment office. When he meets his old supervisor at the supermarket who tells him about the September 11 attacks, he questions the event's realness and suspects that Herr Boehm has been sent by a controlling authority: "And now you want to get me back. But it is too late, Boehm. Tell them that. Tell them Jensen got out and will never get back in again" (*HJ* 125–26).[13]

Hein, who is not only an author but also a practicing psychiatrist, leaves open whether Jensen's behavior is truly that of a mad person. In an attempt to fill his time, he begins to record and analyze the daily TV program for hours, with the help of complicated charts and detailed notes. He arrives at the realization that in order to function properly in the world, one needs to be "normal" and continues to define normality as follows:

> One should go to work.
> One should have a woman or at least frequent sex.
> One should have many friends.
> One should know what is currently fashionable.
> One should know something about music.
> One should be cheerful.
> One should have money.
> One should be beautiful.
> One should make something out of oneself.
> One should have dreams.
>
> Mr. Jensen had to concede that he was not normal. He sighed exhaustedly. (*HJ* 83)[14]

The subjunctive mode in this passage effectively establishes social doctrines and makes it amply evident that Jensen's actual life is incongruous with the consumer habits, moods, and attributes contemporary society considers acceptable or desirable. He is neither attractive nor popular nor successful,

---

**13** "Und jetzt wollen Sie mich wieder zurückholen. Aber dafür ist es zu spät, Boehm. Sagen Sie denen das. Sagen Sie, Jensen ist ausgestiegen und steigt nie wieder ein." *HJ* 125–26.
**14** "Man sollte arbeiten gehen. / Man sollte eine Frau oder zumindest häufig Sex haben. / Man sollte viele Freunde haben. / Man sollte die aktuelle Mode kennen. / Man sollte Ahnung von Musik haben. / Man sollte fröhlich sein. / Man sollte Geld haben. / Man sollte schön sein. / Man sollte etwas mit sich anfangen. / Man sollte Träume haben. / Herr Jensen mußte feststellen, daß er nicht normal war. Er seufzte erschöpft." *HJ* 83.

but rather socially awkward and isolated. Yet the shrewdness of the conclusions Jensen draws about his life, society, and human interaction throughout the novel leaves the reader wondering whether his world truly is illusory, or whether the problem lies with our performance-oriented society that leaves little room for those who operate differently. Jensen consciously refuses to participate in an environment that expects him to function and accomplish things, neither of which he wants to do. In the end, by removing his nametag from the door, he effectively expunges his existence from a world in which he was never comfortable in the first place. The reader, however, is left with the uncomfortable realization that Mr. Jensen most likely would have continued to function within the approved parameters of German society had he not lost his position at the post office. Being forced to idleness leads not only to social isolation but, at least in this case, to psychosis and personal erasure (Cosentino).

## Flotsam of Globalization: Joachim Zelter's *Die Schule der Arbeitslosen* (2006)

In the tradition of dystopian novels such as Aldous Huxley's *Brave New World* (1932) and George Orwell's *1984* (1949), Joachim Zelter's *Die Schule der Arbeitslosen* (2006, The School of The Unemployed) thematizes the topic of unemployment much more scathingly than do Pehnt or Hein. In various interviews the author has identified the novel – which in the meantime also has been produced as a play and shown in different productions around Germany – as a political text written to criticize the ways in which postindustrial societies handle unemployment.[15] Zelter, born in 1962 in Freiburg im Breisgau where he still lives as an independent author, sees the political solutions developed in Germany in the millennial years of high unemployment as inhuman and ineffective and criticizes them by way of satire.

The novel is set in Germany in the year 2016 when unemployment figures have risen to such astronomical heights that the Federal Employment Office (*Bundesagentur für Arbeit*) no longer even publishes them, leading to speculation that ten million people might be unemployed. In order to solve this continuing and long-term problem, the federal government starts a new type of program in which unemployed people between the ages of 20 and 40 from all over Germany voluntarily enter a training facility called Sphericon. They will stay there for a trimester – without access to the outside world or any opportu-

---

15 The interviews can be found on his personal web page www.joachimzelter.de.

nity to go home – in order to restart their lives and ultimately improve their chances of finding a job. Upon entering SPHERICON they have to turn in the tokens of their old identity in the form of I.D.s, insurance and social security cards, which is followed by digging a grave for their old selves on their first day of class.

SPHERICON is organized like a military camp. The students – now called "trainees" – are divided into groups led by a trainer, follow a strict dress code, sleep in bunk beds in common quarters and are instructed to study the school's one-hundred page rule book, which proclaims the slogan "*A New Life*" on every page. Their sole purpose in SPHERICON is to improve their skills as job applicants in every possible way, even if it means reading the obituaries in the paper and calling bereaved families to find out facts about a now vacant job. For seventeen hours a day, five days a week, trainees work on their new biographies, making up education, work experience and skills, following SPHERICON's philosophy that "résumés are a form of practical literature. Like a novel or a drama: exposition, rising action, climax, resolutions ... resolutions galore. A résumé is nothing else."[16] Like the application process, the CV is seen as "a form of art" ("eigene Kunstform," 67) that establishes its own rules; what counts is not a "sense of reality" ("Wirklichkeitssinn") but a "sense of possibility" ("Möglichkeitssinn"). Susanne Heimburger suggests that the novel here references Robert Musil's *Der Mann ohne Eigenschaften* (1930, *The Man Without Qualities*), where "Möglichkeitssinn" promotes a life concept in which various possibilities of human existence can be tested. In the environment of SPHERICON, on the other hand, the utopian quality of a sense of possibility is reduced to the kind of flexibility Richard Sennett describes (Heimburger 142).

As part of their reeducation – the title of the novel clearly references works such as Molière's *L'école des femmes* (1662), Jules Verne's *L'école des Robinsons* (1882), Erich Kästner's *Die Schule der Diktatoren* (1957), and Arno Schmidt's *Die Schule der Atheisten* (1972) – the trainees, like "prisoners" or "drug addicts," are supposed to come to the understanding that they have lived "the wrong way" and reform themselves so that they can become "professional applicants." (*SdA* 12). This process of reinvention is accompanied by a constant propagandistic exposure to slogans ("SPHERICON ... means opening. Opening of all known states. ... Opening of pessimistic 'but'-attitudes. ... There is no but in SPHERICON. SPHERICON means the breaking of the ice in our heads," *SdA*

---

16 "Lebensläufe sind eine Form von angewandter Literatur. Wie ein Roman oder Drama: Exposition, steigende Handlung, Wendepunkt, Lösungen ... Lösungen über Lösungen. Nichts anderes ist ein Lebenslauf." Zelter. *Schule der Arbeitslosen* 67. Quoted henceforth as *SdA* plus page number.

32).[17] The trainees are forced to watch fictitious TV shows called *Job Quest* and *Job Attack*, and listen to nonsensical songs and motivational speeches. Trainees are regularly awoken at night and interviewed aggressively by their respective trainers, the director Ulrich von Benkdorff, and the school psychologist, Dr. Lichtenstein. Their accomplishments are reviewed weekly and rewarded or punished with a system of giving out *Bonus Coins* that range from *Premium* and *Advanced* to *Basic and Basic Minus* and allow shopping for sweets, cigarettes and other personal items. Trainees are also explicitly encouraged to seek sexual adventures in *Weekend Suites I and II* since "promiscuity is an ability in itself" ("Promiskuität ist eine Fähigkeit per se...," *SdA* 102) and indicative of the progress in the application process, according to the school's psychologist.

Only Karla Maier and Roland Bergmann, two trainees of the group Apollo, attempt to subvert the system by holding on to and defending their own biographies. They quickly are reprimanded and publicly humiliated by their trainer Ansgar Fest, yet continue to use their computers to communicate privately about what is happening to them in Sphericon and retreat into the weekend suite to talk to each other instead of having sex. After being punished for transgressing school rules, Roland Bergmann gives up and becomes a model trainee, while an unregenerate Karla is isolated from the group and held in solitary confinement in a basement room, supposedly to protect her from the ire of her fellow trainees (*SdA* 186).

The events in the school come to a head when the Federal Employment Office sends a high representative to inspect the program. Due to Sphericon's success, he grants it a real trainer position for which all trainees are subsequently supposed to compete. This leads to an absurd series of application events pitching the trainees in fierce competition against each other and culminating in a sort of game show:

> ... the candidate of Carnegie – Gert Frommer – he had become a star in the meantime – he had fans all over the school. He entered – as the highlight of the evening – the stage as the last one and sang the song [in English]: *Take me ... Take me all ... All I am ... All I will ... Be ... The right one ... The bright one ... I am ... All what I am ... More what I am ... In my prime ... My prime time ... My prime high life time ... Take me ... Take me all ... Take me home ...* accompanied by guitar music and synthesizer tunes as a play back. (*SdA* 171–72)[18]

---

**17** "Sphericon bedeutet Öffnung. Die Öffnung sämtlicher vertrauter Zustände. ... Die Öffnung pessimistischer Aber-Haltungen. ... Es gibt in Sphericon kein Aber. Sphericon bedeutet das Aufbrechen des Eises in unseren Köpfen." *SdA* 32.
**18** "der Nominierte von Carnegie – Gerd Frommer – war mittlerweile ein Star – er hatte Fans in der ganzen Schule. Er trat – als Höhepunkt des Abens – als Letzter auf die Bühne und sang das Lied: *Take me... take me all ... All I am ... All I will ... Be ... The right one ... The bright one .... I am ... All what I am ... More what I am ... In my prime ... My prime time ... My*

One explicit goal for all trainees is to become bilingual. In the above quotation and throughout the novel, the interspersed passages in English, lingua franca of a globalized world, seem to indicate that its knowledge will lead to professional advancement. But since Frommer and the other contenders produce little more than a collection of trite, nonsensical phrases, the use of multilingualism is revealed as a satirical comment by the author.

Apart from the school officials and Karla Meier and Roland Bergmann, the characters in the novel remain entirely opaque. Zelter displays a world dominated by administrative measures (what Adorno called "verwaltete Welt") where the trainees are controlled day and night. The individual falls silent and the discourse itself takes over, exposing its empty phrases and fatuousness (Preisinger). Emotions, individuality, and personal agency are only encouraged if they lead to new and innovative strategies for the job application, such as in the case of former successful trainees whose photos are displayed in SPHERICON's classrooms: "Criens, 2010 ... was able to send almost 100 e-mails in one night ... application e-mails ... not just e-mails but e-mails with masterpieces of résumés in the attachment ... animated with photos and videos ... spoken résumés ... with added music" (*SdA* 70).[19]

The neglect of the individual is in line with the ideology of the institution whose qualities provide the poetological premise for the novel. Trainer Ansgar Fest remarks:

> "If one were to write a book about SPHERICON, there would be no real human beings, no figures of humans but fragments at the most, or figments of changing resumes ... functions and products of biographical drafts ... combinatory constructs ... future job holders ... job conquerors! And: "Most characters would not even need names. And if they had names, then only in order to exchange and change them at any time..." And: "The language would be the language of SPHERICON: succinct and short, the language of stage instructions. Motions and comments that have been reduced to stage instructions. A language in a constant present." (*SdA* 68–69)[20]

---

prime high life time …Take me … Take me all … Take me home … Begleitet von Gitarrenmusik und Synthesizerklängen als Playback." *SdA* 171–172.

**19** "Criens, 2010 … Konnte in einer Nacht 100 E-mails verschicken … Bewerber E-Mails … Nicht einfach nur E-mails, sondern E-Mails mit Meisterwerken von Lebensläufen im Anhang … Fotoanimiert und videoanimiert … Manchmal sogar gesprochene Lebensläufe … Mit Musik unterlegt." *SdA* 70.

**20** "'Würde man ein Buch über SPHERICON schreiben, es kämen darin keine wirklichen Menschen vor, auch keine Figuren von Menschen, sondern höchstens Fragmente oder Figmente wechselnder Lebensläufe … Funktionen und Produkte biographischer Entwürfe … Kombinatorische Konstrukte … Künftige Stelleninhaber … Stelleneroberer!' Und: 'Die meisten Figuren bräuchten nicht einmal Namen. Und selbst wenn doch, dann nur, um sie jederzeit austauschen und wechseln zu können …' Und: 'Die Sprache wäre die Sprache von

The parameters established in the above passage describe Zelter's narrative concept for the novel. His goal is to sharply delineate the contrast between language use and reality in order to criticize social and economic attitudes that rely on empty rhetorical phrases (Lehman-Wacker and Zelter). The trainee characters remain underdeveloped and flat and do not possess linguistic and intellectual acuity, suggesting that individuals living in neoliberal times (at least those that are unemployed) become reduced to lifeless dummies. The paratactic style of the text makes it less reminiscent of a novel than a report, with short, descriptive, often elliptical sentences. The language is a mixture of the emotionless prose used in bureaucratic institutions and administrations and the anglicized idiom laced with slogans common in coaching and marketing manuals. This is particularly apparent in the book of house rules, also called a "philosophy of life" (*SdA* 26). It is a collection of aphorisms, information, and directives, each of which includes the sentence *"Work is freedom,"* repeated on every page as the motto of the school.

The hardly concealed allusion to the slogan National Socialists put on the gates of concentration camps – *Arbeit macht frei* – is but one of the many references to the Third Reich and its ideologies that underlie the text.[21] When Groener, high-ranking supervisor of a regional office (and very reminiscent of a *Gauleiter*), comes to visit the school, all trainees have to stand outside in the rain to greet his helicopter (*SdA* 118–122), alluding to the endless roll calls inmates were exposed to in the camps. Trainer Ansgar Fest's idea of punishing unsuccessful trainees with exercise on a stationary bike, which, as a side effect, would produce electricity for all of SPHERICON, in effect constitutes a form of forced labor leading to the complete erasure of individualism: "Eight million unemployed ... at some point no longer an immense number, no longer a terrible number ... but a number of energy ..." (*SdA* 185) Finally, the rhetoric and methods of National Socialism shine through in the interrogations of Karla (*SdA* 148–154) and Roland and underscore the inhuman methods used in SPHERICON.

Especially Zelter's historical referencing received mixed reviews; Klaus Ungerer of the *FAZ*, for instance, rejected the interlacing of contemporary problems of capitalism and media society with the language of the Third Reich

---

SPHERICON: knapp und kurz, die Sprache von Regieanweisungen. Bewegungen und Kommentare. Eine Sprache im ständigen Präsens'" (*SdA* 68–69).

**21** Other elements are taken from military jargon. The repeated motto *"Careless Talks Costs Jobs"* (*SdA* 30) alludes to a 1949 poster campaign launched in England against espionage: "Button Your Lip; Loose Talk Can Cost Lives." http://www.homesweethomefront.co.uk/web_pages/hshf_careless_talk_pg.htm. (May 25, 2011).

(34). While the method does lead to a problematic conflation, Zelter, like von Düffel, uses the rhetorical devices of repetition and exaggeration to create a satire that at times seems indiscriminate; it certainly does not enhance the literary qualities of the novel.

What is furthermore crucial for an understanding of the novel is how the German state indirectly sanctions the egregious methods used in SPHERICON. Funded by the government, the school functions as its extension and acts out its policies: "SPHERICON is a center for measures. It implements measures mandated by the respective job centers of the Federal Employment Agency – measures to train unemployed persons. It concentrates all necessary measures into a comprehensive training program. ... *School of Life.*" (*SdA* 6) The absurd and inhumane training program testifies to the fact that the only interest the neoliberal state has in its unemployed subjects is their potential as "human capital." If they cannot be reintegrated into a society where work has taken the place of religion and is the highest priority, then unemployed subjects need to be kept under control at all costs. Despite the rhetoric of optimism displayed in SPHERICON's slogans, the trainees are social pariahs treated by society at large as if they carry "a contagious disease" (*SdA* 13). Their re-education and confinement is a top priority in order to prevent them from turning into groups of unemployed marauders who randomly set fire to gas stations (*SdA* 159), which would threaten the social order of the state.[22]

The ominous signs of the intrinsic inhumanity of the SPHERICON system come to a head in the end, when the freshly graduated trainees are diverted from their homebound Christmas trip to the airport. On a sealed bus – another not so subtle reference to the sealed trains used by the Nazis to transport prisoners to the camps – they are informed that they have earned a "special vacation" in Freetown, Sierra Leone. While the text does not spell out which "final solution" the Federal Employment Office has in store for them, the discrepancies between the rhetoric of a carefree beach vacation and the reality of being locked up in a special part of the airport leads at least trainee Karla to realize "that these are the last steps she takes in Germany, ... that she will enter the plane with the others and fly to Africa and won't ever come back. There are too many trainees. There are too many planes." (*SdA* 204)

It is of course no coincidence that the unemployed are carted off to Sierra Leone, which, like most African countries, remains one of the losers of globali-

---

**22** The mention of marauding groups of unemployed youths conjures images of events in European cities in the aughts, such as the 2005 riots in the Paris banlieues and the 2011 riots across the United Kingdom, following the fatal shooting of Mark Duggan by police after a surveillance operation in London's Tottenham borough.

zation, especially since it is one of the poorest countries on the continent and has been rattled by civil war since 1991.[23] The equation of the unemployed with poor and disenfranchised inhabitants of the Third World is all too obvious; both are human flotsam ("menschliches Strandgut," Wozniak), discarded, without much hope of redemption. Yet this ending takes on another meaning when one considers how ostentatiously Germany is marked as part of the global economic sphere, confirming that its precarious economic situation is due to the effects globalization has had on the country: "He [the regional leader of the federal employment office] spoke of the general situation as if it were a military situation: admittedly, a difficult situation ... the most difficult situation since the war ... an economic war of a global scale ... a *World Wide War...*" (*SdA* 123).[24] The novel thus suggests that it is the economic globalization that has led to out-of-control unemployment figures and has provided the raison d'être for the existence of SPHERICON. Read in this manner, Zelter's text can only lead to the conclusion that the need to remain competitive within the globalized economy justifies the drastic and inhumane measures taken by the German government.

The literary analyses of chapters three and four have shown the ways in which narratives of work and unemployment take up problems of the neoliberal economy and critically react to the changes it has meant not only for the economic sphere but for German society as a whole. Literary texts thus function as a "seismograph of societal development" (Preisinger), disproving that the biggest part of contemporary German literature has not taken note of the societal changes happening all around it, as Enno Stahl has argued (2007, 97). Even where there is no open criticism of neoliberal work processes and practices, what becomes visible are the transformations of the traditional work society Germany has undergone over the last two decades and the raised significance of sectors such as advertizing and consulting that were formally much more marginal.

In all the novels analyzed here, the adversarial effects of living in a neoliberal society under the specter of unemployment are shifted onto the individual and thematized in constructions of subjectivity. An important aspect of this is the exclusion of the private sphere; in the novels hardly any areas of life exist

---

**23** "Timeline: Sierra Leone." http://news.bbc.co.uk/2/hi/africa/1065898.stm (accessed June 18, 2011). Furthermore, the parallels to the time of National Socialism continue here when one remembers the Nazis' "Madagascar Plan" and its provision to ship all the Jews to this African Country.

**24** "Er sprach von der allgemeinen Lage wie von einer militärischen Lage: zugegeben eine schwere Lage... Die schwerste Lage seit dem Krieg ... Ein Wirtschaftskrieg globalen Ausmaßes ... Ein *World Wide War* ..." (*SdA* 123).

outside the sphere of work. If a private sphere remains, it also becomes mediated by work, suggesting that employment, worklessness, money, and economic thinking infiltrate every aspect of social life. We thus experience the normative dimension of the discourse on work around the millennium, namely that work becomes a purpose in itself. The professional position is negotiated in these texts as a category of social identity, making the individual into a marionette of the economic system (Kremer 137). It imparts value and meaning and is thus crucial for building subjectivity. If work falls away, so does the protagonists' identity, as the novels of unemployment analyzed in chapter four confirm.

The texts render the problematic nature of neoliberal workplaces in aesthetically innovative formats while situating themselves firmly in the German literary tradition. Documentary forms, such as the inclusion of interviews in *wir schlafen nicht* and the sober brevity of *Herr Jensen steigt aus* integrate a material aesthetics à la Brecht whose critical thrust has been illustrated by my readings. The use of inner monologue – originally a dramatic form that showcases Düffel's playright pedigree – in *EGO* becomes the means to reveal the shallowness of Philipp's inner life. Finally, narratives of work and unemployment support the argument that satire is often used in transitional times characterized by insecurity and uncertainty (Arntzen 44–45). Satirical elements have regained significance in the aughts and are present throughout the narratives analyzed here.

# 5 Traveling Without Moving? Narratives of (Im)Mobility

"Sometimes, when I am riding the train through Germany, I become angry and solemn. I look out the window, I see red roofs, black trees, and green valleys, I think of my friends and the city I live in, I remember the smell of fresh bread and cold milk and wet asphalt. And then I finally understand that I love Germany, even though I really don't want to, and realize that I can finally stop dreaming of leaving it forever."[1] This passage from Maxim Biller's *Deutschbuch* (2005) is but one of a myriad of texts from the turn of the millennium attempting to discover both Germany and the world. Whether Irina Liebmann offers a poetic travelogue about Germany six years after unification in *Letzten Sommer in Deutschland. Eine romantische Reise* (1997), Wolfgang Büscher circles around Germany's borders in *Deutschland, eine Reise* (2005), or Wladimir Kaminer discovers life beyond Berlin in the provinces in *Mein deutsches Dschungelbuch* (2005), literary travel reports about Germany abound since unification. Especially popular writers, such as Roger Willemsen in *Deutschlandreise* (2002, Travel through Germany), have profited from the escapist wanderlust of the post-Wende decade. The same holds true for fictional literature where travel is omnipresent as well, such as Selim Özdogan's novel *Im Juli* (2000) that was concurrently made into a successful road movie by Fatih Akin. Christian Kracht's *Faserland* (2005) or the prose tales Georg Klein spins about restless Germans in *Von den Deutschen* (2002) also come to mind.[2] One could speculate that unification spurred the need to take stock of the country as a whole, to measure it both spatially and metaphorically in order to ascertain what a subjective or German identity might entail and how it might position itself towards the world at large.

Literature dealing with travel is part of a discourse in society as a whole about German identity and cultural specificity that gained in significance after unification. Through the medium of travel texts united Germany is (re)discov-

---

1 "Manchmal, wenn ich im Zug durch Deutschland fahre, werde ich wütend und ernst. Ich schaue aus dem Fenster, ich sehe rote Dächer, schwarze Bäume und grüne Täler, ich denke an meine Freunde und an die Stadt, in der ich lebe, ich erinnere mich an den Geruch von frischem Brot und kalter Milch und nassem Asphalt. Und dann endlich begreife ich, daß ich Deutschland liebe, obwohl ich es gar nicht will, und mir wird klar, daß ich endlich aufhören kann, davon zu träumen, von hier für immer fortzugehen." "Schweigen über Deutschland." *Deutschbuch* 85.
2 For a survey of travel narratives of the 1990s, see Biernat 174–208. She points out that these travel narratives are written mostly by West German authors and gives some possible reasons on pgs. 192–194.

ered, pointing to attempts of cultural and national repositioning and normalizing that have been broached in other parts of this study. Yet the same can be said about the literary engagement with the global. The basic premise of this chapter is that globalization fundamentally transforms the relationship between the places we inhabit and our cultural practices, experiences, and identities, as John Tomlinson frames it (1999). Also, globalization has changed the character of travel fundamentally, not least because exotic locales that formerly might have been truly unfamiliar to the traveler do not exist any more. Even in our local environment, we are already always cognizant of foreign locales. Every region and every trip, real or virtual, might reflect back upon one's existence, albeit to different degrees (Zank 16), and encounters with foreign places and countries consequently influence German-language authors.

This chapter sets out to analyze some of these narratives of both mobility and immobility. I chose this term deliberately to free the texts from the framework in which one might expect them to be set, namely the more common genre of "travel writing." As "the most resilient of genres," as Graham Huggan describes it, travel writing has a long and rich material and theoretical history. Using the term exclusively would require a discussion of the genre and its conventions, which is not my primary interest here (see Brenner or Lützeler 2005, 94–150). Moreover, the interpenetration of the global and the local implies the need to adapt the genre to new conditions. As Huggan points out, it can no longer rely on classic distinctions such as tourist/"native," foreigner/local, etc. on which it previously depended (4).[3] Travel and tourism now frequently involve staged scenarios in which visitors and locals, aware of their respective roles, perform their respective identities in a "touristic borderzone" (Bruner 17). Along the same lines, sociologist John Urry, a specialist in the field of mobility and tourism, surprisingly suggests that in a world shaped by post-Fordist consumption, "tourism" is effectively coming to an end. In *Consuming Places* (1995) he characterizes people as perpetual tourists who experience mobility either literally or in a simulated fashion, thus questioning the very categories of tourism and tourist (148).

---

**3** Huggan argues "for the imbrication of travel *writing* with other kinds of travel practice, including some of those not previously counted as 'travel' (Holocaust deportation, migrant labor) or 'travel writing' (experimental, ethnography, prose fiction), and including representations of travelers, travel practices, and 'traveling cultures' in the popular audiovisual media, especially television and film." (5) He suggests "travel/writing" to mark the notion's inclusive character. Since my chapter restricts itself to prose fiction, I decided against adopting Huggan's term, but have nevertheless received critical insights from his writing.

Mobility is one of the central aspects that defines and delineates the process of contemporary globalization. It has both material and metaphorical aspects and since the primary focus of the chapter will be on the latter, I want to frame the material side in broad strokes first. The new objects and new technologies globalization brings about are inseparably intertwined with notions of movement, speed, and the compression of time and space, as is visible in technologies such as planes, digital television, computer networks, the Internet, the global stock exchange, and virtual reality. In this context Urry makes a useful distinction between *scapes* and *flows* brought about by globalization. Under *scapes* he subsumes the networks of machines, technologies, organizations, texts and actors, such as corporeal transportation by various means, transportation of objects, wire cables, satellites, fiber-optics cables for computers, televisions, etc. Many of these *scapes* are organized at the global level by transnational organizations such as the UN or the World Bank and their business is conducted in the lingua franca of global institutions, English. *Flows*, on the other hand, consist of streams that move within and across national borders and which individual societies are often unable or unwilling to control – people, images, information, money and waste. For people in the new millennium, these *scapes* and *flows* create new opportunities, activities, and desires, such as relatively cheap international travel, the ability to consume goods and engage in life-styles from across the world, the opportunity to communicate with people in many countries in real time through the Internet, etc. (Urry 2002, 32–36). They also allow us to form transnational networks and what Appadurai calls "imagined worlds," that is, the multiple imaginary spaces that are constituted by imaginations of people spread around the globe (1996, 33). Needless to say, global *scapes* and *flows* also entail global risks, such as epidemics, global climate changes, terrorism, the loss of national sovereignty, displacement and exile, as Ulrich Beck analyzed in his influential studies *Risikogesellschaft* (1986, *Risk Society*) and *Weltrisikogesellschaft* (2007, *World Risk Society*).

In sum, Urry suggests that the development of the various *scapes* and *flows* undermines endogenous social structures and thus the very basis of a sociology that has "society" as its center, not least because the "mobility turn" informs many different disciplines and is, at least in this understanding, post-disciplinary (Urry 2007, 6). The daily permeation of national borders by global processes and flows remake what is commonly understood as the "social," through material transformations that have to do with the described diverse mobilities. Urry arrives at the conclusion that through these mobilities, social life and identities are recursively formed and reconfigured so massively that the discipline of sociology needs to be rethought as one dealing no longer with the "social as society" but the "social as mobility" (2007, 4).

The insight that mobility and travel are at the center of globalization has shaped research in all disciplines.[4] Anthropologist James Clifford might be the writer most associated with making the connection between mobility, travel and culture, and he has influenced my thinking. In his influential study *Routes. Travel and Translation in the Late Twentieth Century* (1997), Clifford argues that cultures need to be rethought as sites of both dwelling *and* travel, meaning they should be seen both in relation to location and place as well as something that is mobile and travelling. Travelers, tourists, migrants, and refuges are physically traversing the globe, bringing their cultures with them, influencing other cultures and people, engendering new cultural formations and identities. Places should be viewed as sites of both residence and travel encounters. Moreover, the idea of culture as travel applies also to the flows of images, ideas, sounds, symbols and objects that circulate the globe and transgress national borders, as explicated by Urry. For the individual subject, travel becomes an engagement with both the familiar and unfamiliar, leading to a blurring between the notions of "home" and "abroad" (see Rojek and Urry). While Clifford acknowledges that travel is marked by gender, class, race, and culture and is often coerced by dependent labor, he advocates for a comparative cultural studies approach to "specific histories, tactics, everyday practices of dwelling *and* traveling: traveling-in-dwelling, dwelling-in-traveling" (36).

Given the ways in which mobilities associated with and produced by social, economic, spatial, and individual changes have altered the cultural landscape of globalized societies, it is not surprising that contemporary German-language literature partakes in the discourse of mobility by producing narratives of mobility. In this chapter I suggest that these texts, in particular, can be read as embodiments of the factors that have shaped our conception of globalization. Subjects and objects in motion, cultural flows, borders, and travel have emerged as central concepts to comprehend the movements of people and goods, images and ideas in a globalized world (Appadurai 2001, 5). For the global Western agents who are no longer tied to a specific place or locale, being mobile on a global scale stands in as an essential component and a signifier for a cosmopolitan mindset. Thus, national borders and local places have ceased to be the clear supports of our identity; after all, globalization transforms the localities we inhabit.

Given this fact, Tomlinson and other theoreticians propose that contemporary globalizing tendencies disrupt the linkage between culture and territory,

---

4 The topic of mobility as related to globalization comes up in almost any study in the social sciences and the humanities dealing with globalization, determined by disciplinary angles and interests. For a feminist perspective, see Kaplan.

leading to our cultural experiences, identities and practices becoming separated from the places we inhabit. Consequently, they suggest that the transformation of culture should not only be grasped in the trope of travel but also in the idea of deterritorialization. This concept, first conceptualized by Deleuze and Guattari in their study on Kafka's writing (*Kafka. Pour une littérature mineure*, 1975) and subsequently widely used in cultural studies, describes "the simultaneous penetration of local worlds by distant forces, and the dislodging of everyday meanings from their 'anchors' in the local environment" (Tomlinson 29). In other words, deterritorialization implies the general weakening of ties between culture and place and the dislodging of cultural subjects and objects from particular locations in space and time (Inda and Rosaldo 14).

The consequences of this development for the individual are far-reaching since deterritorialization naturally affects not only the experience of place but also the understanding of identity. The more social life becomes mediated by the marketing of styles, places, and images, by international travel, and by globally networked media images, the more identities become detached from specific times, places, and histories, and appear free-floating (Hall 1999, 428). But how do narratives of (im)mobility become a medium to reflect upon globalization? How do literary texts negotiate the effects of deterritorialization for identity construction and what do they add to a discourse that has been dominated largely by economic, political, and social contexts? Do they thematize intercultural understanding? What can they tell us about Germany itself?

In Clifford's broad definition, mobility entails a range of more or less voluntarist practices of leaving "home" to go some "other" place. It involves obtaining knowledge and having an "experience" that might be exciting, edifying, pleasurable or estranging (Clifford 66). The mere number of millennial prose texts that one can categorize as narratives of mobility is noteworthy. To give just a small sampling, authors of the younger generation choose ever more exotic settings for their novels and send their globe-trotting protagonists to Iran, Tibet, China, the United States, South America, etc. For example, all of Christian Kracht's novels and prose texts have to do with travel in one way or another, as is especially visible in *Faserland* (1995), set in Germany and Switzerland, and *1979* (2001), set in Iran, Tibet, and China. Thomas Meinecke's *Hellblau* (2003, *Pale Blue*, 2012) spins an intricate transcontinental web between Germany, North Carolina, and Chicago. Daniel Kehlmann's international bestseller *Die Vermessung der Welt* (2005, *Measuring the World*, 2007) tells the lives of Alexander von Humboldt and of mathematician Carl Friedrich Gauss; it is set in Germany, South America, and Russia. Thomas Hettche's

*Woraus wir gemacht sind* (2006, *What We Are Made Of*, 2008) explores the United States after 09/11 and before the Iraq War, while the protagonists in Elke Naters's *Mau Mau* (2002, Go Fish) vacation on an unspecified tropical island. Tanja Dückers's family story *Der längste Tag des Jahres* (2007, The Longest Day of the Year) takes place in Germany and the California desert, while Antje Ravic Strubel's novel *Kältere Schichten der Luft* (2007, Colder Layers of Air) is set in a Swedish summer camp for children.

The potential text corpus is thus greater than that of employment narratives and could have provided material for a separate study. Consequently, the choices made are guided by the attempt to analyze texts that display differing perspectives, while at the same time representing tangible positions on globalization. They range from a focus on the individual and the private sphere that almost excludes an acknowledgement of globalization (Hermann, Hens), to the detached aestheticized perspective of the dandy (Kracht), to a novel that details how travel practices in a globalized world are always permeated with an attempt to escape the existential loneliness of the everyday and the negative logic of capitalism (Berg). With the exception of Berg's *Die Fahrt*, all the novels deal first and foremost with private matters and do not offer explicit commentaries on history, politics, the workplace, socialization or authorities. They confirm that for many German authors, all is still *Ich*, as Nora Fitzgerald has called it; the fixation on subjectivity might be read as an update on the notorious concept of new subjectivity (*Neue Innerlichkeit*) of the 1970s. In German-language literature at the turn of the millennium, the personal is still, or rather once again, political, particularly because the focus on the private realm is inextricably linked to the experience of living in a globalized world. After all, while taking place in a complex interaction of global and local contexts and cultural borrowing, globalization affects the individual most at the local and individual level, contributing to the formation of a glocal subjectivity (Robertson 1992, 1994). Interpersonal relationships are just one of the many sites where the subject negotiates his/her identities and their relation to the surrounding world. While stable liaisons offer a network of support in a global society characterized by increased mobility and homogeneity, they are not immune to the gripping global forces that leave human beings, in Anthony Giddens's words, "fraught with anxieties" (2000, 37). I suggest that the texts analyzed here gain important dimensions when read not simply as subjective stories (*Ich-Geschichten*) but as aesthetic configurations of subjectivity and identity construction that attempt to grasp and verbalize ambivalence towards globalization and the toll it takes on the individual.

# Global Tourists in Judith Hermann's *Nichts als Gespenster* (2003)

In comparison with Judith Hermann's tremendously successful debut of 1998, *Sommerhaus, später (Summerhouse later*, 2001), the reception of *Nichts als Gespenster* (2003, *Nothing But Ghosts*, 2005) ranged from politely restrained to openly scathing. Critics were particularly dismayed at Hermann's protagonists who in seven stories crisscross Europe and the United States, yet scarcely engage with the surrounding world and experience little that is worthy of narration (see Radisch 2003). These travelers are characterized by an "excess of privacy" ("ein Übermaß an Privatheit," Steinfeld 2003) and turn out to be hardly more than sad little *Ich-AGs*, i.e. are obsessively focused on their own matters.[5] In light of the worldwide political development and the spreading "culture of fear" after 09/11, a quote such as the following, taken from an interview with Hermann in 2003, surely caused some irritation:

> The things that have changed for me have to do with my social surroundings. What has happened in Germany or in the world at large has not yet had an impact on my life. Therefore I do not feel that I need to address these matters in my stories.[6]

In her interviews, Hermann often admits that only private matters are the basis for her aesthetic projects. She is also reluctant to serve as a generational spokesperson on the political and social realities of the Berlin Republic (Lenz and Pütz 235). Instead she directs the attention explicitly back to her texts, which are grounded firmly in today's popular culture and describe the hedonistic, apolitical generation of post-1968.

While this is true for both her books, the crossing of national boundaries in favor of an openly displayed globalism is much more pronounced in the second one. In *Sommerhaus später* (1998), most of the characters are tied closely to the bohemian scene of 1990s Berlin. Even though Berlin there, as in other post-unification narratives, is a city "emptied of physical significance" (Brockmann, "Capital" 391) and a metaphor for urban life per se, it remains clearly identifiable and serves as a referential framework for the protagonists.

---

**5** *Ich-AG*, literally "Me Limited Liability Company," is a term coined by the authors of the *Hartz-Gesetze* (Hartz Laws) that came into effect under Hartz II on January 1, 2003. The concept denotes a person in self-employment as part of this government-funded scheme to help unemployed people start their own business.
**6** "Die Dinge, die sich verändert haben, haben mit meinem sozialen Umfeld zu tun, und das, was in Deutschland oder weltweit passiert ist, hat sich noch nicht auf mein Leben ausgewirkt. Insofern habe ich nicht das Gefühl, das in meinen Geschichten unterbringen zu müssen." Hermann in Minkmar and Weidermann.

In *Nichts als Gespenster*, on the other hand, only one of the seven stories, "Ruth (Freundinnen)" [Ruth (Girlfriends)] takes place in Germany, and its partial setting in the capital, an unnamed provincial town, and Würzburg, holds no significance for the story: "Germany, where it is present at all, is just a background, a setting, a home," as Beth Linklater has observed (67). The characters' transnational configuration is mirrored in their relentless exploration of the world beyond Germany's borders. The narratives unfold in Iceland, Venice, Karlovy Vary, Prague, Norway and the United States, emphasizing the significance of global rather than national themes in Hermann's second book.

Traveling is the prominent motif in *Nichts als Gespenster* and the collection's thematic trajectory is communicated in the global mobility of its protagonists. Traveling is, in fact, their preferred way of life. In the title story, the narrator maintains that she and her boyfriend lead rather conventional lives, like many other people: "'They travel and look at the world, and then they come back and work, and after they've earned enough money, they're off again, to somewhere else. Most of them. Most people live like that.'"[7] While this is a rather outlandish claim, the characters are indeed distinctly middle-class, even slightly bourgeois. They seem neither much restricted by national or financial boundaries, nor by familial ties, moving effortlessly in globalized spaces. They present themselves as street-wise, yet lonely globetrotters who are just as much – or as little – at home in Iceland, New York, or on some tropical island as they are in their homeland. Hermann portrays a generation of young urban artists and intellectuals that no longer focus on traditional means of establishing themselves and instead engage in a day-to-day draft form of life that centers exclusively on private concerns and forsakes political, historical, or social considerations.

Thus, Hermann's texts illustrate the postmodern subject's avoidance of fixation that Zygmunt Bauman laid out in his work on identity. Bauman proposes that the modern *pilgrim* – as a seeker of truth and authenticity – has given way to the postmodern metaphorical figures of the *stroller*, the *vagabond*, the *tourist* and the *player* – each of whom is unable to find the commitment and stability that the pilgrim sought and attained (Bauman 1996). Hermann's travelers resonate strongly with a number of ideas in Bauman's configuration of the tourist. Even though they "refuse to partake in the touristy rituals of

---

7 Hermann. *Nothing But Ghosts*, 143. Quoted henceforth in the text as *NBG*, plus page number. "Sie reisen und sehen sich die Welt an, und dann kommen sie zurück und arbeiten, und wenn sie genug Geld verdient haben, fahren sie wieder los, woanders hin. Die meisten. Die meisten Leute leben so." Hermann. *Nichts als Gespenster*, 221. Quoted henceforth as *NAG*, plus page number.

planning, guided sightseeing, exploring, and photographing" (Ganeva 261), they are nevertheless driven by the fear of being bound to a place and fixed in an all too familiar workaday world. In Hermann's stories, the conscious search for newness that Bauman posits as a characteristic of the tourist turns into an aimless drifting, the only tangible outcome of which is the amassing of frequent-flyer miles.

The urge to recognize one's surroundings and the dream of belonging, another important feature Bauman discusses, underlies most of the narratives in *Nichts als Gespenster*. The motto framing it, taken from the popular 1966 song of the Beach Boys, speaks of this dream and marks all the stories as a search to be, for once, in the right place: "Wouldn't it be nice if we could live here / make this the kind of place where we belong." The motto identifies the search for an elusive happiness and the right person as the book's central problems and accentuates the significance of a global popular culture for Hermann's writing, both of which were prevalent in *Sommerhaus, später* as well (see Biendarra 2004). That the sound of the song is emblematic of the carefree Southern Californian lifestyle and, at the same time, remains unmatched by any of the narratives, creates a nostalgia that sets the tone and resonates throughout the book. Its motto deepens the feeling of a quasi-metaphysical homesickness, of being out of place, by reminding the reader of the bygone days of early pop. Hermann's streetwise travelers vacillate between a nostalgic yearning for a place they could call home and the fear of home-boundedness, or, in Bauman's words, "of being tied to a place and barred from exit" (1996, 31).

In *Nichts als Gespenster* it is also striking how Hermann juxtaposes global mobility and a pronounced indifference towards foreign locales. They remain outward props whose only function is to provide an exotic framework for the protagonists' various erotic entanglements (Iceland in "Kaltblau," Karlovy Vary in "Zuhälter," Prague in "Wohin des Wegs," Nevada in the title story) without ever becoming substantial for their experience. The locales provide spaces that magnify or contrast the characters' emotions but do not comment on much outside of the personal realm. The possibility of profound change through mobility is faint since the characters explicitly deny that the foreign topographies they traverse regularly could change them in any way:

> ... the distance, the foreign places, the continents no different from what I can see from my window at home. Four weeks in a strange country. What's the point, I think, what could possibly be different here, what good will it do me – in an absurd way, I feel as though I've already seen it all (*NBG* 106).[8]

---

8 "... die Fremde, die Kontinente nicht anders als jeder Blick aus meinem Fenster, vier Wochen in einem unbekannten Land, wozu, denke ich, was soll da anders sein und was soll

The motifs for their travel remain opaque to the characters, and it is not just rhetorical that they do not seem to know what drives them to visit a specific locale: "what in the world did I want in Paris," asks the narrator in "Ruth", "I went to Corsica – I can no longer remember why Corsica of all places, and it doesn't seem to have been important either," admits another in "Aqua Alta."[9] Cities become entirely interchangeable – "Never mind that we were in Prague. We could just as well have been in Moscow or Zagreb or Cairo" (*NBG* 206).[10] Hermann levels cultural difference when she avoids the narration of local specificities or national characteristics. Along the same lines, the use of foreign languages is never explicitly commented on; while it remains inconclusive in the narratives which language is spoken, the reader assumes that the characters' lingua franca is English since they switch frequently and effortlessly from it to German and vice versa. By assimilating linguistic, local, and national specificities, Hermann marks the protagonists as international and their urban playgrounds as culturally uniform. The narratives suggest that, breaking down ethnic and national boundaries leads to a uniform and deterritorialized culture that is modeled largely after Western capitalist societies but does no longer do justice to cultural heritage. In a neo-romantic vein, some of the stories, such as "Kaltblau" ("Cold-Blue") or "Zuhälter" ("Pimp"), suggest that a return to nature provides a space where a meaningful existence is possible and human interactions can work successfully.[11]

Hermann's tourists displace themselves willingly even though their journeys are undertaken merely with the purpose of fulfilling a vague longing, which remains elusive and incommunicable. They do not pursue travel to obtain knowledge about a different culture or to have the exciting or estranging experience Clifford included in his definition of travel. They rarely even come into close contact with the inhabitants of the foreign places they visit. Instead, they encounter the displaced, for example human remnants of the Cold War in the form of Vietnamese shopkeepers who live in poverty in the deterritorialized space of an Asian cookshop in the middle of Prague:

---

es mir nützen, unsinnigerweise ist mir, als hätte ich alles schon gesehen." "Aqua Alta." *NAG* 135.

**9** "… was um Himmels willen wollte ich eigentlich in Paris?" "Ruth." *NAG* 33. "Ich fuhr nach Korsika – ich kann mich nicht mehr erinnern, warum gerade nach Korsika, es scheint auch nicht wichtig gewesen zu sein …" "Aqua Alta." *NAG* 125.

**10** "Es spielte keine Rolle, daß wir in Prag waren. Wir hätten auch in Moskau oder Zagreb oder Kairo sein können." "Wohin des Wegs." *NAG* 252.

**11** Thomas Borgstedt has explored Hermann's links to the Romantic tradition in *Nichts als Gespenster*. For *Sommerhaus später* see Inge Stephan.

> We ran through a labyrinth of plastic awnings and wooden structures, an ancient woman wearing a turban on her head was bent over a kettle, dogs were tearing at rubbish bins, no daylight at all now, huge puddles, … and then back to the main street, the Moldau, the traffic, the light of the street lamps along the river (*NBG* 211).[12]

The displaced Vietnamese survive, as the narrator notes soberly and rather indifferently, in desolate "dark shacks," where they serve "wild boar goulash with *Knoedel*" and sell knick-knacks, cheaply produced in the Third World, to locals and tourists gone astray. What eludes the female narrator is an awareness of the historical perspective – namely that hiring labor from fellow communist countries such as Vietnam was common practice in the Eastern bloc – and its entwinement with the poverty still prevailing in Central Europe. Instead she unmasks herself and her group of friends as romanticizing hipsters who find the run-down shops of the Vietnamese market infinitely cooler than the openly touristy sites of the Golden City and take pride in seeing only its seedy side.

For Hermann's global tourists, the foreign is assimilated all too easily and the world is structured exclusively by aesthetic criteria, where "tough and harsh realities resistant to aesthetic sculpting do not interfere" (Bauman 1996, 30). Her protagonists favor a distance between themselves and the world, in which they cast their counterparts primarily as the object of aesthetic, not moral evaluation. An encounter with the Other, then, is a strictly inward and reflexive process: Hermann portrays narcissistic *Ich-AGs* who orbit around each other but never truly touch. Traveling remains inconsequential for their social and political sensitization but confirms that, in a globalized world, existential boredom and emptiness can now be experienced anywhere (Ganeva 272).

## Mobile Cosmopolitans in Gregor Hens's *Transfer Lounge* (2003)

Critics hailed Gregor Hens's first novel *Himmelssturz* (2002, A Fall From the Sky), a modern version of Johann Wolfgang Goethe's *Wahlverwandschaften* (*Elective Affinities*), as "the best debut of the year" (Krekeler) and a "masterpiece" (Kraft). Despite this unanimous praise, which subsequently extended to most of Hens's books, this reading offers the first scholarly assessment of an

---

12 "Wir liefen durch ein Labyrinth aus Plastikplanen und Holzgerüsten, über einen Kessel gebeugt eine uralte Frau mit einem Turban auf dem Kopf, Hunde, die an Mülltüten rissen, überhaupt kein Licht mehr, riesige Pfützen … und dann wieder die Straße, die Moldau, der Verkehr, das Licht der Lampen am Fluß. "Wohin des Wegs." *NAG* 257.

author who is considered one of Germany's most promising. While Hermann's characters crisscross Europe, the narrated sites in Hens's collection of fourteen short stories are limited exclusively to Germany and the United States.[13] In *Transfer Lounge. Deutsch-amerikanische Geschichten* (2003, Transfer Lounge. German American Stories), the author portrays people, all of them thirty-something intellectuals, for whom Europe and America become one territory, a single site for their experiences. Unlike Hermann's characters they do not roam the world to escape their ordinary lives but because professional duties, as translators or university professors, or familial commitments require them to travel. Still, the modernist tropes of flight and escape, of crisis and catastrophe play a significant role and become the driving force for some of the plots: leaving for the U.S. or Europe, respectively, allows the characters to break with the memories and snares of family life and relationships gone sour.

The ramifications of an increasingly interconnected, globalized world that requires the individual to be flexible enough to leave home and start afresh in a foreign country are not questioned in the narratives. Hens marks the heightened mobility of a well-educated middle class as a fact and leading a transcontinental life as second nature. Thus, experiences of deterritorialization are a vital piece of the protagonists' identities, which is visible in Hens's treatment of urban as well as rural life. He does not restrict his depictions to the big city; in fact, he takes a particular interest in the vastness of American suburbia and the emptiness of the German province.

Moroever, the interdependencies of mobility that globalization creates become the aesthetic principle of the collection: Arriving, leaving, and temporary stays structure all the stories in *Transfer Lounge*. The typified places of global exchange that the French sociologist Marc Augé has called "supermodern" play an important role. Supermodernity is characterized by an excess of time, space and individuality and marked by the expansion of "non-places" that are non-relational and ahistorical (77–78). Supermarkets, highways and airports, which Augé sees as simulacra of anthropological places, figure prominently in his study, and to experience them is another aspect of a deterritorialized culture. Hens frequently functionalizes these sites, which are more often than not dominated by commercialism and hence "junk-spaces" (Kohlhaas 162), to communicate their dislocating qualities for social relations: a couple finds each other haphazardly in the arrival hall of Grand Central Station, only to part again at the non-descript transfer lounge of JFK airport after a few days of carnal pleasure ("Himmlische Erde"; Heavenly Ground); another couple

---

13 As a German writer and an American university professor at Ohio State University, Hens has an intimate knowledge of both countries.

breaks off a long relationship unceremoniously in the parking lot of a gas
station somewhere in Colorado ("Telluride"); two estranged brothers meet at
a rest stop by the highway outside of Münster ("München '72"; Munich '72).
These places, marked by restlessness and an ephemeral character, are devoid
of history and lack an aura. Hens's narratives poetically illustrate Augé's claim
that non-places are threatening to an individual's subjectivity because they
hinder the building of stable identities and committed social networks. In addition, these sites in Hens accentuate the volatility of the narrated identities.
While his protagonists accept their transcontinental existence without com-
plaint and even need it to maintain their stylized self-construction, they suffer
also from the contradiction between the desire to be heard and the inability
to truly connect in interpersonal communication, leaving them in the numbing
state of limbo that ensues from a deterritorialized existence.

Hermann's stories are often void of true experiences (in the sense of the
German term *Erfahrung*), whereas Hens's narratives are apt examples for a
literature that reworks the modernist tradition and its tropes in the postmodern
constellation (Lützler, *Postmoderne* 32). They are driven by unusual events,
personal crises, and small catastrophes: a young man unexpectedly experiences a blood clot and falls into a coma ("Landgang"; Shore Leave), a train
derails and brings two travelers together ("Heinrich-von-Kleist"), a bridge
crumbles, motivating an internationally renowned city planner to return to
his provincial hometown and renovate his childhood home ("Hubertusgut").
Contemporary history pervades the narratives and situates them at the millennium. "Himmlische Erde", for example, is set in New York City immediately
following the terrorist attacks of September 11, 2001 and the metropolis in
shock is the background of a private encounter. Two strangers spend a few
passionate days together, and as their money runs out, they move higher and
higher towards the sky and finally into a room on the 48th floor of a hotel that
has become the cheapest in light of the pervasive fear of further attacks. In
this homage to Ingeborg Bachmann's radio play *Der gute Gott von Manhattan*
(1957, The Good God of Manhattan) the terror on a global scale has already
taken place and permeates the intimate encounter. The shocks that Hens's
characters live through serve as catalysts through which a discovery of the
innermost self becomes possible and personal weaknesses and shortcomings
palpable. A rupture reveals the cracks in a life continuum; more often than
not, change ensues.

All of the narratives in *Transfer Lounge* are concerned with the authentic
moments in which the opaque surface of well-ordered life shatters to reveal
our own true nature, as one of the protagonists in the story "Heinrich-von-
Kleist" summarizes: "It is about the nanoseconds in which we lose track of

our story and are touched by what we consider our own true nature."[14] This forced authenticity forms the core of Hens's poetic project. What underlies it is the realization that our lives are made up of self-constructed illusions. Identities that appear unified and whole can only exist because subjects construct what Hall calls "narratives of the self" (1990), "Geschichte" and "Geschichten," comforting life stories and histories. Like Kleist in *Das Erdbeben in Chili* (*The Earthquake in Chile*), an author who might have inspired Hens's use of the concept of happenstance (*Zufall*), Hens shows how easily the unexpected tremors emanating from unusual experiences can implode the consistency of the individual's identity construction. It slips into a different state where rationality does not count and risk becomes the governing principle. Similarly to Hermann, Hens conveys that in a globalized world that presents the subject with a myriad of options, it is not wholeness that provides content and meaning but the fragments in which happiness momentarily shimmers.

## Global And Local Violence: Gregor Hens's *Matta verlässt seine Kinder* (2004)

The fragility of identity construction and the ensuing ambivalence come into even sharper focus in Hens's third book *Matta verlässt seine Kinder* (2004, Matta Leaves His Children). In contrast to the stories previously discussed, the action of the novel takes place within the boundaries of Germany. Yet as an account of flight from a well-ordered and stifling life, it fits the definition of travel employed earlier. Here too, the background of the story is the endless traversing of the globe and the ensuing deterritorialized existence, both of which turn out to be the formative factors for the protagonist's identity. They set in motion a drama in which a private world unravels and then literally goes up in flames. As such, I suggest that one should read *Matta verlässt seine Kinder* as a sequel that radicalizes the aesthetic project Hens had begun with *Transfer Lounge*.

The main character Karsten Matta is forty years old and works as a "post-conflict analyst"[15] for a global think tank. For fifteen years he has been traveling the world's hot spots and battlegrounds, writing reports for possible investors. His work requires an ongoing conscious effort to detach himself intellectu-

---

14 "Es geht um die Nanosekunden, in denen wir unsere Geschichte aus den Augen verlieren und von dem berührt werden, was wir als unsere eigene Natur bezeichnen." *Transfer Lounge* 49.

15 *Matta verlässt seine Kinder* 11. Henceforth quoted in the text as *M* plus page number.

ally and emotionally from the poverty, human suffering, and brutalities he has witnessed. Matta has developed various strategies to pacify the memories that haunt him. He attempts to reduce the global misery to abstract numbers ("In Ruanda every line I wrote meant about 4500 deaths"); he is cynical about it ("See you later, friends. I am drinking to the war, once again, I'm drinking to the chaos ...")[16] and tries to see it as a job such as any other that secures a comfortable lifestyle for his wife Rebecca and his two young sons. Yet subconsciously Matta realizes that his work partakes of the well-oiled machinery of war: "It is *a single* war, a global war of annihilation with the most primitive means. It is new and it is different and it is everywhere."[17] Its distinctive new feature is not the depressing concoction of human misery and abjection intrinsic to any armed conflict but the economic interests and ensuing greed that, in a globalized world, ultimately overshadow anything else. As Western governments get involved in wars that are none of their business, these wars become an investment with a stunning profit margin. Matta concludes that, in a deeply perverted way, the Western agents have no real interest to quell the conflicts, despite the lip service they pay to noble values such as democracy, religious freedom, and social justice.

This knowledge, confirmed over many years, is the backdrop for a nervous breakdown and the unraveling of Matta's private life in the text's narrated time, which spans only a weekend. In the beginning of the novel, Matta is preparing for another voyage while waiting for his visa to be processed at the Pakistani embassy in Berlin. The procedure, which he perceives as an abasing and tiresome burden, becomes the trigger for a dramatic chain of events that subsequently leaves all of the characters emotionally or physically damaged. A blood vessel bursts in Matta's left eye and he – quite literally – starts seeing red:

> Fuck Pakistan, he yelled, fuck Karachi, that hell hole, your fucking war, why don't you just stamp your own damn passports, go there yourself and write about the squalor and let yourself be blackmailed, I don't want it, I'm not gonna do it anymore, I won't do you the favor ever again, they will find someone else, but I won't do you the favor again, I am not going to Pakistan or the Balkans or Africa any more, I am not going to write reports on people who slaughter each other, rob each other, rape each other, men who set their women on fire and rape their neighbors' children. As fast and as often and as brutally as possible.[18]

---

**16** "In Ruanda kamen auf jede Zeile, die ich geschrieben habe, etwa 4500 Tote." (*M* 77); "Freunde, bis bald. Ich trinke auf den Krieg, mal wieder, ich trinke auf das Chaos ..." *M* 34.
**17** "Es ist *ein* Krieg, ein globaler Vernichtungskrieg mit primitivsten Mitteln. Er ist neu und er ist anders und er ist überall." *M* 77.
**18** "Scheiß Pakistan, rief er, Scheiß Karatschi, Drecksloch, euer Scheißkrieg, stempelt euch eure eigenen dreckigen Pässe ab, fahrt selbst hin und schreibt über das Elend und lasst

Forsaking his paperwork and even his passport, sweating and raging, Matta storms out of the embassy, drives home, quits his job via e-mail and leaves his bewildered wife and uncomprehending two sons Malte and Chris for good, all in a matter of hours: "I am not coming back, he said. I am not coming back to this life. ... Then he left. Without turning back one more time to look at his family. Without even stroking the children's heads."[19] He drives to Hamburg to meet Malin, his longtime Swedish lover, with whom he envisions a new life. After spending the night at a hotel, they drive south and end up at a restaurant where they coincidentally join a wedding party. The events quickly get out of control and a raging fire breaks out. In an epilogue, written in the utterly dispassionate style of a police report, the reader learns about a terrible car accident but nothing about the fate of Matta and Malin.

A critic for the *Süddeutsche Zeitung*, Hans Peter Kunisch, reads the novel as a "classic tale of breaking out" and Matta as an abnegator of bourgeois family values in the tradition of Max Frisch's Stiller. In fact, most of the reviewers find that the novel's primary subject is the rather traditional motif of a love triangle, "a reasonably suspenseful relationship story with a touch of midlife crisis."[20] While the main character's private tribulations undoubtedly are Hens's thematic focus, the underlying questions are much more complex. The motto by W.G. Sebald that precedes it – the act of violence is too diffuse ("zu diffus ist der Akt der Gewalt") – delineates the nature of Hens's aesthetic project as psychological and sociological. His novel updates a literary tradition that investigates how love is supposed to work in a society in which aggression is an intrinsic quality and the act of violence structural (see Morris). Hens shifts the global violence that penetrates the narratives via Matta's memories into the inside of his protagonist and thereby conceptually defines it as systemic to all human interactions.

Matta serves as the case in point. His marriage with Rebecca only works because of many (unspoken) agreements that require them to tolerate each

---

euch erpressen, ich will es nicht, ich tue es nicht mehr, ich werde euch den Gefallen nicht mehr tun, sie werden einen anderen finden, aber ich werde euch den Gefallen nicht mehr tun, ich fahre nicht mehr nach Pakistan oder auf den Balkan oder nach Afrika, ich berichte nicht mehr über Menschen, die sich gegenseitig abschlachten, die einander ausrauben, vergewaltigen. Männer, die ihre Frauen anzünden und die Kinder ihrer Nachbarn vergewaltigen. Möglichst schnell und möglichst oft und möglichst brutal." *Matta.* Here 18.
**19** "Ich komme nicht wieder, sagte er. Ich komme nicht in dieses Leben zurück. ... Dann ging er. Ohne sich noch einmal nach seiner Familie umzuschauen. Ohne auch nur den Kindern über die Köpfe zu streichen." *M* 42.
**20** "... eine leidlich spannende Beziehungsgeschichte mit midlife-crisis-touch." Mohr. The only critic who acknowledges that the novel is also a "Globalisierungstext" is Hubert Winkels (2004).

other's affairs and white lies. Their marriage is the contractual basis for an open relationship, in which jealousy and demands have as little room as genuine concern does. Both wrongly believe that their sons do not realize the coldness and ensuing tensions between their parents. Their pedagogical methods are governed by consumer ethics (*M* 28, 30), which are supposed to fill the emotional void Malte and Chris experience:

> "The children live reasonably well. The most important thing in their world right now is the playground slide. At home in Berlin it's their toys, books. What matters is that we're there and are constantly buying new stuff and listen to them. Read them something before bedtime. That really isn't a bad childhood."[21]

The novel's title puts the children firmly at the center and evokes the two most vulnerable people who undoubtedly will be scarred by Matta's refusal to continue with his established life. Yet he convinces himself that it will be possible simply "to just disappear from their world" because they are used to his absences anyway (*M* 101). His emotional callousness towards his offspring crystallizes in the image of his kids' tape recorder shattering on the highway after he throws it out of the car window. How Matta deals with leaving his children is the novel's paramount example of the internalized aggression his global professional activity has created.[22] Thus, the text also suggests that global aggression *abandons* an entire generation of children by putting present profit above future well-being.

Matta attempts to convince Malin that the life he constructed with Rebecca is suffocating him and that he is afraid of the manifest tensions between them (*M* 100–101). Yet his relationship with his lover is not free of conflict either. It is characterized by constant power struggles and governed by the phallocentric societal structures Matta continually experiences in his job. He expects Malin to be physically present and emotionally available and tries to bribe her with gifts that he calls "little trinkets from Amazon" ("Amazon-Aufmerksamkeiten," *M* 56), which also serve as (unsuccessful) attempts to control her. Furthermore, Matta and Malin's sexual practices mirror the struggles of the subaltern (female) subjects that are part and parcel of Matta's professional analyses. Consensual yet labeled as a "deadly serious game" ("todernstes Spiel" *M* 68), the couple's love making regularly involves the staging of rape fantasies, in

---

**21** "Die Kinder leben ganz gut. Das Wichtigste in ihrer Welt ist im Moment die Rutsche. Zu Hause in Berlin sind es Spielsachen, Bücher. Was zählt, ist, dass wir da sind und ständig neue Sachen kaufen und ihnen zuhören. Abends etwas vorlesen. Das ist doch keine schlechte Kindheit." *M* 97.
**22** The name "Matta" and the protagonist's mental state resonate with Friedrich Glauser's novel *Matto regiert* (Zurich 1936), in which Matto is designated as the ghost of insanity.

which Matta mutates into a mercenary like the ones he has witnessed countless times in the global war zones (68–69, 78).

In the end of the text different narrative perspectives intersect, offering opposing takes on the events that will lead to the deadly car accident reported in the epilogue. In an interesting aesthetic move, Hens aligns the reader's experience with that of Matta in his professional life. Just as the post-conflict analyst has had to make sense of what he witnessed in the war zones, the reader is presented with encoded and competing versions of the violence happening between Matta and Malin. It becomes the reader's hermeneutic task to figure out whether Matta killed his lover (and possibly Rebecca) or not. The blending of Malin with a female war victim in the narrative, "and there lies a women, a fellow sufferer so to speak, and she coughs and chokes and coughs and chokes,"[23] suggests that Matta's internalized violence has finally overtaken him and found an outlet. Hens's novel illustrates as a case in point how global economic interests galvanize violence and subsequently become so internalized and systemic to the private realm that they implode personal happiness, sanity, and any sense of self.

## Hedonism Gone Global: Christian Kracht's *Der gelbe Bleistift* (1999)[24]

There was a hipster on the plane
There was a sailor too
Big Business men on the plane
Stewardess too (Loudon Wainwright III, *Album II*)

Christian Kracht's *Der gelbe Bleistift* (1999, The Yellow Pencil) is a collection of twenty reports or, more accurately, vignettes about the author's travels, most of them in Asia. All were originally published for a travel column Kracht wrote regularly for the weekly newspaper *Welt am Sonntag*, which explains their briefness of three to fifteen pages. Most of the trips originated in Bangkok where Kracht lived for a few years in the former Yugoslavian embassy and from where he traveled to Azerbaijan, Pakistan, Burma, Hong Kong, Japan, and Vietnam. Born in 1966 as a Swiss citizen, Kracht grew up in the south of France, the United States and Canada and has since resided all over the world.

---

**23** "und da liegt eine Frau, eine Leidensgenossin sozusagen und sie hustet und würgt und hustet und würgt." *M* 134.
**24** I thank Dr. Johannes Birgfeld for his collegiality in providing me with some research materials on Kracht that I could not access in the United States.

He worked as the India correspondent for *Der Spiegel* in New Delhi before moving to Thailand, from which post he went to live in Katmandu, Nepal for a couple of years. He currently lives in Buenos Aires, Argentina. His nomadic life style justifies Klaus Bartels's classification of Kracht's self-stylization as a polyglot, transcultural nomad.[25]

The author's global experiences notwithstanding, the most curious characteristic of these texts might be how little the reader actually learns about the countries, places, and peoples visited.[26] In his foreword to the collection, fellow author Joachim Bessing aptly describes Kracht's method: "His readers only receive a bizarre bouquet of supposedly useless information and observations, then the story breaks off. At exactly the point when our reading habits tell us that it should finally begin."[27] Kracht focuses on details, such as the food and drinks consumed, the weather, architectural details, what airline designs say about the respective nations – the German Lufthansa reminds him of "the cool austerity of waterproof Teflon, meticulously scrubbed autobahns and bad-tempered, tall blondes"[28] – local idiosyncrasies, and the overall brilliance of his traveling partner and her golden Prada sandals. Kracht is not interested in chronological, linear narration. Instead he creates narrative coherence through topography, as Ulla Biernat points out, which in turn produces an endless referential network between the visited places, regions, landscapes, and city quarters (189). Kracht thereby subverts the inherently conservative genre of travel writing, which seeks to repeat and consolidate tropological myths and is motivated by establishing reciprocity with the people and places visited (Holland and Huggan 67–69). Similar to other contemporary German-language authors, Kracht does not privilege the creation of experiences of alterity; he liberates travel literature from the pressure to depict the foreign in original and

---

**25** Kracht's personal web site, www.christiankracht.com, contains no biographical data, and Klaus Bartels rightly points out that personal information about Kracht is available only through the paratexts provided in his books. Since these paratexts are controlled by the author, Bartels suggests that Kracht has fashioned himself into a polyglot, polycultural nomad, the wealthy version of a "third culture kid," i.e. a transcultural person who grew up in different various cultures with a nomad lifestyle. 293–294.

**26** This is equally true for another book Kracht published together with Eckhard Nickel in 1998, *Ferien für immer* (Endless Vacation).

**27** "Seine Leser erhalten von ihm lediglich einen bizarren Strauß vermeintlich unnützer Informationen und Beobachtungen gezeigt [sic], dann bricht die Geschichte ab." Joachim Bessing. "Vorwort." *Der gelbe Bleistift* 14. Henceforth quoted as *GB* plus page number.

**28** "Die deutsche Lufthansa hingegen ist sachlich, außen gelb und nachtblau, innen gelb und grau, und sie vermittelt die kühle Strenge von wasserabweisendem Teflon, von sorgfältig geschrubbten Autobahnen und schlechtgelaunten, hochgewachsenen Blondinen." *GB* 166.

innovative ways and makes room for a more comical or grotesque staging of the experience of strangeness (Biernat 186–187).

Throughout the book, Kracht ironically comments on the expectations generated by the genre, often directly addressing his readers:

> I know what you are thinking, dear reader, oh yes. Herr Kracht makes up everything in his Asia stories. He embellishes too much. He tries to describe the world as more comfortable than it really is. Life in Bangkok simply cannot be an endless tea ceremony on the deck of the *Oriental Hotel.* ... Where are the worldly, the dirt, daily life, and normality? Where are the banal public officials and the even more banal sex tourists, where are poverty and despair? (*GB* 107)[29]

The stories in *Der gelbe Bleistift* do not specifically address many of the economic realities of the countries visited or the social ramifications globalization has had for them. Instead, the reader is presented with entertaining, impressionistic vignettes centered on idiosyncratic aspects, often stemming from popular and consumer culture. An analysis of the collection nevertheless needs to be included in this chapter because Kracht's texts are significant examples of a literature that happily embraces the mobility and time-space compression of the world inherent to globalization, albeit without problematizing how its positive sides are only available to specific social strata.

The following interpretations read *Der gelbe Bleistift* as the literary manifestation of an attitude John Urry calls "aesthetic cosmopolitanism." He argues that a popular appetite for the consumption of foreign places has been emerging in this latest phase of globalization and has become part, not just of the promise of Western liberalism, but of a broader notion of globalized "consumer citizenship." Along with this increased tourist mobility Urry shows how a new type of aesthetic cosmopolitanism is emerging, which entails "a stance of openness towards divergent experiences from *different* national cultures" and "a search for and delight in contrasts between societies rather than a longing for uniformity or superiority." Urry then develops a model of this cultural attitude, which includes "a rudimentary ability to map places and cultures historically, geographically and anthropologically," the willingness to step "outside the tourist environmental bubble," an ability to interpret cultural signs, as well as the capability "to locate one's own society and its culture in terms of a wide

---

**29** "Ich weiß, was Sie denken, lieber Leser, oh ja. Der Herr Kracht erfindet alles in seinen Asien-Geschichten. Er schmückt zuviel aus. Er versucht, die Welt angenehmer zu beschreiben, als sie ist. Das Leben in Bangkok kann doch nicht nur ein endloses Teetrinken auf der Terrasse des *Oriental Hotel* sein. ... Wo bleibt denn da das Weltliche, der Schmutz, der Alltag, die Normalität? Wo blieben die banalen Beamten und die noch banaleren Sex-Touristen, wo bleibt die Armut und die Verzweiflung?" *GB* 107.

ranging historical and geographical attitude" (Urry 1995, 167–170). Interestingly, he links this late 20th century aesthetic cosmopolitanism with the practice of the *Grand Tour* in the late 18th and early 19th century, while acknowledging the ways in which travel was popularized and democratized around 1840.

The idealized cosmopolitanism Urry describes is of course limited to the socio-economic spectrum of (mostly Western) recreational travelers whose affluence and mobility enable their cultural judgment. In his discussion of Urry, John Tomlinson also points out that the aesthetic must not be confused with the ethical; there is no guarantee that the development of general cultural horizons and the honing of semiotic skills will be followed by a sense of responsibility for global totality (Tomlinson 201–202). We will confirm this in *Der gelbe Bleistift*, yet what remains interesting and useful about Urry's model for Kracht's texts is the emphasis on aesthetic aspects, as the following interpretations will illuminate.

Implying that the expectation to reveal something truly meaningful about foreign locales is ultimately absurd, Kracht prefaces his book with a quote by English painter David Hockney, "Surface is an illusion, but so is depth." Hockney's Pop Art paintings, often drawing on images from print magazines, play with the impression of superficiality only to reveal layers of complex meaning. Kracht pursues a similar aesthetic program, conveying his observations to the reader without giving much indication how we might interpret them.

For example, in a story set in Pakistan in 1996, the narrator visits the remote village Darra Adam Khel where "all the weapons in the world are reproduced and sold and tested." (*GB* 66)[30] Ibrahim Khan, a man he met just the previous night, implores him to learn how to fire a bazooka and various other weapons in order to prove that he is "a real man." Although initially "very very scared" Kracht quickly becomes enamored with the weapons he fires, especially the Kalashnikov, which Ibrahim Khan calls "the sword and shield of Islam." (*GB* 74) At the end of the day spent together, Khan gives the narrator a wrapped present, which turns out to be a copy of the Koran. The story makes little mention of the political history of the region, which in the 1990s was still shaped by the Soviet-Afghan War and the instabilities caused by the Taliban taking power in neighboring Afghanistan. As such, the reader is left with colorful impressions but also many questions – why are all these weapons produced in this village? Is Ibrahim Khan an arms dealer? – and confronted with the necessity to fill in her own knowledge of Pakistan and interpret the story's clues.

---

**30** "Irgendwann … Erzählte er mir von diesem winzigen Dorf ganz in der Nähe … in dem alle Waffen der Welt nachgebaut und verkauft und ausprobiert werden." "Der Islam ist eine grüne Wiese, auf der man sich ausruhen kann. Peshawar, 1996." *GB* 66.

Kracht's literary reaction to the places he visits cannot be grasped in the duality of the foreign and the familiar. He always remains distanced from his subjects, positioning himself as an observer who never becomes involved.[31] The first reason for this is class and privilege. Wealthy by birth and seemingly endowed with a limitless trust fund, Kracht travels first-class whenever possible, stays in luxurious hotels, shares with the reader his love for expensive cocktails, and exudes that he basically leads a life of leisure.[32] Naturally, this also limits his encounters with local people, many of whom are equally privileged Western tourists. When he does describe the inhabitants of a country, he arrives at absurd conclusions by overgeneralizing most of the time. A colonial gaze that overlooks everything in an Olympian manner and evaluates and classifies (Lützeler 1998, 235) often tinges his perspective in problematic ways: "The other day we drove through Malaysia. The people here seemed to be unhappier than those in Thailand. The men were sporting mustaches and they seemed pirate-like and mean." (*GB* 87)[33]

The combination of many of the characteristics through which nineteenth century French poet Charles Baudelaire defined the dandy in his essay "The Painter of Modern Life" (1859) – wealthy, blasé, driven by the wish to distinguish himself and be original – is one of the reasons why both Kracht and his literary protagonists have been received as the type's postmodern – or popmodern – version (see Clarke; Tacke and Weyand). In keeping with the aesthetic preferences of new German pop literature, his writing style is light, conversational, and ironic and often functionalized to paint stark pictures that rely on the dichotomy between the privileged and the disenfranchised in developing countries. For example, while he and his companions eat caviar from "ladle-sized spoons" in "the land of the black gold," Azerbaijan, raggedy figures cower in the street, "sniff glue from paper bags and scrape their arms ashamedly with glass chards" (*GB* 36).[34] Needless to say, Kracht's deliberate ignorance of political correctness has not endeared him to those critics who

---

**31** This distance, created through the attitude of the aesthete, is even more pronounced in *Ferien für immer* (1998). See Biernat 196–197.

**32** Kracht has stated repeatedly in interviews that he is very wealthy. While one might question whether this statement is shot through with his usual irony, the fact that his father was the chief representative for the Axel Springer publishing company, Kracht's schooling at the private boarding school Schloss Salem on Lake Constance and his college years at Sarah Lawrence, one of North America's most expensive private colleges, lend it some credence.

**33** "Anderntags fuhren wir durch Malaysia. Die Menschen hier schienen unglücklicher zu sein als in Thailand. Die Männer trugen Schnauzbärte, und sie wirkten piratenartig und böse." *GB* 87.

**34** "Ein paar zusammengekauerte Gestalten hockten am Straßenrand, schnüffelten Klebstoff aus Papiertüten und kratzten sich beschämt mit Glasscherben die Arme auf." *GB* 36.

find his writing amoral and are annoyed about what they perceive as a lack of sincerity (for instance Terkessidis).

Yet Kracht is also acutely aware of his shortcomings and overgeneralizations tied to his privileged position and plays with them ironically. Taking a trip with his mother from Bangkok to Singapore to escape the heat and humidity of the former, he admits

> Having arrived here, you will ask yourself, dear reader, how one can squeeze an entire country like Malaysia into one superficially sketched paragraph? How does one dare to look out a train window, especially on such an ultra-expensive train, and come to such a judgment? You are right, of course ... But we were traveling on the Eastern & Oriental Express that had nothing to do at all with reality. We were travelling through the night in this absurd object that presented slices of Asia to us, nicely portioned into window-size pieces. And if one did not want to look outside, then one would turn her gaze once more towards *Vogue*. ... This had nothing at all to do with Asia (*GB* 88).[35]

In light of the plight of Cambodian workers who are demonstrating for a raise in the minimum wage, Kracht admits in the story "Tristesse Royale," excerpted from the book of the same name: "We were cowardly Preps. And we realized: here in Cambodia, pop culture comes to an end. There was no ironic break between what is and what should be"(*GB* 142).[36] In all his texts, Kracht fashions himself in a specific way that has much to do with the poses that are, in Matthias Waltz's words, part of the topography of the postmodern subject and its socialization. The pose marks the difference between a wonderful peer group and a despised outside world (229–230). In the context of travel, it allows the narrator to keep the foreign at bay with a slightly bored attitude, to treat it as a backdrop throwing the self only into sharper relief.[37]

Irony serves as the stylistic device that enables an attitude of Kantian disinterestedness. In keeping with the type of the dandy, Kracht's style and

---

**35** "Sie werden sich an dieser Stelle fragen, lieber Leser, wie man denn ein ganzes Land wie Malaysia in einen flüchtig skizzierten Absatz zwängen kann? Wie kann man sich erlauben, aus einem Zugfenster zu blicken, in einem arschteuren Zug noch dazu, und dann so ein Urteil fallen? Sie haben recht. ... Aber wir fuhren nun einmal mit dem Eastern & Oriental Express, der mit der Realität nun überhaupt nichts zu tun hat. Wir fuhren mit diesem Unding durch die Nacht, der [sic] uns scheibchenweise Asien vorführte, fein portioniert in zugfenstergroße Ausschnitte. Und wenn man nicht hinaussehen wollte, dann sah man eben wieder in die *Vogue*. ... Mit Asien hatte das nicht das geringste zu tun." *GB* 88.

**36** "Wir waren feige Popper. Und wir erkannten: Here in Kambodscha hört die Popkultur auf. Es gab hier keinen ironischen Bruch zwischen dem, was ist und dem, was sein sollte." *GB* 142.

**37** "Die eigene kleine Medienwelt wird einfach nach Thailand, Kambodscha oder Laos transportiert – das jeweilige Land dient einfach als Kulisse." Terkessidis 63.

approach to his reporting is dictated by looking at the world exclusively as an aesthetic phenomenon, as his poetological remark in the much maligned book *Tristesse Royale* shows: "For me the most worthwhile image remains that of an aesthete with his butterfly net in the jungle. That is the way a reporter must be."[38] Thinking back to the discussion of aesthetic cosmopolitanism, we can now see how it applies to Kracht's writing.

Signs of economic and cultural globalization and Westernization are ubiquitous in *Der gelbe Bleistift*. Pop music plays everywhere the narrator goes – the German 1980s band Modern Talking for example is still enthusiastically covered by a band in the chicest bar in Hanoi. We learn that people in Russia love to wear t-shirts imported from Vietnam displaying the American TV character ALF, and witness an old men in a mud hut playing with a Nintendo game boy. In Baku, old busses that have been imported from Schleswig-Hostein for public transportation still display the route "Husum-Niebüll," and the *Wild West Bar* "looks exactly like a dive in the Nevada desert. Dolly Parton and Hank Snow jangled from the speakers ... and Russian waitresses wore red-and-white checkered cowboy shirts and brought grilled cheese sandwiches for seventeen dollars a piece" (*GB* 39).[39] Kracht observes most places as sites where a global consumer culture rules, introducing the reader to the hybrid nature of contemporary global culture organized around music and fashion. While this culture is commercial and commodified, it also possesses an inherent cosmopolitan potential, as Tomlinson points out (200).

While Kracht stylizes himself as the distant observer who does not judge, what critics so far have failed to notice is his vehement criticism of globalizing effects. When it comes to global spaces ruled by hyper-capitalism, his dislike is scathing. For example, in Hong Kong the architecture of the city makes it impossible not to walk into shopping malls, thus "shopping becomes the first and last reason to exist; moving through space here only serves emptying the credit card" (*GB* 91).[40] Singapore, characterized in the story's title as "Disneyland with Corporal Punishment," is in Kracht's eyes the most horrible city he knows, particularly due to the cultural blandness globalized spaces so often

---

**38** "Für mich bleibt das erstrebenswerteste Bild das des Ästheten im Urwald mit seinem Schmetterlingsnetz. Das ist für mich der Reporter, wie er sein muss." *Tristesse Royale* 84.
**39** "Das *Wild West* war ein großer Holzschuppen am ölverseuchten Strand vor den Toren Bakus, der genauso aussah wie eine Schrabbelkneipe in der Wüste von Nevada. Aus den Boxen schepperte Dolly Parton und Hank Snow ... und russische Kellnerinnen trugen rotweiß karierte Cowboy-Hemden und brachten Grilled Cheese Sandwiches für siebzehn Dollar das Stück." *GB* 39.
**40** "Einkaufen wird so zum ersten und letzten Existenzzweck; die Fortbewegung durch den Raum dient nur dem Leeren der Kreditkarte." *GB* 91.

entail. He writes: "But what makes Singapore so particularly perfidious is that every place there looks like Frankfurt, or Disneyland. Just as modern, respectable, and bleak, promising the exact same clinical, calculated fun" (*GB* 116).[41] The social politics present in these "global cities" – which, according to sociologist Saskia Sassen, are nodal points of cross-border networks, information and communications technologies – in Kracht's mind lead to conservative ethics, reactionary aesthetics, and places devoid of contemplation and art.

Kracht's negative characterization of Frankfurt is in line with criticism leveled against Germany as a whole. His extensive travels must also be marked as an attempt to escape from Europe, specifically Germany (see Langston, Schumacher), to disappear towards a zero point, as he formulates in *Tristesse Royale*.[42] While Switzerland generally is a largely positive contrasting backdrop in *Der gelbe Bleistift* – the author is often reminded of his home country and finds many similarities between it and the countries visited – the Germans are always the tourists he seems to loath most. They are also the ones missing out on economic opportunities with regards to globalization: "It won't work, nope, I don't feel like it, I am not responsible, those seem to be the sentences with which the Germans wanted to catapult themselves into the new century,"[43] he remarks ironically with regard to the nonexistent German investments in the oil rich Caucasus region.

Kracht shows the reader a version of Asia that is void of cultural conflict. The condition for travel narratives like his is in fact a world fundamentally shaped by globalization, as a process that creates uniformity in urban living spaces and tourism and intensifies and commodifies communication and transport. The experience of the foreign as something that is familiar because it has already been experienced virtually, as well as the possibility to feel at home anywhere in the world thanks to international hotel standards, mobile phones, and the Internet or, alternatively, the option to not interact with the foreign culture at all, are the preconditions for Kracht's travel praxis and the literature emanating from it (Birgfeld 411). This is not only true for *Der gelbe Bleistift* but for Kracht's entire oeuvre. In his travel vignettes as well as in his

---

**41** "Klar, in China gibt es Massenhinrichtungen mit Genickschuß, und anderswo ist es noch viel schlimmer. Was Singapur aber so besonders perfide macht, ist, daß es dort überall so aussieht wie in Frankfurt, oder in Disneyland. Genauso modern-bieder, öde und genau denselben klinischen, vorher exakt abgezirkelten Spaß verheißend." *GB* 116.

**42** "Deshalb verschwinde ich auch immer nach Asien – kein Re-Modeling, sondern mein eigenes Verschwinden hin zum Nullpunkt." *Tristesse Royale* 153.

**43** "Es klappt nicht, nee, keine Lust, oder ich bin nicht zuständig, das schienen die Sätze zu sein, mit denen sich die Deutschen ins nächste Jahrhundert hinüberkatapultieren wollen." *GB* 38.

novels, especially *1979* (2001) and *Ich werde hier sein im Sonnenschein und im Schatten* (2008, I Will Be Here In Sunshine And Shade), he presents the reader with phenomena of the surface. What seems familiar and real is distorted to such a degree that the created space becomes an alternate one. This oscillating, exotic world functions as a projection screen that allows taking flight from the truisms of a neoliberal Western society and its inherent consumerism.

## No Happiness on Earth: Sibylle Berg's *Die Fahrt* (2007)

Sibylle Berg's fifth novel *Die Fahrt* (2007, The Journey), a sprawling work of three hundred and forty five pages and eighty chapters, offers a stark contrast to the works previously analyzed in this chapter. Whereas most of these texts comment only implicitly on the effects globalization has on the individual, Berg presents an explicit criticism of the abject sides of global capitalism. She suggests that in a globalized world, personal happiness exists neither for privileged Westerners nor for people on the periphery, albeit for very different reasons.

Sibylle Berg, born in 1962 in Weimar, immigrated to West Germany in 1984. She is not only a novelist but also a prolific playwright and works for various journalistic venues, such as *Die Zeit* and *Der Spiegel*. She now lives in Zurich. Her fifth novel *Die Fahrt* is less a traditional novel than a patchwork of travel narratives (Jacobsen) that encompasses a total of thirty-six characters and takes place on all seven continents except Africa. Its structural frame rests on five people whose original residence is Berlin. Frank, Pia, Helena, Ruth, and Miki know one another at least tangentially – as neighbors or acquaintances – and reappear throughout the text in various locales. They serve as anchors for other characters and their respective stories, all told by a heterodiegetic narrator. The macro structure of this narrative network is reminiscent of Ingo Schulze's *Simple Storys* and has its origin not in literature, but the cut-up technique used in film by auteurs such as Jim Jarmusch in *Mystery Train* (1989) or Robert Altman in *Short Cuts* (1992) (see Baßler 81). The author arranges the individual stories, which are between one and ten pages long, into a loose structure whose sequence is interchangeable.

As announced by the novel's title, its central focus is on issues of mobility, which is critically illuminated as a product and enactment of globalization (Jeremiah 138). Four of the five Western "anchor characters" are constantly on the move, traveling to far-away places in search of something that they themselves cannot clearly articulate. Their original place of residence or nationality seem arbitrary at best and, similarly to the characters in Hermann's *Nichts als*

*Gespenster* and Hens's *Transfer Lounge*, they do not feel a strong connection to their country of origin: "Frank had never had a homeland [*Heimat*] ... One does not find that on the Internet or by desperately traveling around."[44] While some have primary reasons for moving from one country to another – Ruth follows a boyfriend from Berlin to Tel Aviv, Miki receives a financially lucrative job offer in Hong Kong she cannot refuse – their often boundless travel is not to get to know the world or its people but primarily to escape their lives, "to roam through some unknown city in order to pass the time, until something happened that generally was not any better."[45] Similarly to Hermann's protagonists, most do not even enjoy traveling. Yet even if they did not already hate their touristic adventures from the outset like Frank, who panics on a plane to Shanghai and storms out at the last minute (*F* 116–119), all eventually come to the realization that travel does not enrich their lives in any meaningful way: "It was a shifting of consumption. Not Prada pieces but countries and misery and hostels were consumed, the life of strange people was being shopped, shoved into big plastic bags" (*F* 242).[46] Echoing this, in a podcast conversation for the 2007 Frankfurt Book Fair about *Die Fahrt*, Berg expresses her belief that life in Western capitalism attempts to mold people into an ideal of normality ("Normalitätsideal") that most people aspire to reach but fail (Buchmesse podcast). Tourism, "another word for what would cause the world's downfall," (*F* 44) is an attempted escape in order to find something that remains futile at home.

Another important factor in the Western characters' quests is age. Most are over forty years old, and they constantly remind the reader that this stage of life is characterized by stasis, disappointed hopes, loneliness, and indifference:

> She [Miki] was too old to get upset, to foam at the mouth, to be for or against something, she just couldn't care less, the end was too close, too predictable, it was clear that everything would die off with her, without significance. How do I hang in there for another 40 years? (*F* 211)[47]

---

**44** "Eine Heimat hatte Frank nie gehabt. ... Heimat findet man nicht im Internet oder durch verzweifeltes Herumgereise." *Die Fahrt* 17. Henceforth quoted in the text as *F* plus page number.

**45** "Da man durch irgendeine unbekannte Stadt stromerte, einzig um Zeit herumzubringen, bis irgendwas passierte, was dann in aller Regel auch nicht besser war." *F* 261.

**46** "Es war eine Verlagerung des Konsumierens. Nicht Prada-Teile, sondern Länder und Elend und Herbergen wurden konsumiert, fremder Leuts Leben wurde geshoppt, in große Plastiktaschen gestopft." *F* 242.

**47** "Sie war zu alt, um sich aufzuregen, um zu schäumen, um für oder gegen etwas zu sein, dazu schien ihr alles zu egal, zu nah das Ende, zu absehbar, dass alles mit einem sterben würde, ohne Bedeutung. Wie halte ich noch 40 Jahre durch?" *F* 211.

By displaying their apathetic acceptance that life beyond forty is little more than one slow decline towards death, the characters consistently undermine the rhetoric of never-ending youthfulness so ubiquitous in a capitalist consumer society and expose it as mendacious.[48]

The repetitiveness of themes such as aging, stasis, and indifference irritated *Zeit* critic Rolf-Bernhard Essig:

> Practically all of the characters are fearful, suffer from their existence and extreme boredom, and cannot stand the lack of perspective and senselessness. They hate people in particular, and themselves. All pace round, all are crying, all just want to get away without ever finding anything on their travels but ugliness always and everywhere, giant cockroaches and the insight that home at least was more bearable than foreign countries.[49]

While critics like Essig and Moritz complained that Berg recycled some of her previous material in *Die Fahrt*, I would argue that repetitiveness and hyperbole are not aesthetic shortcomings but go hand in hand with the irony and sarcasm present in all of her work, making up her specific aesthetic style. This is especially true in this novel that deals with global social problems clearly important to the author: she drives her point home over and over again. Furthermore, an exaggerated dose of blood and gore, deviant sexual behavior, violence and the grotesque are present in most of the texts, leading one scholar to claim that Berg must be full of contempt for her characters (Ujma 76). To be sure, in most of her texts she does terrible things to the protagonists, not even shying away from castrating them due to "a mean-spirited mood the author was in."[50] In her aptly titled debut, *Ein paar Leute suchen das Glück und lachen sich tot*

---

48 The protagonists in Berg's books age with the author, as Petra Günter has stated. I would add that Berg's treatment of age is an important topos in both her literary and stage work and in the construction of her public persona. In interviews she regularly suggests that she is much younger than she actually is. Her ironic play on the topic notwithstanding, she reveals her anxieties about aging: "Ich habe noch nicht herausgefunden, wie das geht, in Würde alt zu werden. ... Außerdem wird der Körper nun mal nicht schöner, und ich bin eitel und ein blöder Formalästhet." (I still have not found out how that works, to age with dignity ... Apart from that, a body does not become more beautiful over time, and I am vain and a stupid aesthete). In Tabert 21.
49 "Praktisch alle Figuren haben Angst, leiden an ihrer Existenz und extremer Langeweile, ertragen die Perspektiv- und Sinnlosigkeit nicht. Sie hassen vor allem andere Menschen und sich selbst. Alle tigern herum, alle weinen, alle wollen nur weg, ohne im Reisen etwas anderes zu finden als immer und überall Hässlichkeit, riesige Kakerlaken und die Erkenntnis, dass es daheim noch erträglicher war als in der Fremde."
50 "Bert legt sich auf Raul. Er dringt direkt in ihn ein. Bert fickt Raul, der seinen Schwanz durch eine fiese Laune der Autorin bei der Transformation in ein prima Leben verloren hat." Berg. *Amerika* 196.

(1997, Some People In Search of Luck Die of Laughter) whose form is similar to *Die Fahrt*, only one of ten characters survives; four are murdered, two commit suicide, two die in a car crash, one dies of thirst in the desert (see Link 25). However, I would argue that these extreme measures against the protagonists are made possible by the fact that none are psychologically rounded but mere composites of Western traits. In both *Ein paar Leute*... and *Die Fahrt* Berg composes types whose fates are interchangeable because their motives and interests also are; they lack perspective and are narcissistic and ungrateful in their constant complaining about their privileged life. This is also apparent in the title of *Die Fahrt*; the singular seems strange since the reader encounters a myriad of journeys crisscrossing the globe. Yet although the scenarios span vastly different experiences, from being kidnapped in the Burmese jungle to surviving a tsunami in Sri Lanka to being lost and penniless in Bombay, the singular title suggests that the experiences of the Western characters are, in all their diversity, ultimately very uniform: metaphorically speaking, they all experience one *Fahrt*.

This critical stance also grounds the novel's evaluation of the social, spatial and economic effects of globalization. Similarly to the texts by Kracht analyzed in this chapter, many of the narratives illustrate how globalization changes the physical environment and leads to a culture of visual sameness. Especially urban spaces in Europe and Southeast Asia are now organized around the abstract nominal of commercialism. In cities such as Vienna, which is traditionally known for its architectural treasures, the pedestrian zone aptly illustrates this development:

> Ruth ... now stood at a loss in the pedestrian zone and gazed at all the stores that looked like everywhere else ... Mango and Zara, H & M and Douglas and Schlecker and Nordsee and Tally Weijl and Esprit and Benetton, and did this never stop? These chains everywhere that all sold the same crap from Bangladesh and hordes of people wore it and all looked alike with highlights in their hair, and just now the world cup was on. The globalized world population staggered through the summer and played nationalism. But German flags and Iranian flags flew peacefully and cheerfully, flags wherever one looked, and all were finally someone, a great We (*F* 224).[51]

---

**51** "Ruth stand [...] ratlos in der Fußgängerpassage und sah all die Läden an, die aussahen wie überall. ... Mango und Zara, H&M und Douglas und Schlecker und Nordsee und Tally Weijl und Esprit und Benetton, und hörte das nie auf? Diese Ladenketten überall, die überall den gleichen Dreck aus Bangladesh verkauften, und Horden von Menschen trugen das und sahen sich ähnlich mit Strähnchen im Haar, und gerade war Fußballweltmeisterschaft. Die globalisierte Weltbevölkerung taumelte durch den Sommer und spielte Nationalismus. Aber so friedvoll und so heiter wehten Deutschlandfahnen und Irakfahnen, Fahnen, wohin man sah, und alle waren endlich wer, ein Wir." F 224.

*Die Fahrt* shows how capitalist endeavors, specifically neoliberalist business practices, have a leveling effect and inevitably lead to cultural and social homogenization. They motivate people to consume the same things, chase the same dreams, and react the same way to their environment. Interestingly, the only country in the novel exempt from the negative sides of globalism is the one spared by it, " a country, more or less left alone by the world, anybody would benefit from this." (*F* 311) Due to its rough climate, Iceland has little tourism and lacks the consumerist infrastructure generally accompanying it, such as hotel chains, chain stores, and advertising billboards. Instead the country lives by an organic rhythm determined by nature, weather and tides, a feeling of community between the relatively few inhabitants, and folklore, such as the Icelandic belief in elves. At least this is how Frank perceives it when he visits the island on a business trip (*F* 308–312). Subsequently he decides to stay "forever," encounters Ruth again with whom he had fallen in love in Berlin and spends a few happy weeks with her before dying of cancer in the closing story. The opening one is also set in Iceland, and it is not coincidental that two narratives whose focus is on how illness brings an end to otherwise happy relationships frame the text. Berg's "cheerful cynicism" ("heitere Zynikerin," Dawidowski 52) notwithstanding, these framing narratives underline the moral of the novel, namely that a harmonious relationship away from the globalized world is the only way to personal happiness, at least for privileged Westerners.

One dimension of globalization is that it introduces greater complexity and heterogeneity into societies. As a result, national cultures become less homogenous and stable as the result of the growth of minority nationalities, yet also progressively more multicultural and polyethnic. However, in *Die Fahrt*, increasing "contact zones" (Mary Louise Pratt) between people of different national and ethnic origin do not necessarily lead to a "global ecumene" that is a space of interaction, growing dialogues and mutual understanding, as social anthropologist Ulf Hannerz theorized. The novel instead comments critically on the hybridization of cultures, in this example in London:

> A shitty street amidst a gigantic quarter that looked like a screwed-up mixture of Bombay, Dhaka, and Marrakesh. Some English workers ... faded into the mass of veiled kaftan wearing people... So this is what the world was supposed to look like? Like a dirty bazaar? Great idea, thought Pia, damn multiculturalism if that means that one will have to wear a veil soon (*F* 317)[52]

---

[52] "Eine Scheißstraße inmitten eines riesigen Viertels, in dem es aussah wie in einer verunglückten Mischung aus Bombay, Dhaka und Marrakesch. [...] So also sollte die Welt aussehen? Wie ein dreckiger Basar? Super Idee, dachte Pia, scheiß auf multikulturell, wenn es bedeutete, dass man sich bald verschleiern musste." *F* 317.

Pia's outright resentment and the racist undertone of her rant illustrate the prevailing fear of many white, middle-class Germans when confronted with people of a different ethnic or religious background; it reads like a layman's commentary on what Huntington in his highly controversial book described as a looming "clash of civilizations."[53] Yet the stereotyping is also present in people on the periphery, namely in the Third World (see "Amita, Bombay," *F* 146). The locals in exotic countries show just as much contempt for the visiting Western tourists, not least because they often move around without showing respect for local traditions and customs: "'We come here and take their places in the ashram away from them, we are dressed indecently', Helena looked at her shifted jeans mini-skirt, 'and we let them work for us. They are just waiting for us to let ourselves go'" (*F* 144).[54] The novel marks the stereotyping of any Other as a universal human behavior, thereby relativizing the attitudes of both well-to-do Westerners and marginalized Southerners. Berg's aesthetic approach is one that openly uses clichés and stereotypes in order to unmask them as inadequate in social and political discourse. Nevertheless, I would contend whether this truly is a "nuanced approach" to the issue of multiculturalism as Jeremiah has argued (141) since Berg forgoes any of its positive aspects and relies instead on highlighting it as constant, low-grade cultural warfare.

A central theme of *Die Fahrt* – and in my mind the main argument for calling it a novel of globalization – is its commentary on mobility. The novel pointedly illustrates the exclusions of a large part of the world from upward economic and social movement. Three narratives about three different women in the Third World render this insight in particularly vivid colors. Each stands on its own, i.e., is not motivated by a contact with one of the anchor characters. The stories read more like factual travel reports than literary fiction, giving testimony to the research the author did in various locations for an entire year.[55] The first one of Juana, a thirty-six year old women living in the Andes,

---

**53** Huntington supports the homogenization thesis when he argues that the cultural fault lines between seven or eight major civilizations, namely Western, Japanese, Confucian, Islam, Hinduism, Slavic-Orthodox, Latin America and African will widen in the post-Cold War period. Differences between them will be highlighted and eventually lead to an increase in cultural conflicts. His thoughts experienced a renaissance after September 11, 2001, yet critics have pointed out all along that civilizations are not monolithic but complex and diverse and draw upon a range of cultures and influences.

**54** "'Wir kommen hierher und nehmen ihnen ihre Plätze im Ashram weg, wir laufen mit unzüchtigen Sachen rum', Helena blickte auf ihren verrutschten Jeansminirock, 'und lassen sie für uns arbeiten. Sie warten nur darauf, dass wir uns gehenlassen.'" *F* 144.

**55** Berg tells in the aforementioned podcast for the Frankfurt Book Fair how she traveled for a full year to do her own research for the novel. After not having left her house for twelve years, she felt she needed a "reality check" to see whether the world was really like she

illustrates how progress is a two-sided coin that generates both happiness and discontent. Having recognized that any advancement for the farmers in the mountainous regions of Peru will depend on women, the mayor of Marco encourages them to start playing soccer. While Juana experiences the community and camaraderie on the team as an escape from the "constant hard labor necessary to survive" (F 98) and make her temporarily happy, her newfound hobby also breeds discontent:

> And in a hundred years Juana's children might have gone to college, and all would live in high rises with electricity and would speculate on the stock market and eat sushi at night. But until this came to pass, Juana would have to play a lot of soccer, be tired and cold during the day and ask herself every once in a while what kind of shitty life she had. Now that she had an idea how things could be different (F 100).[56]

Berg leaves little doubt that limited opportunities contribute forcefully to the plight of women in the Third World and suggests that they especially are the "losers of globalization." (F 148) Yet the stories also acknowledge women's proactive efforts towards upward mobility, which is often what lifts them and their families out of the most abject poverty.[57] In another story, Amarita migrates from her village in the countryside where there is no doctor or school to Bombay (now called Mumbai) in search of a better life. She must quickly realize that the only option for her is to work as a cleaning lady in a restaurant, but even this income provides only enough for her to live on the street. Nevertheless, her newfound freedom and empowerment lead her to start learning English, in order to one day become a flight attendant: "Something new had entered her life. Something like hope." (F 151) While it is unclear how realistic Amarita's dream is, education clearly is one of the few means to achieve upward mobility.

What might be attainable in Mumbai, India's richest city with the highest GDP in South, West, and Central Asia, proves utopian in neighboring Bangladesh, the third poorest country in the world after China and India. The longest chapter of the novel provides the story of Parul, a young woman in Barisal

---

imagined it. Apart from two unspecified places, she claims to have been to all the locales in the novel.

**56** "Und in hundert Jahren würden Juanas Kinder vielleicht studiert haben, und alle würden in Hochhäusern leben, mit Strom, und würden an der Börse spekulieren und abends Sushi essen. Doch bis es soweit ware, müsste Juana noch viel Fußball spielen, am Tag müde sein und frieren und sich ab und zu fragen, was das eigentlich für ein beschissenes Leben war. Jetzt, wo sie eine Ahnung hatte, wie es anders gehen könnte." F 100.

**57** This is the guiding idea behind microloan programs for women in many developing countries. See Zarkirova.

whose life illustrates the enormous challenges women face in Southern Asia. Since she is "just a girl" (*F* 319), she receives no formal education and is brought up by her mother in the mindset of being "a second class human being" (*F* 321). Her parents marry her off to a man twenty years her elder when she is only thirteen. After a devastating flood, the couple moves to a slum in the city. A mother of four at the age of twenty-five (not counting the children who died prematurely), Parul lives in abject poverty and is subjected to daily abuse by her husband, experiencing no love, security, comfort or happiness whatsoever. When he finally takes a new wife after a few years and tells her to leave, she resists him for the first time, "she screamed for every year of her life, and she did not stop when her husband started to beat her." After the violent abuse, he leaves her "in front of the hut like a pile of trash," (*F* 329) leading the reader to believe that she most likely will be dead by morning.

The story chastises in the most vivid and unsentimental way the low social position of Bangladeshi women who are subject to a rigid patriarchal system that grants females few human rights (see *Women in Bangladesh*). As opposed to the Western tourists most stories deal with, the narratives from South Asia and the post-communist countries of Eastern Europe (see "Olga, Bishkek, Kyrgyztan;" "Helena, Ukraine") measure aesthetically what Zygmunt Bauman calls "the top and bottom of the freedom scale" (1998, 87). In his work on globalization, he suggests that access to mobility is one of the most stratifying factors in today's world and profoundly shapes our social experience. He argues that the mobile "tourists" of the first world live in a perpetual present where space does not matter because it can easily be navigated. Residents of the second world on the other hand, whom Bauman calls "vagabonds," live in space, "heavy, resilient, untouchable ... their time is void; in their time, nothing ever happens" (1998, 88–89). Whereas "tourists move because they find the world within their (global) reach irresistibly *attractive,* the vagabonds move because they find the world within their (local) reach unbearably *inhospitable. The tourists travel because they want to*; the vagabonds because they *have no other bearable choice*" (1998, 92–93). Berg's story echoes exactly this when she writes, "Whenever Amarita looked at foreigners she felt an envy that almost left her breathless. THEY COULD LEAVE. And she would never be able to go anywhere. She had not even really made it to the city" (*F* 148).[58] Parul's forced move from one slum to a slightly better one also illustrates outside impediments on mobility. And for Olga, happiness depends on finding a Western man

---

**58** "Wann immer Amarita Fremde ansah, hatte sie einen Neid in sich, der ihr fast den Atem nahm. DIE KONNTEN WEG. Und sie würde nie irgendwohin können. Sie hatte es ja noch nicht einmal richtig in die Stadt geschafft." *F* 148.

who might take her away from the poverty and squalor of Kyrgyzstan: "Half of the people in her city lived below the poverty line, 60 percent were unemployed and since communism did not exist any more, one was not even told lies anymore. There was nothing to hope for, there was only the present, and that was wretched" (*F* 228–29).[59]

As my analyses have shown, Sibylle Berg's *Die Fahrt* truly differs from the other texts analyzed in this chapter, especially from the literary manifestations of an aesthetic cosmopolitanism in Kracht's *Der gelbe Bleistift*. While both authors share an interest in the opaque surfaces of consumerism, Berg's criticism has little in common with Kracht's detached irony. Her characters are marked by deterritorialization, like those in Hermann and Hens, but the realistic narration of her female vagabonds and their abject poverty varies greatly from the distanced, aestheticized experiences recounted in *Nichts als Gespenster*. I thus agree with Jeremiah's assertion that *Die Fahrt* "proposes and practices a relational nomadic ethics" (143) since the vanishing point of Berg's aesthetic project, while shot through with misanthropy, is that of a moralist who recognizes the world for what it is instead of for what it should be. Berg's writing is from the outset a critical reading of existing social conditions, power and gender relations, and capitalist relations of production that utilizes cynicism as a distancing means in order to pursue its enlightened project (Degler 126).

## Retreating to the Province: Florian Illies's *Ortsgespräch* (2006)

"Ich wollte einfach dorthin zurück, wo ich meine Kindheit verbracht hatte, wodurch mein Spezifisches bis ins Innerste vermittelt war. Spüren mochte ich, daß, was man im Leben realisiert, wenig anderes ist als der Versuch, die Kindheit einzuholen."
Theodor W. Adorno, "Auf die Frage: Was ist deutsch?"(1965)

This chapter would not be complete without presenting a final juxtaposition to the texts analyzed so far. As we have seen, they showcase either the indifference of global tourists vis-à-vis foreign locales and cultures or the wariness with which these globetrotters approach globalized spaces. Yet a number of books, especially of the non-fiction variety, perform the opposite move and

---

**59** "Die Hälfte der Menschen in ihrer Stadt lebte unter der Armutsgrenze, 60 Prozent waren arbeitslos, und seit es den Kommunismus nicht mehr gab, wurden einem noch nicht einmal mehr Lügen erzählt. Da war nichts zum Daraufhoffen, da war nur das Jetzt, und das war erbärmlich." *F* 228–229.

focus on the local homeland and emotional ties to Germany. While the idea of *Heimat* – a word whose English translation "homeland" does not carry the same weight as in German and is thus a challenging concept for the self-analytical speaker (Blickle 4) – has been important to German self-perceptions over the last two centuries, my argument is that it gains particular significance in the aughts. Literature dealing with ideas of *Heimat* and provincial life signifies a second important strand in the German-language reaction to globalization. As I suggested in the beginning of this chapter, there seems to be a need after unification to measure the country both spatially and metaphorically in order to ascertain what a subjective and/or German identity might entail. As a result, a consciousness of *Heimat*, often in the form of nostalgia for East German things and ways of life (*Ostalgie*), has been visible particularly in East Germany (see Berdahl). Ingo Schulze's novel *Simple Storys*, analyzed in chapter two, comes to mind as one example; others include Jana Hensel's *Zonenkinder* (2002; *After The Wall*, 2004; the East German counterpart of Illies's *Generation Golf*), Claudia Rusch's *Meine freie deutsche Jugend* (2003, My Free German Youth) and, more recently, Uwe Tellkamp's *Der Turm* (2008, The Tower) and Judith Zander's *Dinge, die wir heute sagten* (2010, Things We Said Today). The primary focus of these and other novels is not the province per se, but a reflection on social life in the former GDR and/or in newly unified Germany.

Some critics have also suggested that the multicultural experience of the World Soccer Cup held in Germany in the summer of 2006 served as a catalyst for a renewed love for the fatherland and *Heimat* (see Kurbjuweit and Allgöver; Schediwy).[60] *Ortsgespräch* echoes this by drawing a direct line between the sporting event and the renewed interest in the homeland.[61] A number of non-fiction texts provide further evidence, spanning the gamut from hardly concealed advertisement (*Das Beste an Deutschland. 250 Gründe, unser Land heute zu lieben*; The Best of Germany. 250 Reasons to Love Our Country Today) to real and imagined travels throughout Germany (Wolfgang Büscher's *Deutschland, eine Reise;* Germany, A Trip) to essays about the country and its mental state (Richard Wagner's *Der deutsche Horizont. Vom Schicksal eines guten Landes; The German Horizon. About the Fate of a Good Country*), all published in 2006.[62]

---

**60** See also the prolonged discussion on H-Net, the global network for German historians, which is still available in the archive under the key word "world cup 2006."

**61** "Was die Fußball-WM fürs Nationale war, könnte dieses Buch für die lange Zeit verlorene Naturbegeisterung der Deutschen werden. Für ihre Romantik, ihr Heimatgefühl." Lottmann 154.

**62** René Aguigah provides an overview of this literature in an interesting essay in *Literaturen*.

Florian Illies's *Ortsgespräch* (2006, Local Call) is thus but one example for a larger trend in which the globalized world exists only on the periphery. In telling the story of his historic hometown Schlitz in Upper Hesse, Illies withdraws into the familiar sphere of *Heimat*, which he conflates with the German province[63] as well as with memories of his childhood. Writing in a breezy journalistic style, he introduces the reader to the town's colorful inhabitants and the community building routines that regulate their life, providing much anecdotal evidence for "the cliché that in Schlitz, time is standing still."[64] Illies's goal is to advocate for the province as a "deceleration oasis" ("Entschleunigungsoase," *O* 197) that gives the individual the opportunity to calm down, relax and reboot in a world that seems to spin ever faster, where time is continuously shortened by the practices that are supposed to save time, such as e-mail, mobile text messaging, and coffee to go (*O* 15):

> Decrease your speed. That was – from the perspective of the suitcase pulling city slicker who changed cities, partners and jobs – for a long time a paralyzing nightmare. But this is slowly changing. Why should the one who is attached to a certain place be thought of as backwards instead of the one restlessly rushing about, one wonders slightly exhausted. Were the sedentary ones not always superior to the nomads?[65]

Illies's name has come up before in this study as the author of *Generation Golf*, published in 2000. That work presents a nostalgia-tinged evaluation of growing up middle-class in prospering 1970s and 1980s West Germany. Offering little more than anecdotal evidence about his cohort, the author waxes poetic about consumer items of his childhood like Playmobil and Nutella, popular television shows, and public figures such as soccer players and politicians. Nevertheless, he claims to have identified decisive traits of his generation, and many readers actually loved the book for providing them with identificatory possibilities, which was evident in the readers's reviews of *Generation Golf* on Amazon.de. Professional critics took less kindly to Illies's over-generalizations, elitism and superficiality. Yet despite receiving its share of acid criticism, the book provided a handy descriptor for the generation born between 1965 and 1975 that has showed staying power, not only in this study, but also in the

---

63 This bothers Albert Meier who points out that the term "province," imported from centralist France, historically does not work for a federalist system such as Germany (161).

64 *Ortsgespräch* 41. Henceforth quoted in the text as *O* plus page number.

65 "Das Tempo drosseln. Das war – aus der Perspektive des rollkofferziehenden Großstädters, der Städte, Partner, Arbeitsplätze wechselte – lange ein lähmender Alptraum. Doch langsam ändert sich das, denn warum sollte eigentlich unbedingt der Ortsgebundene der Rückständige sein und nicht der Umherhetzende, so fragt man leicht erschöpft. Waren die Sesshaften den Nomaden nicht immer überlegen?" *O* 41.

public discourse and in literary and sociological scholarship. Sociologist Markus Klein shows for instance that the Generation Golf is a clearly distinguished birth cohort characterized by a process of averting from postmaterial values (see also McCarthy). This is due in part to the resuscitation of thinking in generational categories that gained significance in the wake of unification both in the public sphere and German cultural studies (see Anz, Weigel). Illies's *Generation Golf* added significantly to this millennial discourse, not least because it has a generational conflict at its center. One way to read the book is as an attempt to break the grip that the generation of 1968 still has on united Germany, as is most obvious in a comment on Christian Kracht's *Faserland*. Illies praises the author for having had the courage to call the beliefs of this cohort "ridiculous:" "The distancing vis-à-vis the predecessor generation with their moral haughtiness became an important maxim for us. After all, we knew few of them; most, I believed, had become social studies teachers or were pictured on the wanted posters of the Red Army Faction that hung in every post office."[66] Illies's identificatory reading of Kracht suggests that the latter is the founding figure of a new, collective identity that mocks the social engagement of their predecessors as outdated and out of touch with reality.

In *Generation Golf* Illies had identified in his own cohort "a curious disposition to be retrospective," which he named as the reason for writing a memoir at the age of 28.[67] Six years later, *Ortsgespräch* reads as a logical continuation of the professed proximity to familial and geographic roots, which would also be showcased in Illies's following two books.[68] Given that he lives in Berlin as a very successful journalist – he was editor-in-chief of the famous *Berliner Seiten* of the *FAZ* between 1999 and 2002 and the arts and leisure editor for *Die Zeit* until spring 2011; he now publishes the art and lifestyle magazine *Monopol* and is a partner at the Berlin auctioning house Griesebach – one could question whether Illies's longing for the province is indeed real. Does he merely offer a performance of "a longing for a longing," as Wolfgang Schneider

---

**66** "Die Abgrenzung gegen die Vorgängergeneration mit ihrer Moralhoheit war für uns früh eine entscheidende Lebensmaxime. Wir kannten ja relativ wenige von ihnen, die meisten waren, so glaubte ich, Gemeinschaftskundelehrer geworden, oder hingen auf den RAF-Fahndungsplakaten in den Postämtern." *Generation Golf* 177.

**67** "Wir haben, obwohl kaum erwachsen, schon jetzt einen merkwürdigen Hang zur Retrospektive, und manche von uns schreiben schon mit 28 Jahren ein Buch über ihre eigene Kindheit, im eitlen Glauben, daran lasse sich die Geschichte einer ganzen Generation erzählen." *Generation Golf* 197.

**68** Illies published *Anleitung zum Unschuldigsein* in 2001 and *Generation Golf Zwei* in 2003, neither one of which was as successful as his first book.

suggests?[69] It is indeed important to acknowledge that Illies is one of the savvy media workers described earlier in this study who know the rules and processes in the literary field and take advantage of their own hybrid position in it. In Illies's case, this concerns his dual roles as employed journalist and freelance author. Strategic considerations most likely guide the choice of subject to a certain extent.[70] This is especially visible in his third book, *Generation Golf Zwei,* with which he tried unsuccessfully to repeat his debut hit.

Trendsetting and marketing ploys notwithstanding, my argument is that Illies consciously positions the homey province as a last refuge to a globalized world. While acknowledging that globalization is now a given reality that has brought many attractive things into the life of the western consumer, he also implies that it has changed life in Germany for the worse. Within the spectrum of the discourse on globalization he comes down on the side of (early) critics who argue that it is an equalizer stifling local diversity and customs, aptly captured in George Ritzer's catch phrase of "McDonaldization."

Commenting on the visible and very real changes most urban and non-urban areas in Germany have undergone, Illies's first point of contention concerns commerce. The strip mall, so ubiquitous in the U.S., has arrived in Germany as well, mostly on the outskirts of towns. It represents the dying off of independent businesses that do not stand a chance versus stores such as Schlecker, a drugstore chain: "The words are always the same: 'Going-out-of-business sale'... with those five words, in black, sometimes red, most often yellow print, globalization is signposted in the black-red-gold German province" (*O* 150).[71]

His second criticism is how globalization leads to a culture of homogeneity, essentially levels differences and makes the world a more boring place (*O* 129). Typical of Illies's writing style that is always focused on the punch line, his examples for the most part underplay the complex intertwining between the global and the local that has been the focus of many studies on globalization.

---

**69** "Ironisch abgefedert zelebriert der Autor eine Sehnsucht nach der Provinz, die er vermutlich selbst nur in sehr beherrschbarem Mass hat. Eigentlich handelt es sich eher um die Sehnsucht nach einer Sehnsucht." Schneider.

**70** This leads Hanna Leitgeb to speculate: "Wir stellen uns vor: eine lange Phase quälenden Kopfzerbrechens mit Freundin und Agenten darüber, was denn aus der Illies-Feder als Nächstes den Nerv der Zeit treffen könnte" (We imagine a long phase of the author racking his brain, together with his girlfriend and agent, what he might pen next that would capture the spirit of the times). Hanna Leitgeb. "Der Verlust der Unschuld. Florian Illies und das Gewissen der Generation Golf." 26.

**71** "Die Worte sind immer die gleichen: ‚Total Räumungsverkauf wegen Geschäftsaufgabe'... mit diesen vier Worten, in schwarz, manchmal rot, meistens gelb, wird der schwarz-rot-gelben Provinz die Globalisierung ausgeschildert." *O* 150.

Illies, on the other hand, assumes that the local environment is only passively affected by globalizing factors, instead of actively adopting products to the tastes and sensibilities of local markets. In this context, it becomes obvious that *Ortsgespräch* has no interest in presenting a nuanced perspective or even the "theory of the province" that fellow author David Wagner wished for. Writing a book with mass-appeal about the character of the German province requires a certain degree of overgeneralization as a stylistic device. Consequently Illies fearlessly uses clichés commonly associated with provincial life. Throughout the text he comments on the lush landscape of Upper Hesse, the beautiful half-timbered architecture of Schlitz with its five castles, and the cleanliness, inflexibility, and small town mentality of its inhabitants. He employs Romantic topoi such as German beech groves (*O* 87) and the affinity for nature and environmental protection to illustrate the superiority of small-town life over the big cities. While *taz* critic Kolja Mensing saw "neo-conservatism for the simple minded" in this, Joachim Lottmann took the opposite stance when he predicted in a review in the *Spiegel* that *Ortsgespräch* would be read in all of Germany and lead to a romantic return to nature and the homeland. But Illies is an intelligent enough writer to subvert his romantic sentimentality with a healthy dose of irony, which is an aesthetic strategy used successfully in all of his books. His disclaimer in the beginning, "Of course everything in this book is a pack of lies" ("erstunken und erlogen") signals to the reader from the outset that she might want to take his observations with a grain of salt.

*Ortsgespräch* offers a salient commentary on globalizing effects precisely because that is not its central goal. Although it focuses on the local instead of the global, Illies, similar to the narratives of Hermann, Hens, and Berg, echoes German wariness in the face of globalization and offers an implicit critique of it.[72] He just goes about it differently: his text celebrates experiences commonly associated with a time before globalizing factors, especially in the form of neoliberalism and new technologies, reshaped our lives. As in *Generation Golf* and *Generation Golf Zwei*, Illies's perspective is that of an upper middle-class child who grew up privileged and materialistic, yet with an underdeveloped political consciousness. His anecdotes of *Heimat* reference a supposedly sim-

---

**72** In this context I disagree with Meier's position: "Globalisierungkritik ist mit Illies' Interesse an der eigenen Heimatregion offensichtlich nicht verbunden, weil der entsprechende Modernisierungsdruck wertneutral zur Sprache gebracht wird, ohne den Zustand 'vor der Globalisierung' als das Bessere auszuspielen." 163. (Illies's interest in his home region obviously is not connected to a critique of globalization because the pressure to modernize is expressed in a neutral way, without pitting the conditions "before globalization" against those after globalization.)

pler time when the prosperous welfare state in the West provided a sense of security and a carefree childhood; thus providing what Emily Jeremiah has called "a refuge from globalization" (140).

In the context of the effects unification had on Germany as a whole, Julia Hell and Johannes von Moltke reflect on the ways in which post-unification nostalgia has materialized in the visual arts, cinema, and literature. One of their central arguments is that nostalgic convergence is not limited to the territory of the former GDR, since "Germany's new postfordist arrangements, with their ever-mounting pressures to take risks, are transforming lives in East and West," leading to various nostalgias that all serve as a "refusal of the present" (87). To be sure, this rejection is much less pronounced in Illies's *Ortsgespräch* than it is in the examples analyzed by Hell and von Moltke (among them Sven Regener's novel *Herr Lehmann* and Oskar Roehler's film *Die Unberührbare*). Illies, not least due to his professional background as a journalist, is situated firmly in the twenty-first century and appreciates the technological advances globalization has brought. Yet yearning for the qualities commonly associated with "home," such as community, cordiality, and loyalty, is also present here, as the very beginning of the text shows. The zoom from the universal perspective to the province also signals an awareness of the glocal, i.e. the intertwinement of the global and the local that shapes our lives:

> I am sitting in Berlin at my computer, "Google Earth" is the name of the program, the images are coming from outer space, high-resolution satellite photos with which one can zoom close to every place on earth. ... But the most exciting thing is to travel back. Hitchhiking back to the galaxy of the homeland. Why do we like to use the most advanced technologies to dig back into the past ... to find out whether our home is still standing, like back when we left it? The satellites send comforting messages: it is still standing.[73]

While technological advances here and in other passages are recognized as useful, Illies also implies that human beings continue to look for retreat spaces precisely *because* changes brought about by globalization leave them feeling disconnected from their spatial environment and their social communities:

> Surely we will at some point stop the nonsense of gulping cappuccino on the run from light-brown paper cups, as if we were running a marathon and could not stop in between.

---

**73** "Ich sitze in Berlin an meinem Computer, "Google Earth" heißt das Programm, die Bilder kommen aus dem All, hochaufgelöste Satellitenfotos, mit denen man sich an jeden Ort der Erde heranzoomen kann ... Doch am aufregendsten ist es, zurückzureisen. Per Anhalter in die Galaxis Heimat. Warum nur nutzt man die fortschrittlichste Technik so gerne, um sich zurückzugraben in die Vergangenheit ... um herauszufinden ... ob die Heimat noch so steht – so, wie man sie einst verlassen hat? Die Satelliten senden beruhigende Botschaften: Sie steht." *O* 9–10.

In these times longing for a deceleration oasis like the Schwarzer Grund 17 keeps growing. What is served there are Capri Sun, Auerhahn beer and seltzer water from dimpled glass bottles. And whoever wants coffee has to sit down.[74]

This slightly regressive focus on a romantic and often idealized retreat space does suggest longing for a more rooted type of experience. Yet whether one wants to go so far as to call this stance "anti-modern" depends on the individual reader's attitude vis-à-vis the benefits and drawbacks that globalization entails for the individual – and thus one's disposition towards (unfettered) progress. Illies knows of course that slowing down the development he describes is not likely, making a reversal to the habits still practiced in the province impossible. So he hides the inherent nostalgia that goes hand in hand with his walk down memory lane behind the ironic stance he takes. In this context, I agree with Meier who marks the irony as a solution to the aporia inherent to reflecting on the province. As something that is in the past of the observer but nevertheless exists as a counter draft to the existence in the metropolis, the province causes a longing whose absurdity is always already recognized; a "meta longing" (Meier 162) that is aware of its own artificiality but nevertheless powerful. Or, in Illies's words: "A longing for a longing for the countryside."

Literary critics such as Jochen Förster bemoaned that in the first years of the millennium young German authors were too exclusively concerned with their subjective condition, asserting that their ahistorical, de-politicized narratives could not do justice to the complexities of today's world (Förster 29). This rather generalized assessment owes much to an understanding of realistic writing, literature's societal significance, and political engagement that is anchored in the ideals of 1968 and dominates at least the older and middle-aged generations of critics. For them, a discursive phenomenon such as relevant realism (*Relevanter Realismus*) discussed in chapter two, which calls for prose that lives up to its alleged societal responsibilities is much more likely to satisfy.[75] Yet for a different subset of younger writers, it is precisely the absence of "history" and "politics" that illustrates both, namely the state of

---

**74** "Und sicher wird man irgendwann mit dem Unsinn aufhören, Cappuccino immer im Laufen aus hellbraunen Pappbechern zu schlürfen, als sei man beim Marathon und dürfe zwischendurch nicht anhalten. In diesen Zeiten wächst die Sehnsucht nach Entschleunigungsoasen wie der im Schwaren Grund 17. Zu trinken gibt es dort noch heute Capri-Sonne, Auerhahn-Bier und Sprudel aus genoppten Glasflaschen. Und wer Kaffee will, muss sich setzen." *O* 16.
**75** Matthias Politycki, Martin R. Dean, Thomas Hettche, and Michael Schindhelm published their manifest "Was soll der Roman?" in 2005 in *Die Zeit*.

contemporary German society as they perceive it. As the literary case studies in this chapter have shown, subjectivism and the reflection of global issues are presented here and by no means prove mutually exclusive.

Even though only Berg and Illies thematize globalization explicitly, all the stories share certain features that speak mostly of its alienating forces. These are contained in the characters' sense of displacement and inability to relate to others in successful communication, and through the narrative structure shown to be systemic to their post-national cosmopolitanism. The protagonists' unrelenting travel conveys a search for a bygone sense of place and identity that the experience of globalization has called into question, maybe even eradicated. The postmodern life strategies of these global tourists tend to render all human relations fragmentary and discontinuous, and the resulting alienation figures most prominently in interpersonal relationships, which are marred by ambivalence, indecisiveness and cruelty. For these German-language authors, living in a globalized, deterritorialized world entails the fissure of stable identities and functioning social networks.

The literary portrayal of globalized subjects in their intimate realms, influenced and shaped by powers largely beyond their control, is thus not a retreat from contemporary issues. On the contrary, it is a form of creative engagement that demonstrates as a case in point how, despite the problems it breeds, globalization promotes new aesthetic and cultural forms (Lützeler 2005, 35). Hermann, Hens, Kracht, and Berg combine re-interpretations and re-writings of the German literary tradition with Anglo-American formats, as well as depictions of contemporary lifestyles with global popular culture. Thus, they contribute to what Brigitte Weingart has called the poetics of normalization (167–168). Their prose translates the fusion of different cultural traditions into an aesthetic syncretism, one well suited to grasp the fragmentation of identities and the demand for new cultural identifications that the global subject is confronted with on a daily basis: in New York, Rio, Tokyo, in beautiful apartments and run-down summer houses alike.

# 6 Coda: Piles of Authenticity: Narrating 09/11

"Objects which in themselves we view with pain, we delight to contemplate when reproduced with minute fidelity: such as the forms of the most ignoble animals and of dead bodies." Aristotle. *Poetics.* 4th chapter

"Many things are over. The narrative ends in the rubble, and it is left to us to create the counter-narrative." Don DeLillo (34)

In the decade after the terrorist attacks on New York and Washington, D.C., "09/11" became a forceful and ever-present trope that continues to influence our lives in a variety of ways. Not a week goes by without the announcement of more deaths in America's war on terror. An ominous feeling of new threats overshadows our lives and has created a culture of fear in the American public that political spin-doctors and the media fuel in equal measure. Thus, the dictum uttered by George W. Bush in the immediate aftermath of 09/11 – nothing will be as it used to be, the world will forever be changed – has proven itself to be the writing on the wall. Although this notion is somewhat of a cliché, it does carry significance due to its sheer omnipresence; it marks our understanding of September 11 as a caesura of *global* significance, as Jan Philipp Reemtsma has pointed out (330).

If the world has changed, has the literary perception of it changed with it? This question prompted me to undertake an extensive survey of texts in German and English that directly address the fateful September morning and its aftermath. Naturally, Anglo-American writers were affected more directly by the events and have published a number of narrative texts in recent years. In Ian McEwan's *Saturday* (2005), Jonathan Safran Foer's *Extremely Loud And Incredibly Close* (2005), Jay McInerney's *The Good Life* (2006), John Updike's *Terrorist* (2006), and Don DeLillo's *Falling Man* (2007), respectively, 09/11 is the background event that sets the plot in motion and serves as a catalyst for the characters. Frédéric Beigbeder's *Windows On The World* (2004), on the other hand, is set in the World Trade Center in the hour before the first plane hit the first tower. My investigation was motivated by a desire to understand how the event of 09/11 inscribed itself into the cultural memory of the West. How have authors approached it? Has it changed their topics and aesthetics? Should we really read "09/11" as the marker for the end of the "fun society" (Spaßgesellschaft) and the beginning of a "new seriousness" (neue Ernsthaftigkeit), as many critics suggested?

As already laid out in previous chapters, Germany in the years between 1990 and 2000 was concerned primarily with the aftermath of unification and in the process of negotiating "competing versions of a new German 'normality'" (Taberner 2005 xxi) which, as literary scholars have shown, is reflected in the literature of those years. An intense examination of the (Nazi) past, the old *Bundesrepublik* and the GDR stands on a par with renderings of the hedonistic, apolitical life-style of a younger *Generation Golf*, as embodied in many texts of new German pop literature. September 11, however, put an end to the German illusion that the effects of living in a globalized world were largely limited to and could be dealt with primarily in the economic realm. The proclamations of solidarity uttered in the immediate aftermath of 09/11, succinctly captured in the newspaper headline "We are all Americans" proved to be prophetic as subsequent terrorist attacks unfolded around the world. Although the bombings in Madrid (March 11, 2004) and London (July 7, 2005), to name just two in Western Europe, did not attain the same phantasmic qualities that September 11 holds, they confirmed that the strikes would not be limited to the United States as the capitalist super-state but were attacks on an entire Western collective. Consequently, pertinent ideas of how this collective operates in its public as well as its political state changed, leading to the realization that terrorist acts concern us less as individuals or as nationals of a particular country, and more as part of a group that does not stop at national boundaries (Schmidt 162). The events of 09/11 have heightened the awareness that terror has become just as much a globalized phenomenon as our economy and consumer habits.

While this is certainly true for the political level and was mirrored in the emotional responses of many concerned and shocked non-Americans, German literary responses only reflected this in the first phase immediate following 09/11. Even though many texts by a younger generation of authors now engage more critically with contemporary realities than they did in the late 1990s, coming to terms with September 11 in German-language literature for the most part does not entail reflecting on the kind of fear Ingeborg Bachmann called "non-disputable, sheer terror, the massive attack on life."[1] My argument is that 09/11 instead becomes a trope for the complex ramifications of globalization that presents authors with the opportunity to engage with the conflicting effects and the marks that globalization in its many forms leaves on the individual and the collective. Whether this topical engagement constitutes a return to a politically more committed literature is the vanishing point of my interest in this topic.

Ina Hartwig, literary critic for the *Frankfurter Rundschau*, strongly argued that the terrorist attacks had indeed changed the literary landscape. Six

---

[1] "Die Angst ist nicht disputierbar, sie ist der Überfall, sie ist [der] Terror, der massive Angriff auf das Leben." Bachmann. *Der Fall Franza* 406.

months after 09/11 she stated at a symposium on "War and Literature" at the *Deutsche Literaturkonferenz* in Leipzig:

> September 11 is irresistible for writers. The subject and the catastrophe, the social and the world order, the inwardness and the reality of the media, these are the big topics on the horizon of the respective small literary attempts. Because we would have to discuss whether one should even consider it literature.[2]

Hartwig's assessment is reflected in the relatively large number of texts in the first phase of an artistic engagement with 09/11. These contributions often have an immediate and spontaneous character. Many appeared in literary magazines and the *Feuilleton* or online as blogs. For example, journalist Else Buschheuer kept her New York diary www.else-buschheuer.de (which is no longer available online) during a six-months internship at the now defunct German-language Jewish newspaper *Aufbau*. The text was originally published as an online diary/blog from June to November 2001 before it appeared as a book, which is clearly divided into two distinct parts, pre- and post 09/11. While the first 100 pages from June 30 to September 10 read like the impressions of a wide-eyed, slightly naïve first- time visitor to the Big Apple, the second, longer section that spans the time from September 11 to November 4 chronicles Buschheuer's breathless, at times hysterical attempts to come to terms with the personal terror that she experienced while living in the immediate vicinity of Ground Zero. The decision to retain all of the real time online entries unedited in the printed edition (including the frequent typos) is, we can assume, due to the author's and the editor's idea that they reflect an unmediated, spontaneous authenticity. Unfortunately, this also makes for a reading that remains entirely superficial in its analysis:

> 09/12/01 12:36 AM NYC TIME: "Incapable of turning off the TV [because how should I know then where the next plane will come crashing down?] incapable of closing my eyes [immediately the burning towers start sliding down, for you as well? Will it remain this way?] incapable to log off the Net [maybe it'll be the last time?]." – 09/12/01 2:50 AM NYC TIME: When NBC is showing the video of the second tower collapsing, and I recognize the screams I heard in front of my window, I can't breathe. There are two really high

---

2 "Der 11. September ist unwiderstehlich für die Schriftsteller. Das Ich und die Katastrophe, das Soziale und die Weltordnung, die Innerlichkeit und die Medienwirklichkeit: Das sind die großen Themen am Horizont dieser kleinen literarischen Versuche. Denn ob es sich um Literatur handelt, muss erst diskutiert werden." Hartwig 166.

shrill screams of two women on the video. That was ... how long ago? ... twenty hours? ... the last thing I thought I'd hear during my life time.[3]

A more interesting contribution is Kathrin Röggla's account *really ground zero. 11. september und folgendes*, which was published in 2001. Some of the texts collected here first appeared as installments in German newspapers (mostly in the Berlin newspaper *taz*) while Röggla was on a fellowship in New York City, where she witnessed the terrorist attacks first-hand. In the book, she organizes her short texts into twenty-two chapters that are accompanied by her own black and white photographs. *really ground zero* is the rather unmediated attempt to artistically and intellectually process the piles of authenticity ("haufen an authentizität")[4] brought about by the smoldering ruins of the World Trade Center. The texts record the somber mood in the American population, the hyperbolic production of politics through and in the media and, most importantly, the changes in language and policies that the American government advanced in its attempt to gain a handle on the national trauma.

Large parts of *really ground zero* are transcripts of televised C-Span reports, reminiscent of Rainald Goetz's *Fernsehmitschriften* in his three-volume edition *1989*, published in 1993. Like Goetz, Röggla integrates her media protocols into the text without further comment and generally avoids the inclusion of direct emotional responses to what she observes. Her distanced account lacks the somewhat hysterical identification with the victims that Buschheuer displays. Instead, Röggla shows the attempts of a traumatized American public "to reassure oneself of reality in small communicative gestures full of redundancies and repetitions."[5] In the process, she identifies and analyzes a form of speech that she characterizes as "rhetoric without substance," the blending of religious and political speech known as jingoism (*rgz* 35).[6]

---

**3** "12.09.01. 12:36AM NYC TIME: "Unfähig, den Fernseher auszuschalten [woher soll ich dann wissen, wo das nächste Flugzeug runterkommt?] unfähig, die Augen zu schließen [dann rutschen sofort die brennenden Türme zusammen, bei Ihnen auch? bleibt das jetzt so?], unfähig, aus dem Netz zu gehen [vielleicht ist es das letzte Mal?]." – 12.09.01 2:50AM NYC TIME: Wenn sie bei NBC das Video vom zweiten Turmeinsturz zeigen, auf dem ich die Schreie von vor meinem Fenster wiedererkenne, krieg ich keine Luft. Da sind zwei ganz hohe schrille kreischende Frauenschreie drauf. Das war vor... wie lange ist das her? ... zwanzig Stunden? ... das Letzte, was ich in meinem Leben zu hören glaubte." Buschheuer 153–154.
**4** Röggla. *really ground zero* 108. Quoted henceforth in the text as *rgz* plus page number.
**5** "... sich einer realität zu versichern in kleinen kommunikativen gesten voller redundanzen und wiederholungen". *rgz* 8.
**6** Jingoism is by definition a form of chauvinist patriotism; one uses whatever means necessary to safeguard a country's national interest and bullying other countries in the process.

The emphasis on linguistic analysis was one of the reasons many critics reacted negatively to *really ground zero*. They felt that the author was avoiding reality and instead favored the flight into the abstractions of rhetoric. Yet these criticisms neglect the thrust of her project, which was to travel "from the pile of authenticity to the pile where terms take on a different meaning."[7] It also marginalized Röggla's keen awareness of the difficult relationship between reality, authenticity, and fiction, which she addresses first in the opening sentence, "So now I have a life. A real one" (*rgz* 6). The common differentiation between fact and fiction simply collapses in light of the events that seemed like the enactment of a dream or a scene from a movie, as many critics noted (Köhler, for instance).

Röggla's decision not to describe the smoking crater of Ground Zero has to do with her notion that she could only fail if she tried to aestheticize and give form to something that at the time felt like a living nightmare. In its attempt to record "ideology at work" as Röggla calls it,[8] *really ground zero* identifies the linguistic rearmament as an indispensable tool to prepare the American public for the ensuing political action of the invasions of Afghanistan and Iraq. A decade later, it provides an insightful analysis locating the inception of a political rhetoric that continues to shape the American media landscape and the public sphere to this day.

One can think of *really ground zero* as casting a spotlight, as a moment in time in which the author freeze-frames the particular historical juncture of 09/11 and the individual and national trauma emanating from it, or, in Röggla's own words "[...] the attempt to gain an overview over this pile of ideologemes, vocabulary that has been broken open, changes in context, rhetorical operations, biased translations."[9] Critics however found the literary approach inappropriate: "In trying to be not just journalism but literature, Kathrin Röggla's book celebrates its own linguistic and perception problems and that has a disgusting quality when the ruins are still smoldering."[10] Neglect of the fact that *really ground zero* was an essayistic attempt is a poignant example for the expectation that authors should or could be the ones to explain significant historical and global developments, as well as for the disappointment when

---

7 "... vom haufen der authentizität zum haufen der begriffsverschiebungen". *rgz* 109.

8 "man kann der ideologie bei der arbeit zusehen." *rgz* 108.

9 "der versuch, aus diesem haufen an ideologemen, aufgebrochenem vokabular, kontextverschiebungen, rhetorischen operationen, schrägen übersetzungen, einen überblick zu bekommen." *rgz* 100.

10 "Kathrin Rögglas Buch, indem es Literatur sein will und nicht nur Journalismus, feiert wortreich seine Sprach- und Wahrnehmungsschwierigkeiten, und das hat, wenn die Trümmer noch rauchen, etwas Abstoßendes." Scheel 157.

they do not live up to these expectations. The author as "grand wizard," as Thomas Meinecke has called it, is a very German idea and a remaining aberration, despite the tarnished reputations of the old generation of intellectual figureheads.[11] As an exercise in linguistic analysis, *really ground zero* complements the critical, explicitly political impetus of Röggla's larger oeuvre, which, as detailed in chapter three, is formally quite diverse. It examines across various genres and poetic modes what living in a globalized, post-national polity governed by neo-liberalism means for society as a whole, as well as for the subject formation and identity construction of the individual.

The second phase of the narration of 09/11 is, of course, still ongoing. However, the improved aesthetic quality of the texts that have been published since 2003 indicates that any historical experience needs time to be processed psychologically and intellectually and requires what Andrea Köhler has called an aesthetic incubation period ("ästhetische Inkubationszeit," 237). The first longer pieces on 09/11 did not appear until a few years ago, and it was left to already established writers – such Ian McEwan and Martin Amis in Britain, or Don DeLillo and John Updike in the U.S. – to write more ambitious, novel-length narratives. What links these novels to comparable German texts is the focus on individual life stories and situations in which the characters have to deal with the aftermath of the terrorist attacks and somehow rebuild their more or less fractured lives. This still confirms the position of *Zeit* critic Thomas E. Schmid who wrote in 2002 that writers had recorded the changed global situation mostly in their emotional and intellectual reactions (161).

Katharina Hacker can justifiably lay claim to having written the first German 09/11 novel with *Die Habenichtse* (*The Have-Nots*, 2007), published in 2006, leading Wilhelm Amann to call it a "socially committed society novel," a genre renewed in the context of globalization processes (212). This might be one of the reasons why it was recognized with the *German Book Prize* for best novel the same year.[12] The book has since been translated into English and

---

11 I am thinking of Günter Grass's participation in the SS, which he revealed in passing in *Beim Häuten der Zwiebel* (2006, *Peeling the Onion*, 2007), as well as Erwin Strittmatter's controversial membership in the SS during World War Two and his activities as an informant for the East German *Staatssicherheit*.

12 Hacker was born in 1967 in Frankfurt/Main and studied philosophy, history, and Jewish Studies in Freiburg. She resided and worked in Israel for a few years before returning to Berlin, where she now lives as a freelance writer. She is a prolific author and translator who has published poems, essays, and a number of novels, among them *Der Bademeister* (2000, *The Lifeguard*, 2002, also translated into Russian), *Eine Art Liebe* (2003, Some Kind of Love), and most recently *Die Erdbeeren von Antons Mutter* (2010, The Strawberries of Anton's Mother), the second part in a trilogy. This and other information about Hacker can be found on her web site http://www.katharinahacker.de.

Italian; being published in the former language generally opens the door to other translations as well.[13] At least fourteen other translations are in preparation for *Die Habenichtse*, among them Chinese, Vietnamese, and Hebrew. Hacker's international profile is the best indication that the goal of the *Book Prize*, namely to create interest in German-language authors, reading, and the leading medium ("Leitmedium") book beyond national borders, has been reached.[14] Since its founding in 2005 by the German Publishers and Booksellers' Association (*Börsenverein des Deutschen Buchhandels)*, the annual prize has meant critical and commercial success for the winners; Hacker indicated in an interview with *Deutsche Welle* that the prize money of 25,000 Euros finally ended her ongoing financial insecurity and allowed for a more relaxed existence (Wojcik).

Although the realistically written novel *Die Habenichtse* focuses on an anamnesis of interpersonal relationships, it is, so my thesis, really one about the effects of globalization on the human psyche. Hacker characterizes the private realm as the decisive locus where the political unfolds, much like Ian McEwan in *Saturday* and Don DeLillo in *Falling Man*.[15] Even if they are not aware of it, 09/11 and the subsequent war in Iraq serve as a catalyst for the novel's two main characters in their private sphere; a catalyst that brings out their psychological imbalances, callousness and inner emptiness and leads to the unraveling of lives that seem "perfect," at least on the surface.

Throughout the global plot structure of *Die Habenichtse* media spheres and private life are closely linked; the events of September 11 are narrated only parenthetically in the second chapter:

> Prominently mounted on a low brown shelf unit, the television sent shadows flickering across the parquet floor, shadows of the collapsing towers, of people letting go of the buildings and leaping to their deaths. On the dining table, glasses and plates had been set out for at least thirty guests, but most had not turned up.[16]

---

**13** One should note that the licensing of German-language books has been rising again after a slump in 2009 and 2008 (in 2010, 30% more international licenses were sold than in 2008). In 2010, a total of 8,191 licenses were sold to foreign countries, with China having risen to most important partner (789 licenses), followed by Spain (646 licenses) and Poland (578 liceses). http://www.boersenverein.de/de/portal/Wirtschaftszahlen/158286 (March 30, 2012).
**14** http://www.deutscher-buchpreis.de/de/352668.
**15** "Wie fast alle anderen Schriftsteller, die sich mit dem 11. September beschäftigt haben, wählt auch Don DeLillo den Ort des Persönlichen und Privaten, um sich dem letztlich doch vor allem politischen Schock des Ereignisses zu nähern; ihm als Einzigem gelingt es aber, das Private plausibel zu machen eben als den Platz, wo das Politische greifbar wird." Diez.
**16** *The Have-Nots* 15, English translation by Helen Atkins (subsequently cited as *HN* plus page number). "Der Fernseher thronte auf einem niedrigen braunen Regal, über das Parkett flackerten die Schatten der in sich zusammenstürzenden Türme, der Menschen, die sich von

Belying the incidental depiction is the fact that the fates of Isabelle and Jakob, the novel's main characters, are intricately interwoven with September 11, 2001 from the outset. It is the day of their encounter at said party in Berlin, after not having been in touch since they had had a brief romance as students in Freiburg a decade prior. They fall in love, marry a short time later, and move to London in the spring of 2003. Jakob is a lawyer who specializes in questions of restitutions, both for victims of the Nazi regime and those expropriated in the GDR. The job Jakob starts in London should have gone to Robert, his friend and colleague who died in the attacks on the World Trade Center while on business in New York. Jakob was there as well, but had moved his appointment in order to be able to meet Isabelle at the party in Berlin: "He had been spared: Isabelle, he thought, had saved him." (*HN* 28)[17]

Jakob's and Isabelle's lives in London unfold against the backdrop of the beginning war; they arrive right before Britain sends its troops into Iraq in late March 2003. Similarly to Ian McEwan's *Saturday*, which shares its locale with *Die Habenichtse*, the narrative is interlaced with reports from newspaper articles, descriptions of anti-war protests and conversations about the war between friends. Yet the political realities only find entry into the novel in the form of the hysterical rhetoric of media reports, but are not accepted by Isabel and Jacob as something that truly means a change, except for their own private life, as Reinhäckl notes (133):

> He thought of September 11th, a year and a half ago, of his helpless agitation that had had nothing to do with New York, and of Bush's speech, "nothing the way it was before." Nothing had changed. There were "sleepers" waiting to carry out acts of terrorism, there had been the war in Afghanistan, houses destroyed, human beings burned to death, bodies hastily buried, and in remote, inaccessible mountains there were still Taliban or al-Qaeda fighters, names and things that meant no more to people here than the intrigues and dramatic crises in a television soap ... Only for Robert's parents, Jakob reflected, had everything really changed; and for himself. He had found Isabelle, and was going to move to London. (*HN* 111)[18]

---

den Fassaden lösten und in den Tod sprangen. Gläser und Teller für mindestens dreißig Gäste standen auf dem Eßtisch, aber die meisten waren nicht gekommen." *Die Habenichtse* 9. Subsequently cited as *H* plus page number.

**17** "Er war verschont geblieben.... Isabelle hatte ihn gerettet." *H* 22.

**18** "Er dachte an den 11. September vor anderthalb Jahren, an seine hilflose Aufregung, die mit New York nichts zu tun hatte, an Bushs Rede, *nichts, wie es war*. Nichts hatte sich verändert. Es gab Schläfer, es hatte den Afghanistan-Krieg gegeben, es gab zerstörte Häuser, verbrannte Menschen, hastig beerdigte Tote und in unwegsamen Bergen weiter Taliban- oder Al-Quaida-Kämpfer, Namen und Dinge, die für sie hier nicht mehr bedeuteten als die Verwicklungen und Dramen einer Fernsehserie ... Nur für Roberts Eltern, dachte Jakob, hat sich alles geändert, und für ihn selbst. Er hatte Isabelle gefunden, er würde nach London gehen." *H* 92.

Just like they fail to acknowledge that they "owe" their posh London life to the tragic death of Robert in the Towers, the couple does not admit that the politically charged and angry atmosphere in the capital might influence their existence. Jakob laughs off suggestions to buy supplies in order to be prepared for a possible terrorist attack and posits that "September 11th had come to represent merely the watershed between an imagined carefree 'before' and the anxious, aggressive wailing and moaning that was now increasing by the day." (*HN* 111)[19]

Hacker's treatment of her characters suggests that Jakob's and Isabelle's emotional detachment is not due to the particular personal situation they find themselves in but intrinsic; grounded in having grown up as part of the *Generation Golf* cohort described earlier, as privileged middle-class children in prosperous 1980s West Germany who never developed a historical consciousness or a sense of social and political engagement. They have everything a person could wish for – both are educated, have interesting jobs (Isabelle co-owns a graphic design firm), make enough money, and are at the center of a group of caring friends. In short, they lead an incredibly privileged, cosmopolitan existence as globalized citizens, yet they seem to suffer from a form of emotional Asperger's syndrome; they lack the ability to truly communicate with each other and are incapable of meaningfully relating to the world that surrounds them and the individuals in it; they are stand-ins for a generation that has forgotten what makes life worth living, as Heike Hermann puts it. Thus they appear as the real *Habenichtse*, the have-nots that give the novel its title.

The frequent outbursts of violence that Jakob and Isabelle experience – a mugging on the street, a beaten child, a murdered cat, an interrupted attempt at group sex – are symptomatic for the slow unraveling of their shared life. Hacker illustrates this further by narrating their relationships with various other protagonists in Berlin and London, three of whom are have-nots in a different sense. The relationship to Jim, a petty drug dealer and addict to whom Isabelle feels strangely attracted despite his physical abuse of her, sheds light on her general passiveness and her ambivalent emotions towards her straight-laced husband. *Zeit* critic Verena Auffermann sees her as a magnet for brutality and danger, yet I would argue that the encounter with their direct neighbors, a family that lives in emotional and material squalidness, illustrates Isabelle's own cruel streak. Together with her physical characteristics, it identifies her as the literary type of a *femme fragile*.[20]

**19** "Der 11. September war inzwischen nichts als die Scheidelinie zwischen einem phantasierten, unbeschwerten Vorher und dem ängstlichen, aggressiven Gejammer, das sich immer weiter ausbreitete." *H* 93.
**20** About the type, see Thomalla. I disagree here with Christian Sieg who sees Isabelle's non-reaction to the children's abuse as a symptom of being psychologically overtaxed.

The site of these encounters is the Lady Margret Road in London's Kentish Town, a place that, in the sense of Doreen Massey, is characterized by an intersection of networks of social relations and movements, incoherent, progressive, yet also full of internal conflicts. In other words, this street is a global place in that a mobile elite crosses paths with the disenfranchised who are chained to their current location due to a lack of economic and cultural capital, leading Amann to suggest that the novel probes the validity of Pierre Bourdieu's sociological field theory in literary form (218). Specifically, the Victorian house Jakob has rented on Lady Margret Road becomes the location for a catastrophe fueled by the young couple's apathy. The classical topos of the house on the one hand embodies the different social strata that are represented in Kentish Town, yet on the other hand it also shows that social indifference characterizes all the characters, independent of their social status (Reinhäckl 133).

Through the eyes of two neglected children, Sara, a bed-wetting girl who is violently beaten by their alcoholic father, and her teenage brother Dave, Hacker tells a depressing story of abuse and utter hopelessness. For weeks Isabelle, who works at home, deliberately ignores the shouting, bumping, and crying on the other side of the wall of her beautiful house. Yet one morning she watches Sara playing in the yard, enwrapped in an imaginary play-fight with a dragon and impaired by hunger. Sara hits her cat Polly hard with a stick and injures her gravely. Immediately thereafter, the child succumbs to her emotional distress about the brutal act, falls to the ground and starts to vomit violently. Reluctantly, Isabelle finally decides to intervene and climbs the fence, thereby not only crossing the fence of the two yards but also the symbolic threshold of class and privilege. Yet she quickly changes her mind, feeling unsure what to do,

> It would be easy to help the child up on to the wall, and here she was already, close beside her, her breath slightly sour-smelling, with both her arms stretched upwards. But it was the cat that Isabelle lifted up and put on the wall, before starting to look for some hold for herself ... Sitting on top of the wall, she looked down at the girl, who was making no attempt to follow her. In speechless horror she was staring at Isabelle, and now there was no trace of anything childlike in her face, only hopelessness and suffering; Isabelle couldn't help laughing. (*HN* 255)[21]

---

However, Sieg has a point when he writes: "Das Ausblenden des Leidens der eigenen Freunde wird in *Die Habenichtse* zum Symbol der Verdrängung von globalen Problemen." 43. (Suppressing the suffering of their [Isabelle's and Robert's] own friends becomes a symbol for suppressing global problems in *The Have-Nots*.)

**21** "Es wäre ein leichtes, dem Kind heraufzuhelfen, und da war das Mädchen schon, dicht neben ihr, atmend, säuerlich riechend, beide Arme nach oben gereckt. Aber Isabelle hob die Katze auf, setzte das Tier oben ab und fing an, nach einem Halt für sich selbst zu suchen...

The outburst of aggression that leads Isabelle to abandon Sara overnight in the yard and subsequently abuse her cat is one of the various loci of the novel where private life intersects with politics, where the violence that is normally clad in the coat of world history becomes personal. Hacker's narrative operates on the premise that an event such as the terrorist attacks, which Jean Baudrillard called in *The Spirit of Terrorism* an epoch-making break defying all attempts of explanation, cannot be thought through and rationally reflected upon. Instead, Hacker foregrounds the ambivalence, cruelty and fragmentation of human relations that living under the threat of globalized terror might bring forth. She thereby updates and continues the tradition of a focus on subjectivity in realistic writing that Max Frisch had defended in the period of the Cold War and the nuclear arms race when he wrote, "It is not the time for personal narratives. But human life is fulfilled or falls short within an individual human being, nowhere else."[22]

Hacker's *Habenichtse* adds another interpretive layer to the anamnesis of the *Generation Golf* born between 1965 and 1975. The emotional and psychological state of Isabelle and Jakob, as well as their apolitical stance is remarkably similar to the literary renderings of other characters, some of which I analyzed earlier in this study, such as the bloodless, ghostly shells in Judith Hermann's *Sommerhaus, später* and *Nichts als Gespenster*, the globalized, international travelers in Gregor Hens's short stories and his novel *Matta verläßt seine Kinder* and the discontented Western tourists in Sibylle Berg's *Die Fahrt*. Additional examples include Julia Franck's cruel female characters in *Bauchlandung* (Belly Flop, 2000) and Antje Rávic Strubel's bunch of wild camp counselors in *Kältere Schichten der Luft* (Colder Layers of Air, 2007). These and other authors depict a generation absorbed by private concerns, exasperated by its freedoms and helpless when faced with political and social questions of a global nature. In their focus on the globalized subject in the private sphere, Hacker and others record the severe irritations and the fragmentations of identities brought by a glocalized existence. The very fact that more texts like *Die Habenichtse* are emerging indicates that the satiated, hedonistic *Lummerland* captured ad nauseam in the late 1990s might indeed be burned down (abgebrannt), at least as a literary topic, at least for the moment.

───────────

Oben auf dem Mauersims sitzend, schaute sie nach dem Mädchen. Es unternahm keinen Versuch, ihr zu folgen. Mit sprachlosem Entsetzen starrte es Isabelle an, alles Kindliche war aus seinem Gesicht verschwunden, es gab nur noch Ausweglosigkeit und Leid darin; Isabelle mußte lachen." *H* 229.
**22** "Es ist nicht die Zeit für Ich-Geschichten. Und doch vollzieht sich das menschliche Leben oder verfehlt sich am einzelnen Ich, nirgends sonst." *Mein Name sei Gantenbein* 142.

An underlying skepticism runs as a thread through the novels analyzed in this study. Literary texts express what sociological studies on globalization might omit, namely the deep-seated weariness many people feel when confronted with the effects of globalization in their own lives. Literature refracts the very real anxieties Germans feel with regard to their changing country and a changing Europe. Many still identify globalization with an act of expropriation from their own culture since the global flows of images, ideas, sounds, symbols, and object crisscross national boundaries and alter existing cultures in the process. It is an ongoing task to negotiate these effects as Germany continues to change in the process of globalization and Europeanization, despite the current uncertainties about the future of the European Union that have been coming to the fore at the end of the first millennial decade.

Transnational migrants, as well as the many non-ethnic Germans and newly German residents will continue to change the face of the country. Germany is already a globalized space where people from many different countries live next to each other. It will remain their shared project to bring about the "new cosmopolitanism" Ulrich Beck has called for (2007, see also Beck and Grande) so that they can actually live *together*. Even if there were no other argument to be made in this context, it is clear that Germany needs its immigrants given its demographic development of low birth rates and an aging population. One would hope that this realization would lead to further changes in political and social discourse. Instead of fanning anti-immigration sentiments by declaring multiculturalism to be dead, as Angela Merkel did in September 2010, it would behoove politicians and intellectuals alike to promote a more open society and actually live the politics of integration.

Naturally, German-language authors will continue to reflect these larger developments and contribute through their literary texts what an essay or a newspaper article cannot, namely create moments of intensity, surprise, alienation, and beauty through aesthetic form. Given how much the make-up of German society has changed, texts by transnational, transcultural writers – Herta Müller, Richard Wagner, Rafik Schami, Terézia Mora, Zsuzsa Bánk, Marica Bodrožić, Saša Stanišić, Olga Grjasnowa, Julya Rabinowich, María Cecilia Barbetta, Ilija Trojanow, Dimitré Dinev and Feridun Zaimoğlu, to name just a few – will play an ever more significant role in the future. They will continue to add their voices to the multitude of the cultural choir and further enrich the diversity of German-language literature. But that is a different story and shall be told another time.

# Works Cited

Unless otherwise noted in the citation, Internet links were checked last for availability on
June 24, 2012.

"Merkel erklärt Multikulti für gescheitert." *Der Spiegel*. October 16, 2010.
http://www.spiegel.de/politik/deutschland/0,1518,723532,00.html (July 31, 2011).

"National Endowment for the Humanities. *Reading on the Rise*." January 12, 2009.
http://graphics8.nytimes.com/packages/pdf/books/ReadingReport.pdf.

"Ist Fremd-Sein ein Problem, ein Thema oder ein Marktvorteil? Vier nicht ganz deutsche
Autoren – Terézia Mora, Imran Ayata, Wladimir Kaminer und Navid Kerman – im
Literaturen-Gespräch." *Literaturen* 4 (2005): 26–31.

Ablass, Stefanie. "Ökonomisierung des Körpers: Interdependenzen von ökonomischer und
physischer Sphäre im Wirtschaftsroman." *Literatur der Jahrtausendwende. Themen,
Schreibverfahren und Buchmarkt um 2000*. Evi Zemanek and Susanne Krones, eds.
Bielefeld: Transcript, 2008. 163–177.

Adorján, Johanna and Hellmuth Karasek. "Ich glaube an Heldentaten." Interview with Julia
Franck. *Der Tagesspiegel*. December 10, 2000. W 1.

Aguigah, René: "Wanderers Nachtlieder. Neues von der Heimatfront: Florian Illies und
Wolfgang Büscher, Nicol Ljubic und Adam Soboczynski suchen, was die deutsche Welt
im Innersten zusammenhält." *Literaturen* 10 (2006): 98–106.

Albert, Michel. *Capitalism versus Capitalism: How America's Obsession with Individual
Achievement and Short-Term Profit Has Led It to the Brink of Collapse*. New York:
Four Walls Eight Windows, 1993.

Amann, Wilhelm, Georg Mein, and Rolf Parr, eds. *Globalisierung und Gegenwartsliteratur.
Konstellationen – Konzepte – Perspektiven*. Heidelberg: Synchron, 2010.

Amann, Wilhelm. "Global Flows – Local Culture? Katharina Hacker: *Die Habenichtse*."
*Globalisierung und Gegenwartsliteratur. Konstellationen – Konzepte – Perspektiven*.
Wilhelm Amann, Georg Mein, and Rolf Parr, eds. Heidelberg: Synchron, 2010. 209–222.

Anz, Thomas, ed. *'Es geht nicht um Christa Wolf.' Der Literaturstreit im vereinten
Deutschland*. Frankfurt a.M.: Fischer, 1995.

Anz, Thomas. "Epochenumbruch und Generationswechsel? Zur Konjunktur von
Generationenkonstrukten seit 1989." *Schreiben nach der Wende: Ein Jahrzehnt
deutscher Literatur 1989–1999*. Gerhard Fischer and David Roberts, eds. Tübingen:
Stauffenburg, 2001. 31–48.

Anz, Thomas. "Generationenkonstrukte. Zu ihrer Konjunktur nach 1989." *Konkurrenzen,
Konflikte, Kontinuitäten. Generationenfragen in der Literatur seit 1990*. Andrea Geier and
Jan Süselbeck, eds. Göttingen: Wallstein, 2009. 16–29.

Appadurai, Arjun. *Modernity at Large. Cultural Dimensions of Globalization*. Minneapolis/
London: University of Minnesota Press, 1996.

Appadurai, Arjun. "Grassroots Globalization and the Research Imagination." *Globalization*.
Arjun Appadurai, ed. Durham and London: Duke UP, 2001. 1–21.

Arntzen, Helmut. *Satire in der deutschen Literatur: Geschichte und Theorie*. Darmstadt:
Wissenschaftliche Buchgesellschaft, 1989.

Assmann, Aleida and Ute Frevert. *Geschichtsvergessenheit – Geschichtsversessenheit.
Vom Umgang mit deutschen Vergangenheiten nach 1945*. Stuttgart: DVA, 1999.

Assmann, Aleida. *Erinnerungsräume. Formen und Wandlungen des kulturellen
Gedächtnisses*. Munich: Beck, 1999.

Auffermann, Verena. "Hyänen leuchten unter gelben Hyazinthen. Über die hohe Kunst des Schaumschlagens: Rainer Merkels gelungene Expedition in unsere Dienstleistungswelt." *Süddeutsche Zeitung*. October 10, 2001.

Auffermann, Verena. "Schlimme brave Welt. Katharina Hackers überzeugender Zeitroman 'Die Habenichtse.'" *Die Zeit*. March 16, 2003 [Literaturbeilage].

Augé, Marc. *Non-Places. Introduction to an Anthropology of Supermodernity*. Trans. John Howe. London, New York: Verso, 1995.

Bachmann, Ingeborg. *Der Fall Franza*. Unvollendeter Roman. *Werke*. Christine Koschel, Inge von Weidenbaum and Clemens Münster, eds. Vol. 3. Munich/Zürich: R. Piper & Co, 1982. 339–482.

Baßler, Moritz. *Der neue deutsche Poproman. Die neuen Archivisten*. Munich: C.H. Beck, 2002.

Bartels, Gerrit. "Die Lachnummer im Hinterzimmer. Trommeln und Lügen: Joachim Lottmann verabschiedete sich im Berliner 'Kurvenstar' feierlich von der Popliteratur." *taz, die Tageszeitung*. July 21, 2003.

Bartels, Klaus. "Die zwei Körper des Dichters. Stefan Georges Arbeit an seinem öffentlichen Gesicht." *Autorinszenierungen. Autorschaft und literarisches Werk im Kontext der Medien*. Christine Künzel and Jörg Schönert, eds. Würzburg: Königshausen & Neumann, 2007. 25–46.

Bartels, Klaus. "Fluchtpunkt Katmandu. Globaler Nomadismus bei Christian Kracht." *Unterwegs. Zur Poetik des Vagabundentums im 20. Jahrhundert*. Hans Richard Brittnacher and Magnus Klaue, eds. Cologne, Weimar, Vienna: Böhlau, 2008. 291–302.

Bartmer, Rose. „Die Debütanten und der Markt." *Sprache im technischen Zeitalter* 162 (July 2002): 193–205.

Baudelaire, Charles. "The Painter of Modern Life." *The Painter of Modern Life and Other Essays*. 2nd edition. London: Phaidon, 1995. 1–42.

Baudrillard, Jean. *The Spirit of Terrorism and Requiem for the Twin Towers*. Trans. Chris Turner. London: Verso, 2002.

Baumann, Zygmunt. "From Pilgrim To Tourist – Or A Short History Of Identity." *Questions of Cultural Identity*. Stuart Hall and Paul DuGay, eds. London: Sage, 1996. 18–35.

Baumann, Zygmunt. *Globalization. The Human Consequences*. New York: Columbia UP, 1998.

Baumann, Zygmunt. *Liquid Modernity*. Cambridge/Malden: Polity Press, 2000.

Baumann, Zygmunt. *Society Under Siege*. Oxford: Blackwell, 2002.

Beck, Stefan. "Introduction." *Surviving Globalization? Perspectives for the German Economic Model*. Stefan Beck, Frank Klobes, and Christoph Scherrer, eds. Dordrecht: Springer, 2005. 1–14.

Beck, Stefan and Christoph Scherrer. "Explaining the Dynamics of Red-Green Economic Reforms." *Surviving Globalization? Perspectives for the German Economic Model*. Stefan Beck, Frank Klobes, and Christoph Scherrer, eds. Dordrecht: Springer, 2005. 201–253.

Beck, Ulrich. *Risikogesellschaft*. Frankfurt a.M.: Suhrkamp, 1986.

Beck, Ulrich. *What Is Globalization?* Trans. Patrick Camiller. Cambride/Malden: Polity, 2000 [German edition 1997].

Beck, Ulrich. "The Cosmopolitan Society and its Enemies." *Theory, Culture & Society* 19.1–2 (2002): 17–44.

Beck, Ulrich. *Weltrisikogesellschaft. Auf der Suche nach der verlorenen Sicherheit*. Frankfurt a.M.: Suhrkamp, 2007.

Beck, Ulrich "Ein neuer Kosmopolitismus liegt in der Luft. Sieben Thesen für eine bessere Welt." *Literaturen* 11 (2007): 6–12.

Beck, Ulrich and Edgar Grande. *Das kosmopolitische Europa. Gesellschaft und Politik in der Zweiten Moderne.* Suhrkamp, Frankfurt am Main 2000.

Becker, Jurek. "Die Wiedervereinigung der deutschen Literatur." *Spätmoderne und Postmoderne. Beiträge zur deutschsprachigen Gegenwartsliteratur.* Paul Michael Lützeler, ed. Frankfurt a.M.: Fischer, 1991. 23–26.

Becker, Jürgen and Ulrich Janetzki, eds. *Helden wie ihr. Junge Schriftsteller über ihre literarischen Vorbilder.* Quadriga: Berlin, 2000.

Behrendt, Eva: "'Ich will niemanden abhalten, Schulden zu machen.' Die Autorin Kathrin Röggla über ihr neues Stück ‚draußen tobt die dunkelziffer.'" *Theater Heute* 07 (2005): 40–43.

Beigbeder, Frédéric. *£ 9.99. A Novel.* Trans. Adriana Hunter. London: Picador, 2002.

Berdahl, Daphne. "'(N)Ostalgie' for the Present: Memory, Longing, and East German Things." *Ethnos* 64.2 (1999): 192–211.

Berg, Sibylle. *Amerika. Roman.* Frankfurt a.M.: Goldmann, 2001 (originally Hamburg: Hoffmann und Campe, 1999).

Berg, Sibylle. *Die Fahrt. Roman.* 2nd edition. Cologne: Kiepenheuer & Witsch, 2007.

Berg, Sibylle. "Sibylle Berg: *Die Fahrt* – Buchmesse Podcast." October 12, 2007. http://www.literaturcafe.de/sibylle-berg-buchmesse-podcast-2007/ (July 14, 2011).

Berghahn, Klaus and Wolfgang Müller. "Tätig sein, ohne zu arbeiten? Die Arbeit und das Menschenbild der Klassik." *Arbeit als Thema in der deutschen Literatur vom Mittelalter bis zur Gegenwart.* Reinhold Grimm and Jost Hermand, eds. Königstein: Athenäum, 1979. 51–73.

Berman, Russel A. "The Humanities, Globalization, and the Transformation of the University." *Profession* (2007): 210–217.

Berthold, Norbert and Rainer Fehn. "Unemployment in Germany: Reasons and Remedies." *Structural Unemployment in Western Europe. Reasons and Remedies.* Martin Werding, ed. Cambridge, MA/London: The MIT Press, 2006. 267–292.

Bertschik, Julia. "'Junge Talente.' Über Jobs und Müßiggang in der Gegenwartsliteratur." *Arbeit – Kultur – Identität. Zur Transformation von Arbeitslandschaften in der Literatur.* Dagmar Kift and Hanneliese Palm, eds. Essen: Klartext, 2007. 69–83.

Bertschik, Julia. "Neue Popliteratur International. Zur globalen Vernetzung popkulturellen Wissens." *Globalisierung und Gegenwartsliteratur. Konstellationen – Konzepte – Perspektiven.* Wilhelm Amann, Georg Mein, and Rolf Parr, eds. Heidelberg: Synchron, 2010. 241–257.

Bessing, Joachim. *Wir Maschine. Roman.* Munich: DTV 2003 [first published Stuttgart: Deutsche Verlagsanstalt, 2001].

Bessing, Joachim et al. *Das popkulturelle Quintett mit Joachim Bessing, Christian Kracht, Eckhart Nickel, Alexander v. Schönburg und Benjamin von Stuckrad-Barre.* Berlin: Ullstein, 1999.

Beste, Ralph et al. "Wir sind eine Welt." *Der Spiegel* 38 (2001): 32–35.

Biendarra, Anke S. "Der Erzähler als 'popmoderner Flaneur' in Christian Krachts Roman *Faserland.*" *German Life and Letters* 55:2 (April 2002): 164–79.

Biendarra, Anke S. "Gen(d)eration Next. Prose by Julia Franck and Judith Hermann." *Studies in Twentieth and Twentieth-First Century Literature* 28:1. Winter 2004: 211–239.

Biendarra, Anke S. "Ich bin wie der Thelonius Monk im Bebop – einer, der anders spielt." Interview with Thomas Meinecke. *Literaturkritik.de* (July 2007): http://www.literaturkritik.de/public/rezension.php?rez_id=10946.

Biendarra, Anke S. "Schriftsteller zu sein und in seinem Leben anwesend zu sein, ist für mich eins." Interview with Terézia Mora. *Transit* 3:1 (2007). http://german.berkeley.edu/transit/2007/biendarra.html.

Biendarra, Anke S. "Jedes Buch ist ein eigenes Projekt, das eine eigene Form findet." Interview with Gregor Hens. *Glossen* 27 (2008). http://www.dickinson.edu/glossen/heft27/Interviews/Biendarra-Hens.html.

Biendarra, Anke S. "Schreiben ist wie ein schöner Zustand, der mich verwandelt." Interview with Antje Rávic Strubel. *Glossen* 27 (2008). http://www.dickinson.edu/glossen/heft27/Interviews/Biendarra.html.

Biendarra, Anke S., ed. *Closing Borders, Bridging Gaps? Deutscher Pop an der Jahrtausendwende. Literatur für Leser* 2 (2008).

Biendarra, Anke S. and Sabine Wilke. "'Man muss den literarischen Stil immer aus dem Stoff entwickeln.' Interview mit Ingo Schulze." *GDR Bulletin* 26 (1999): 25–29.

Biernat, Ulla. *"Ich bin nicht der erste Fremde hier." Zur deutschsprachigen Reiseliteratur nach 1945.* Würzburg: Königshausen & Neumann, 2004.

Biller, Maxim. "Soviel Sinnlichkeit wie der Stadtplan von Kiel. Warum die deutsche Literatur nichts so nötig hat wie den Realismus. Ein Grundsatzprogramm" (first published in: *Die Weltwoche.* July 25, 1991). *Maulhelden und Königskinder. Zur Debatte über die deutschsprachige Gegenwartsliteratur.* Andrea Köhler and Reinhard Mohr, eds. Leipzig: Reclam, 1998. 62–71.

Biller, Maxim. "Feige das Land, schlapp die Literatur. Über die Schwierigkeiten beim Sagen der Wahrheit". *Die Zeit* 16. April 13, 2000. 47–49.

Biller, Maxim. *Deutschbuch.* Munich: Deutscher Taschenbuch Verlag, 2001.

Biller, Maxim and Sven Gächter. "'Handke ist lächerlich.' Maxim Biller über die Defizite der deutschen Literatur, die Rolle seiner Generation, das deutsche Feuilleton und den unvermeidlichen Marcel Reich-Ranicki." *Profil* 19 (1995). 90–93.

Birgfeld, Johannes. "Christian Kracht als Modellfall einer Reiseliteratur des globalisierten Zeitalters." *Akten des XI. Internationalen Germanistenkongresses Paris 2005.* Vol. 9 [Kulturkonflikte in der Reiseliteratur]. Annakutty V. K. Findeis, Hans-Wolf Jäger, and Françoise Knopper, eds. Bern: Peter Lang 2007. 405–411.

Blickle, Peter. *Heimat. A Critical Theory of the German Idea of Homeland.* Rochester, NY: Camden House, 2002.

Blumenkamp, Kathrin. "Authentizität in literarischem Text und Paratext. Alexa Hennig von Lange und Amélie Nothomb." *Literatur der Jahrtausendwende. Themen, Schreibverfahren und Buchmarkt um 2000.* Evi Zemanek and Susanne Krones, eds. Bielefeld: Transcript, 2008, 345–360.

Bogdal, Klaus-Michael. "Klimawechsel. Eine kleine Meteorologie der Gegenwartsliteratur." *Baustelle Gegenwartsliteratur. Die neunziger Jahre.* Andreas Erb, ed. Opladen: Westdeutscher Verlag, 1998. 9–31.

Bogdal, Klaus-Michael. "Deutschland sucht den Superstar. Über die Chancen der Gegenwartsliteratur in der Mediengesellschaft." *Deutschsprachige Gegenwartsliteratur seit 1989. Zwischenbilanzen – Analysen – Vermittlungsperspektiven.* Clemens Kammler and Torsten Pflugmacher, eds. Heidelberg: Synchron, 2004. 85–94.

Bohrer, Karl Heinz. "Die Ästhetik am Ausgang ihrer Unmündigkeit." *Merkur* 44 (1990): 851–65.

Böttiger, Helmut. "Die Literatur selbst als Event." *neue deutsche literatur.* July/August 1999: 164–171.

Borchert, Margret and Gerrit Landherr. "The Changing Meanings of Work in Germany."
*Advances in Developing Human Resources* 11.2 (2009): 204–217.

Borgstedt, Thomas. "Judith Hermann und die Neuromantik der Gegenwart."
*Gegenwartsliteratur* 5 (Fall 2006): 207–232.

Bourdieu, Pierre. "Der Korporativismus des Universellen. Die Rolle des Intellektuellen in der
modernen Welt." *Pierre Bourdieu. Die Intellektuellen und die Macht.* Irene Dölling, ed.
Hamburg: VSA-Verlag, 1991. 41–65.

Bourdieu, Pierre. *The Field of Cultural Production. Essays on Art and Literature.* Randall
Johnson, ed. Cambridge/Malden: Polity, 1993.

Bourdieu, Pierre. *Contre-feux: Propos pour servir à la résistance contre l'invasion néo-*
*liberale.* Paris: Liber, 1998. (Engl. *Acts of Resistance: Against the Tyranny of the Market.*
New York: The New Press, 1999).

Brandt, Sabine. "Schluß mit dem Geschrei. Günter de Bruyn über die deutsche Nation."
*Frankfurter Allgemeine Zeitung.* October 8, 1991. L 9.

Brenner, Peter. *Der Reisebericht: Die Entwicklung einer Gattung in der deutschen Literatur.*
Frankfurt a.M.: Suhrkamp, 1989.

Brinkmann, Rolf Dieter. *Der Film in Worten. Prosa, Erzählungen, Essays, Hörspiele, Fotos,*
*Collagen 1965–1974.* Reinbek: Rowohlt, 1982.

Bruner, Edward M. *Cultures on Tour: Ethnographies of Travel.* Chicago: University of Chicago
Press, 2005.

Brockmann, Stephen. "After the Wall: German Intellectuals and the Opening of the Border."
*The Berlin Wall: Representations and Perspectives.* Ernst Schürer, Manfred Keune and
Philip Jenkins, eds. New York et al.: Peter Lang, 1996. 281–292.

Brockmann, Stephen. *Literature and German Reunification.* Cambridge: Cambridge UP, 1999.

Brockmann, Stephen. "The Written Capital." *Monatshefte* 3 (1999): 376–395.

Brown, Rebecca. "Daniel Kehlmann, *Die Vermessung der Welt*: Measuring Celebrity through
the Ages." *Emerging German-Language Novelists of the Twenty-First Century.* Lyn
Marven and Stuart Taberner, eds. Rochester/New York: Camden House, 2011. 75–88.

Bubis, Ignaz. "Wer von der Schande spricht. Niemand darf die Erinnerung an die Verbrechen
des Nationalsozialismus auslöschen. Eine Rede zum 9. November." *Frankfurter*
*Allgemeine Zeitung.* November 10, 1998. 47.

Bude, Hein. *Generation Berlin.* Berlin: Merve Verlag, 2001.

Bude, Hein and Andreas Willisch, eds. *Das Problem der* Exklusion. *Ausgegrenzte,*
*Entbehrliche, Überflüssige.* Hamburg: HIS-Verlagsgesellschaft, 2006.

Bürger, Jan and Hanna Leitgeb. "Die ungeheure Belästigung. Ein Gespräch mit den
Schriftstellern Durs Grünbein und Thomas Meinecke über die intellektuelle Situation
nach dem 11. September 2001." *Literaturen* 12 (2001): 13–19.

Buschheuer, Else. *www.else-buschheuer.de. Das New York Tagebuch.* 1st ed. Cologne:
Kiepenheuer & Witsch, 2002.

Butler, Judith. *Excitable Speech: A Politics of the Performative.* New York: Routledge, 1997.

Caemmerer, Christiane, Walter Delabar, and Helga Meise, eds. *Fräuleinwunder literarisch.*
*Literatur von Frauen zu Beginn des 21. Jahrhunderts.* Frankfurt a.M.: Peter Lang, 2005.

Carpenter, Susan. "*Twilight* Has a Strong Internet Connection. Stephenie Meyer grew her
books' readership with a constant, open, grateful and helpful online presence."
*Los Angeles Times* December 29, 2008. http://articles.latimes.com/2008/nov/29/
entertainment/et-twilightnet29 (March 14, 2012).

Carr, Nicolas. "Is Google Making Us Stupid?" *The Atlantic.* July/August 2008.
http://www.theatlantic.com/doc/200807/google (March 14, 2012).

Chilese, Viviana. "Menschen im Büro: Zur Arbeitswelt in der deutschen Literatur." *Gedächtnis und Identität. Die deutsche Literatur nach der Vereinigung.* Fabrizio Cambi, ed. Würzburg: Königshausen & Neumann, 2008. 293–304.

Clarke, David. "Dandyism and Homosexuality in the Novels of Christian Kracht." *Seminar* 41.1 (2005): 36–54.

Clifford, James. *Routes. Travel and Translation in the Late Twentieth Century.* Cambridge, MA/ London: Harvard UP, 1997.

Cosentino, Christine: "Jakob Heins *Herr Jensen steigt aus*: Anmerkungen zum 'schmalen Grad dazwischen'." *Glossen* 28 (2008) http://www2.dickinson.edu/glossen/Heft28/ index.html.

Dallach, Christoph: "Vampire sind attraktiv, klug und cool." Interview mit Stephenie Meyer. *Spiegel Online* June 11, 2008. http://www.spiegel.de/kultur/literatur/ 0,1518,558826,00.html (March 14, 2010).

Damrosch, David. "World Literature, National Contexts." *Modern Philology* 100.4 (2003): 512–531.

Dath, Dietmar. *Deutschland macht dicht. Eine Mandelbaumiade.* Mit Bildern von Piwi. 1st ed. Frankfurt a.M.: Suhrkamp, 2010.

Dawidowski, Christian. "Ausgestellte Körpermenschen. Über Sibylle Berg." *Theater fürs 21. Jahrhundert.* Heinz Ludwig Arnold and Christian Dawidowski, eds. Munich: Text & Kritik, 2004. 52–69.

Dean, Martin R., Thomas Hettche, Matthias Politycki, and Michael Schindhelm. "Was soll der Roman? Manifest für einen Relevanten Realismus." *Die Zeit* 25 (2005).

De Bruyn, Günter. *Jubelschreie, Trauergesänge. Deutsche Befindlichkeiten.* Frankfurt a.M.: Fischer, 1991.

Degler, Frank. "Figurationen des Abschieds: Sibylle Bergs Experimentalpoetik u-topischer [sic] Neuanfänge." *Gegenwartsliteratur* 8 (2009): 122–147.

Deiritz, Karl and Hannes Kraus. *Der deutsch-deutsche Literaturstreit oder 'Freunde, es spricht sich schlecht mit gebundener Zunge.' Analysen und Materialien.* Hamburg, Zürich: Luchterhand, 1991.

DeLillo, Don. "In the Ruins of the Future. Reflections on Terror and Loss in the Shadow of September." *Harper's Magazine* (December 2001): 33–40.

Dettmer, Marcus et al.: "Ära der Unsicherheit." *Der Spiegel* 12 (2010): 82–94.

Deupmann, Christoph. "Narrating (New) Economy: Literatur und Wirtschaft um 2000." *Literatur der Jahrtausendwende. Themen, Schreibverfahren und Buchmarkt um 2000.* Evi Zemanek and Susanne Krones, eds. Bielefeld: Transcript, 2008. 151–161.

Diederichsen, Diedrich. "Ist was Pop?" (1997). *Der lange Weg nach Mitte. Der Sound und die Stadt.* Cologne: Kiepenheuer & Witsch, 1999. 272–286.

Diez, Georg. "Nähe. Distanz. Kälte. Wie es Don DeLillo in seinem großartigen Roman *Falling Man* gelingt, auf den Schock des 11. September eine Antwort zu finden." *Die Zeit.* May 17, 2007.

Dirke, Sabine von. "Sleepless in the New Economy: Money, Unemployment and Identity in the Literature of Generation Golf." *Über Gegenwartsliteratur. Interpretationen und Interventionen.* Mark W. Rectanus, ed. Bielefeld: Aisthesis, 2008. 141–156.

Dirke, Sabine von and David Coury, eds. *Globalization, German Literature and the New Economy.* Special issue of *Seminar* 47:3 (September 2011).

Döbler, Katharina. "Ich entscheide heute, was sie morgen wollen. Frédéric Beigbeder schreibt einen Werbetext für sich selbst, nennt ihn Roman und hat Erfolg." *Die Zeit.* June 13, 2002.

Döring, Christian, ed. *Deutschsprachige Gegenwartsliteratur. Wider ihre Verächter.* Frankfurt a.M.: Suhrkamp, 1995.

Dougherty, Carter. "German Unemployment Reaches 12.6%." *International Herald Tribune.* March 1, 2005. International Business Section: 8.

Düffel, John von. "Auslaufmodell Ich. Über die neuen Leiden des modernen Mannes." *Wasser und andere Welten. Geschichten vom Schwimmen und Schreiben.* 1st edition. Cologne: Dumont, 2002. 84–97.

Düffel, John von and Franziska Schößler. "Gespräch über das Theater der neunziger Jahre." *Theater fürs 21. Jahrhundert.* Heinz Ludwig Arnold and Christian Dawidowski, eds. Munich: Text & Kritik, 2004. 42–51.

Düffel, John von, Tessa Müller and Lisa-Maria Seydlitz: "'Das sind echte Märchen.' Interview mit John von Düffel. March 15, 2008." *Lit07.de – Magazin für Literaturkritik und kritische Öffentlichkeit.* http://www.lit07.de/cms/content/magazin/interview/seydlitz-mueller-von-dueffel-maerchen.html (August 15, 2010).

Düffel, John von. *EGO. Roman.* 3rd edition. Munich: Deutscher Taschenbuch Verlag, 2008.

Durrani, Osmand. "'Alles wird besser, nichts wird gut.' Reflections on the incompatibility of the better and the good." *The New Germany. Literature And Society After Unification.* Colin Good, Kevin Hillard, and Osman Durrani, eds. Sheffield: Sheffield Academic Press, 1995. xi-xxiv.

Eggerstorfer, Wolfgang. *Schönheit und Adel der Arbeit: Arbeitsliteratur im Dritten Reich.* Frankfurt a.M.: Peter Lang, 1988.

Eligon, John. "Rowling Wins Lawsuit Against Harry Potter Lexicon". *New York Times.* September 8, 2008. http://www.nytimes.com/2008/09/09/nyregion/09potter.html?_r=1.

Ellis, Bret Easton. *American Psycho. A Novel.* 1st ed. New York: Vintage Books, 1991.

Ellis, Bret Easton. *Glamorama.* New York: Alfred A. Knopf, 1998.

Epstein, Joseph. "Celebrity Culture." *The Hedgehog Review. Critical Reflections on Contemporary Culture* 7.1 (2005): 7–20.

English, John F. and John Frow. "Literary Authorship and Celebrity Culture." *A Concise Companion to Contemporary British Fiction.* John F. English, ed. Malden/Oxford: Blackwell, 2006. 39–57.

English, John F. *The Economy of Prestige. Prizes, Awards, and the Circulation of Cultural Value.* Cambridge/London: Harvard UP, 2005.

Emmerich, Wolfgang. *Proletarische Lebensläufe. Autobiographische Dokumente zur Entstehung der Zweiten Kultur in Deutschland.* Vol. 1. Reinbek: Rowohlt, 1974.

Emmerich, Wolfgang. *Kleine Literaturgeschichte der DDR.* Erweiterte Neuausgabe. Berlin: Aufbau, 2005.

Erhart, Walter. "Generationen – zum Gebrauch eines alten Begriffes für die jüngste Geschichte der Literaturwissenschaft." *Literaturwissenschaft und Wissenschaftsforschung.* Jörg Schönert, ed. Stuttgart: Metzler, 2000. 77–100.

Ernst, Thomas. "Weblogs. Ein globales Medienformat." *Globalisierung und Gegenwartsliteratur. Konstellationen – Konzepte – Perspektiven.* Wilhelm Amann, Georg Mein, and Rolf Parr, eds. Heidelberg: Synchron, 2010. 281–302.

Ervasti, Heikki and Takis Venetoklis. "Unemployment and Subjective Well-being: An Empirical Test of Deprivation Theory, Incentive Paradigm and Financial Strain Approach." *Acta Sociologica* 53.2 (June 2010): 119–138.

Essig, Rolf-Bernhard. "Die äußeren und die inneren Slums. Sibylle Berg's neuer Roman *Die Fahrt* stellt grundsätzliche Fragen." *Die Zeit* 41 (2007). L 22.

Fäßler, Peter E. *Globalisierung. Ein historisches Kompendium.* Cologne/Weimar/Vienna: Böhlau, 2007.

Fang, Karin. *Romantic Writing and the Empire of Signs: Periodic Culture and Post-Napoleonic Authorship.* Charlottesville: University of Virginia Press, 2010.

Feather, John. *Communicating Knowledge: Publishing in the 21st Century.* Munich: K.G. Saur, 2003.

Ferris, Suzanne and Mallory Young, eds. *Chick Lit. The New Woman's Fiction.* New York: Routledge, 2006.

Fetscher, Justus. "Kalkül der Verschwendung. Goethes Ökonomien." *Ökonomien der Armut. Soziale Verhältnisse in der Literatur.* Elke Brüns, ed. Munich: Fink, 2008. 79–103.

Fischer, Ernst. *Literarische Agenturen – die heimlichen Herrscher im Literaturbetrieb?* Wiesbaden: Harassowitz, 2001.

Fitzgerald, Nora. "For Young German Writers, All Is Ich". *New York Times.* July 25, 2003. Art & Leisure Section I. 5–6.

Florida, Richard. *The Rise of the Creative Class.* New York: Basic Books, 2002.

Förster, Jochen. "'Wovon erzählt dieses Buch?' Ist doch egal: Spannend an Judith Hermanns neuem Band *Nichts als Gespenster* ist vor allem seine Rezeption." *Die Welt.* February 4, 2003. 29.

Förster, Nikolaus. *Die Wiederkehr des Erzählens: Deutschsprachige Prosa der 80er und 90er Jahre.* Darmstadt: Wissenschaftliche Buchgesellschaft, 1999.

Foucault, Michel. *Überwachen und Strafen. Die Geburt des Gefängnisses.* Trans. Walter Seitter. Frankfurt a.M.: Suhrkamp 1994 [orig. *Surveiller et punir: La naissance de la prison.* 1975].

Foucault, Michel. *Der Wille zum Wissen. Sexualität und Wahrheit I.* Frankfurt a.M.: Suhrkamp, 1983 [orig. *Histoire de la sexualité, I: La volonté de savoir.* 1976].

Foucault, Michel. "Body/Power" [Interview 1975]. *Power/Knowledge. Selected Interviews and Other Writings 1972–1977.* Colin Gordon, ed. New York: Pantheon, 1980. 55–62.

Foucault, Michel. "Truth and Power" [Interview 1975]. *Power/Knowledge. Selected Interviews and Other Writings 1972–1977.* Collin Gordon, ed. New York: Pantheon, 1980. 109–45.

Foucault, Michel. *Sicherheit, Territorium, Bevölkerung. Geschichte der Gouvernementalität I.* Vorlesung am Collège de France 1977–1978 and *Die Geburt der Biopolitik. Geschichte der Gouvernementalität II.* Vorlesung am Collège de France 1978–1979. Frankfurt a.M.: Suhrkamp, 2004.

Fox, Susannah and Mary Madden: "Riding the Waves of 'Web 2.0.'" *Pew Internet and American Life Project.* October 5, 2006. http://www.pewinternet.org/Reports/2006/Riding-the-Waves-of-Web-20.aspx (March 10, 2010).

Freund, Wieland, Martin Hielscher, and Thomas Hettche. "Zurück in die Wirklichkeit. Ein Schriftsteller und ein Lektor diskutieren über die neue deutsche Literatur." *Die Welt.* November 24, 2001. http://www.welt.de/print-welt/article489029/Zurueck_in_die_Wirklichkeit.html (November 21, 2011).

Friebe, Holm and Sascha Lobo. *Wir nennen es Arbeit. Die digitale Bohème oder Intelligentes Leben jenseits der Festanstellung.* Aktualisierte Taschenbuchausgabe 2008. Munich: Heyne, 2006.

Frisch, Max. *Mein Name sei Gantenbein. Roman* (1964). *Gesammelte Werke in zeitlicher Folge.* Jubiläumsausgabe in sieben Bänden. Hans Mayer and Walter Schmitz, eds. Vol. V. 5–320. Frankfurt a.M.: Suhrkamp, 1986.

Fuchs, Anne. "From 'Vergangenheitsbewältigung' to Generational Memory Contests in Günter Grass, Monika Maron and Uwe Timm." *German Life and Letters* 59.2 (April 2006): 168–89.

Ganeva, Mila. "Female Flâneurs: Judith Hermann's *Sommerhaus, später* and *Nichts als Gespenster.*" *Gegenwartsliteratur* 3 (2004): 250–277.

Genette, Gérard. *Paratexts. Thresholds of Interpretation.* Cambrigde: Cambrige UP, 1997.

Gentry, Francis. "Arbeit in der mittelalterlichen Gesellschaft. Die Entwicklung einer Theorie der Arbeit vom 11. bis zum 14. Jahrhundert." *Arbeit als Thema in der deutschen Literatur vom Mittelalter bis zur Gegenwart.* Reinhold Grimm and Jost Hermand, eds. Königstein: Athenäum, 1979. 3–28.

Ghezzi, Luigi. "Homepages von Schriftstellern. Zur Konstruktion einer literarischen Identität im Netz." *Literatur.com. Tendenzen im Literaturmarketing.* Erhard Schütz and Thomas Wegmann, eds. Berlin: Weidler, 2002. 24–41.

Giddens, Anthony. "The Globalization of Modernity." *The Consequences of Modernity.* Palo Alto: Stanford UP, 1990. 63–78.

Giddens, Anthony. *Runaway World. How Globalization is Reshaping Our Lives.* Routledge: New York, 2000.

Glass, Loren."Buying In, Selling Out: From Literary to Musical Celebrity in the United States." *The Hedgehog Review.* Spring 2005: 21–35.

Gleba, Kerstin and Eckhard Schumacher, eds. *Pop seit 1965.* Cologne: KiWi, 2007.

Goetz, Rainald. "Subito." *Hirn* [1986]. Frankfurt a.M.: Suhrkamp, 2003. 9–21.

Goetz, Rainald. *Abfall für alle. Roman eines Jahres.* Frankfurt a.M.: Suhrkamp, 1999.

Goldman-Mellor, Sidra, Katherine Saxton, and Ralph Catalano. "Economic Contraction and Mental Health." *International Journal of Mental Health* 39.2 (2010): 6–31.

Grass, Günter. *Deutscher Lastenausgleich. Wider das dumpfe Einheitsgebot. Reden und Gespräche.* Frankfurt a.M.: Luchterhand, 1990.

Grass, Günter. *Ein Schnäppchen namens DDR. Letzte Reden vorm Glockengeläut.* Frankfurt a.M.: Luchterhand, 1990.

Grass, Günter. *Ein weites Feld.* Roman. Göttingen: Steidl, 1995.

Grasskamp, Walter. "Das verborgene Gesicht. Zu Literatur und Fotografie." *Merkur* 4 (2005): 304–317.

Graves, Peter. "Karen Duve, Kathrin Schmidt, Judith Hermann: 'Ein literarisches Fräuleinwunder'?" *German Life and Letters* 55:2. (April 2002): 196–207.

Gray, Richard, T. *Money Matters: Economics and the German Cultural Imagination, 1770–1850.* Seattle: University of Washington Press, 2008.

Greiner, Ulrich. "Die deutsche Gesinnungsästhetik. Noch einmal: Christa Wolf und der deutsche Literaturstreit. Eine Zwischenbilanz." *Die Zeit.* November 2, 1990.

Greiner, Ulrich. "Menschen wie Tauben im Gras." *Die Zeit.* March 26, 1998 [Buchmessenbeilage].

Gropps, Rose-Maria. "Dieses Buch ist kein Buch." [Interview with Elfriede Jelinek]. *Frankfurter Allgemeine Zeitung* April 17, 2007. http://www.faz.net/s/Rub1DA1FB848C1E44858CB87A0FE6AD1B68/Doc~E4087C7695B4D4949A901CF77A8BE1A8A~ATpl~Ecommon~Scontent.html.

Grunenberg, Antonia. "Das Ende der Macht ist der Anfang der Literatur. Zum Streit um die Schriftstellerinnen in der DDR." *Aus Politik und Zeitgeschichte.* B 44 (1990): 7–26.

Günter, Petra. "Sibylle Berg." *Kritisches Lexikon zur deutschsprachigen Gegenwartsliteratur (KLG)* 10 (2006): 1–8.

Gupta, Suman. *Globalization and Literature.* Cambridge/Malden: Polity, 2009.

Habermas, Jürgen. "Nochmals: Zur Identität der Deutschen. Ein Volk von aufgebrachten Wirtschaftsbürgern?" *Die nachholende Revolution. Kleine politische Schriften VII.* Frankfurt a.M.: Suhrkamp, 1990. 205–224.

Hacker, Katharina. *Die Habenichtse*. Roman. Frankfurt a.M.: Suhrkamp, 2006.

Hacker, Katharina. *The Have-Nots*. Trans. Helene Atkins. New York: Europa Editions, 2007.

Haines, Brigid. "German-language writing from eastern and central Europe." *Contemporary German Fiction. Writing in the Berlin Republic.* Stuart Taberner, ed. Cambridge: Cambridge UP, 2007. 215–229.

Hall, Stuart. "Cultural studies: two paradigms." *Media, Culture and Society* 2.1 (1980): 57–72.

Hall, Stuart. "Kulturelle Identität und Globalisierung." *Widerspenstige Kulturen. Cultural Studies als Herausforderung*. Karl H. Hörning and Rainer Winter, eds. Frankfurt a.M.: Suhrkamp, 1999. 393–441.

Händler, Ernst-Wihelm. *Wenn wir sterben*. Roman. 4$^{st}$ edition. Frankfurt: Frankfurter Verlagsanstalt, 2002.

Hage, Volker. "Literarisches Fräuleinwunder: Junge Schriftstellerinnen sind die Überraschung des Frühjahr-Buchmarkts." *Der Spiegel*. March 22, 1999: 7, 244–46.

Hage, Volker. "Die neuen deutschen Dichter. Die Enkel von Grass & Co." *Der Spiegel*. October 11, 1999: 244–254.

Hager, Heinke. "Literaturagentur." *Das BuchMarktBuch. Der Literaturbetrieb in Grundbegriffen*. Erhard Schütz, ed. Reinbek: Rowohlt Encyclopädie, 2005. 217–220.

Hagestedt, Lutz and Joachim Unseld, eds. *Literatur als Passion. Zum Werk von Ernst-Wilhelm Händler*. 1$^{st}$ edition. Frankfurt: Frankfurter Verlagsanstalt, 2006.

Han, Byung-Chul. *Müdigkeitsgesellschaft*. Berlin: Matthes und Seitz, 2010.

Hannerz, Ulf. "Notes on the Global Ecumene." *Public Culture* 1.2 (1989): 66–75.

Hartling, Florian. *Der digitale Autor: Autorschaft im Zeitalter des Internets*. Bielefeld: Transcript, 2009.

Hartwig, Ina. "Literatur am Nullpunkt. Der 11. September und die Ich-Prüfungen der Schriftsteller. Eine vorläufige Bestandsaufnahme." *Neue deutsche Literatur*. 50.544 (2002): 164–169.

Harvey, David. *The Condition of Postmodernity: An Inquiry Into The Origins of Cultural Change*. Cambridge: Blackwell, 1990.

Heimburger, Susanne. "Zur Literarisierung von Arbeitswelt in Anne Webers *Gold im Mund* und *Liebe Vögel* und Joachim Zelters *Schule der Arbeitslosen*." *Narrative der Arbeit – Narratives of Work. Limbus. Australian Yearbook of German Literary and Cultural Studies*. Vol. 2. Freiburg i.Br.: Rombach, 2009: 133–146.

Hein, Jakob. *Herr Jensen steigt aus*. Roman. 5$^{th}$ paperback ed. Munich/Zurich: Piper, 2010.

Held, David, Anthony G. McGrew, David Goldblatt, and Jonathan Perraton. *Global Transformations: Politics, Economics, Culture*. Cambridge: Polity, 1999.

Hell, Julia and Johannes von Moltke: "Unification Effects: Imaginary Landscapes of the Berlin Republic." *The Germanic Review* 80.1 (2005): 74–95.

Hennig von Lange, Alexa. "Eine neue Frauenbewegung müsste den Mann mitbedenken." *Die Zeit* August 24, 2006. http://www.zeit.de/2006/35/Feminismus-Hennig-von-Lange (March 14, 2010).

Hens, Gregor. *Transfer Lounge. Deutsch-amerikanische Geschichten*. Hamburg: Mare Bibliothek, 2003.

Hens, Gregor. *Matta verlässt seine Kinder*. Roman. Frankfurt a.M.: Fischer, 2004.

Henwood, Doug. *After the New Economy*. New York: The New Press, 2003.

Hermann, Heike. "Nur ein Stich in der Seele. Katharina Hackers Roman 'Die Habenichtse' über die Armseligkeiten und Sehnsüchte einer Generation." *Literaturkritik.de*.

10. October 2006. http://www.literaturkritik.de/piblic.rezension.php?rez_id=9945 (October 4, 2006).

Hermann, Judith. *Sommerhaus, später.* Erzählungen. Frankfurt a.M: Fischer, 1998.

Hermann, Judith. "Kann ich die sein, für die man mich hält? Von den Ehrungen, die der Literaturbetrieb verleiht, und ihren Wirkungen – Eine Dankesrede." *Die Welt.* October 1, 1999. 34.

Hermann, Judith. "Rede zum Förderpreis des Bremer Literaturpreises." *Dokumentation der Rudolf-Alexander-Schröder-Stiftung.* Bremen, 1999.

Hermann, Judith. *Nichts als Gespenster.* Erzählungen. Frankfurt a.M.: Fischer, 2003.

Hermann, Judith. "Meine Generation – was ist das eigentlich? In einem Interview gibt die Schriftstellerin Judith Hermann erstmals Auskunft über ihr langes Schweigen und ihr neues Buch 'Nichts als Gespenster'." *Frankfurter Allgemeine Sonntagszeitung.* January 19, 2003. http://www.faz.net/s/RubCC21B04EE95145B3AC877C874FB1B611/ Doc~EE7500780A1F64D81AF8C7D52F7D9AC07~ATpl~Ecommon~Scontent.html.

Hermann, Judith. *Nothing But Ghosts.* Stories. Trans. Margo Bettauer Dembo. London/ New York: Fourth Estate, 2005.

Herrmann, Leonhard. "Ausstieg aus der Wirklichkeit." *Kreuzer.* March 1, 2006.

Hertfelder, Thomas. "'Modell Deutschland' – Erfolgsgeschichte oder Illusion?" *Modell Deutschland: Erfolgsgeschichte oder Illusion?* Thomas Hertfelder and Andreas Rödder, eds. Göttingen: Vandenhoeck & Ruprecht, 2005. 9–27

Herzinger, Richard. "Jung, schick und heiter. Im schönen Schein der Marktwirtschaft: Der Literaturbetrieb entwickelt sich zur neuen Sparte der Lifestyle-Industrie." *Die Zeit* 13 (1999).

Hettche, Thomas. "Nova Huta." *Zuerst bin ich immer Leser. Prosa schreiben heute.* Ute-Christine Krupp and Ulrike Janssen, eds. Frankfurt a.M.: Suhrkamp, 2000. 40–55.

Hettche, Thomas and Jana Hensel. Eds. *Null. Literatur im Netz.* 1st ed. Cologne: DuMont, 2000.

Hielscher, Martin. "Literatur in Deutschland – Avantgarde und pädagogischer Purismus. Abschied von einem Zwang" [Gekürzte Fassung]. *Neue Rundschau* 106.4 (1996).

Hielscher, Martin. "Andere Stimmen – andere Räume. Die Funktion der Migrantenliteratur in deutschen Verlagen und Dimitré Dinevs Roman 'Engelszungen'." *Literatur und Migration.* Text & Kritik (Sonderband). Heinz Ludwig Arnold, ed. Munich: Edition Text & Kritik, 2006: 196–210.

Hoch, Jenny. "Mobbing ist psychologische Kriegsführung. Interview mit Annette Pehnt." *Spiegel Online.* November 8, 2007.

Hochhuth, Rolf. "McKinsey kommt. Schauspiel in fünf Akten mit fünf Epilogen." *Neue Dramen, Gedichte, Prosa.* Reinbek: Rowohlt. 1st ed. 2006. 874–945.

Hoffmann, Reiner. "Globalization and Labor Markets: A View From Germany in the European Union." *Responses to Globalization in Germany and the United States. Seven Sectors Compared.* Carl Lankowski, ed. AICGS Research Report No. 10. American Institute for Contemporary German Studies 1999. 47–66.

Hohendahl, Peter Uwe. "Soziale Rolle und individuelle Freiheit. Zur Kritik des bürgerlichen Arbeitsbegriffes in Fontanes Gesellschaftsromanen." *Arbeit als Thema in der deutschen Literatur vom Mittelalter bis zur Gegenwart.* Reinhold Grimm and Jost Hermand, eds. Königstein: Athenäum, 1979. 74–101.

Hohendahl, Peter Uwe. "Wandel der Öffentlichkeit. Kulturelle und politische Identität im heutigen Deutschland." *Die Nation. Transatlantische Perspektiven zur Geschichte eines Problems.* Claudia Mayer-Iswandy, ed. Tübingen: Stauffenburg, 1994.

Holland, Patrick and Graham Huggan. *Tourists with Typewriters. Critical Reflections on Contemporary Travel Writing*. Ann Arbor: University of Michigan Press, 1998.

Houellebecq, Michel. *Extension du domaine de la lutte*. Engl. *Whatever*. Trans. Paul Hammond. Serpent's Tail, 1998

Houellebecq, Michel. *Les Particules élementaires*. Engl. *Elementary Particles*. Trans. Frank Wynne. Vintage 2001.

Huggan, Graham. *Extreme Pursuits. Travel/Writing in an Age of Globalization*. Ann Arbor: University of Michigan Press, 2009.

Huntington, Samuel. *The Clash of Civilizations and the Remaking of World Order*. London: Touchstone, 1997.

Illies, Florian. *Generation Golf. Eine Inspektion*. 13th edition. Berlin: Argon, 2000.

Illies, Florian. *Ortsgespräch*. 1st edition. Munich: Karl Blessing Verlag, 2006.

Inda, Jonathan Xavier and Renato Rosaldo. "Tracking Global Flows." *The Anthropology of Globalization. A Reader*. Jonathan Xavier Inda and Renato Rosaldo, eds. 2nd ed. London: Blackwell, 2008. 3–46.

Jacobsen, Dietmar. "Kein Glück. Nirgends. Sibylle Berg erzählt von Menschen 'unklaren Alters mit einer großen Lebensmüdigkeit.'" November 11, 2007. http://www.poetenladen.de/jacobsen-sibylle-berg.htm (July 4, 2011).

Jäger, Andrea. "Das Reich der Notwendigkeit. Die Gründerzeitliteratur der DDR arbeitet am Mythos Arbeit." *Deutsche Gründungsmythen. Jahrbuch Literatur und Politik 2*. Matteo Galli and Heinz-Peter Preußer, eds. Heidelberg: Universitätsverlag Winter, 2008. 157–168.

Jay, Paul. "Beyond Discipline? Globalization and the Future of English." *PMLA* 116.1. Special Topic: Globalizing Literary Studies (January 2001): 32–47.

Jeremiah, Emily. *"Die Fahrt*: Literature, Germanness, and Globalization." *Emerging German-language novelists of the twenty-first century*. Lyn Marven and Stuart Taberner, eds. Rochester: Camden House, 2011. 133–147.

Jeremias, Ralph. "The Truth About the German 'Job Miracle': A Report on the Inner Life of a 'Job Wonderland'." *Working USA. The Journal of Labor and Society* 13.4 (December 2010): 507–519.

Kacandes, Irene. "German Cultural Studies: What Is At Stake?" *A User's Guide to German Cultural Studies*. Scott Denham, Irene Kacancdes, and Jonathan Petropoulos, eds. Ann Arbor: University of Michigan Press, 1997. 3–28.

Kaes, Anton. "New Historicism and the Study of German Literature." *The German Quarterly* 62.3. (1989): 210–219.

Kaiser, Céline and Alexander Böhnke. "Interview with Kathrin Röggla." http://www.kathrin-roeggla.de/text/schlafen_interview.htm.

Kaplan, Caren. *Questions of Travel: Postmodern Discourses of Displacement*. Durham: Duke UP, 1996.

Karolle-Berg, Julia and Katya Skow. "From *Frauenliteratur* to *Frauenliteraturbetrieb*. Marketing Literature to German Women in the Twenty-First Century." *German Literature In A New Century*. Katharina Gerstenberger and Patricia Herminghouse, eds. New York/Oxford: Berghahn, 2008. 220–236.

Kasaty, Olga Olivia. "Ein Gespräch mit Kathrin Röggla. Berlin, 1. Juni 2005." *Entgrenzungen. Vierzehn Autorengespräche*. Munich: Text & Kritik, 2007. 257–287.

Klein, Naomi. *No Logo*. New York: Picador, 2000.

Klein, Markus. "Gibt es die Generation Golf? Eine empirische Inspektion." *Kölner Zeitschrift für Soziologie und Sozialpsychologie*. 55.1 (2003): 99–115.

Klobes, Frank. "The Dynamics of Industrial Restructuring." *Surviving Globalization? Perspectives for the German Economic Model.* Stefan Beck, Frank Klobes, and Christoph Scherrer, eds. Dordrecht: Springer, 2005. 69–92.

Kluge, Alexander: „Die schärfste Ideologie: daß die Realität sich auf ihren realistischen Charakter beruft" (1975). *In Gefahr und größter Not bringt der Mittelweg den Tod. Texte zu Kino, Film, Politik.* Christian Schulte, ed. Berlin: Vorwerk 8, 1999. 127–134.

Knipphals, Dirk. "Unter der Oberfläche aus Kitsch und Blabla. Thomas Hettche, Rainer Merkel und Norbert Niemann schreiben vertrackte Gesellschaftsromane." *taz, Die Tageszeitung.* October 10, 2001.

Knischweski, Gerd and Ulla Spittler. "Remembering the Berlin Republic. The Debate about the Central Holocaust Memorial in Berlin." *Debatte: Journal of Contemporary Central and Eastern Europe* 13.1 (2005): 25–42.

Köhler, Andrea and Reinhard Moritz, eds. *Maulhelden und Königskinder. Zur Debatte über die deutschsprachige Gegenwartsliteratur.* Leipzig: Reclam, 1998.

Köhler, Andrea. "'Is that all there is?' Judith Hermann oder Die Geschichte eines Erfolges." *Aufgerissen. Zur Literatur der 90er.* Thomas Kraft, ed. Munich/Zurich: Piper, 2000. 83–89.

Köhler, Andrea. "Ground Zero." *Merkur* 3 (2002): 234–239.

Kohlhaas, Rem. "Junk-space. Logan Airport: A World-Class Upgrade for the 21$^{th}$ Century." *Content.* Cologne: Taschen, 2004. 162–171.

Kormann, Eva. "Jelineks Tochter und das Medienspiel. Zu Kathrin Rögglas *wir schlafen nicht.*" *Zwischen Inszenierung und Botschaft. Zur Literatur deutschsprachiger Autorinnen ab Ende des 20. Jahrhunderts.* Ilse Nagelschmid et al., eds. Berlin: Frank & Timme, 2006. 229–245.

Kracht, Christian. *Faserland.* Roman. Cologne: Kiepenheuer & Witsch, 1995.

Kracht, Christian. *Der gelbe Bleistift.* 3rd edition. Cologne: Kiepenheuer & Witsch, 1999.

Kracht, Christian. "Ich weine oft. Christian Kracht im Gespräch." *Der Tagesspiegel.* July 1–2, 2000.

Kraft, Thomas. "The show must go on. Zur literarischen Situation der neunziger Jahre." *Aufgerissen. Zur Literatur der 90er.* Thomas Kraft, ed. Munich/Zurich: Piper, 2000. 9–22.

Kraft, Thomas. "Schiefer Haussegen. Gregor Hens' Roman *Himmelssturz.*" *Neue Zürcher Zeitung.* August, 17 (2002): 35.

Krause, Tilman and Matthias Politycki. „Nicht alles Deutsche ist schwer verdaulich. Wir brauchen ein Forum für den Aufbruch der deutschen Literatur" [Interview]. *Die Welt.* December 30, 1998. 11.

Krekeler, Elmar. "Schöner Wohnen. Gescheitert. Gregor Hens hat mit *Himmelssturz* das beste Debüt des Jahres geschrieben." *Die Welt.* July 13, 2002: 4.

Kremer, Christian. *Milieu und Performativität. Deutsche Gegenwartsprosa von John von Düffel, Georg M. Oswald und Kathrin Rögggla.* Marburg: Tectum Verlag, 2008.

Krumbholz, Martin. "Das glückliche Leben. Elke Naters' Roman *Königinnen.*" *Neue Zürcher Zeitung.* March 2, 1999. 36.

Krumbholz, Martin. "Wann haben Sie das letzte Mal gedacht? Die Vorteile der Unsensiblen: Elke Naters' zweiter Alltags-Roman *Lügen.*" *Süddeutsche Zeitung.* August 27, 1999. 15.

Künzel, Christine. "Einleitung." *Autorinszenierungen. Autorschaft und literarisches Werk im Kontext der Medien.* Christine Künzel and Jörg Schönert, eds. Würzburg: Königshausen & Neumann, 2007. 9–23.

Kuhn, Johannes. "Zocker, Zirkus, Dreistigkeit." *Der Spiegel.* March 10, 2007.
    http://www.spiegel.de/wirtschaft/0,1518,470879,00.html.
Kulish, Nicholas. "Growth of German Economy Bolsters Its Stance on Recession."
    *The New York Times.* August 14, 2010. A1 and A 6.
Kunisch, Hans-Peter. "In klassischer Novellenform: Gregor Hens erzählt in *Matta verlässt
    seine Kinder* eine Ausbruchsgeschichte." *Süddeutsche Zeitung.* April 20, 2004.
Kurbjuweit. Dirk, Kristina Allgöwer et al. "Deutschland, ein Sommermärchen." *Der Spiegel.*
    June 19, 2006. 68–81.
Lakshmi, Rama. "India's Cheeky 'Chick Lit' Finds An Audience." *The Washington Post.*
    November 23, 2007.
Langston, Richard. "Escape from Germany: Disappearing Bodies and Postmodern Space in
    Christian Kracht's Prose." *The German Quarterly* 78.4 (Winter 2005): 50–70.
Lash, Scott and John Urry. *Economies of Signs and Space.* London: Sage, 1994.
Lehmann-Wacker, Sigrid. "'Die völlige Irrationalität der Bundesagentur darstellen.' Gespräch
    mit Joachim Zelter anlässlich der Uraufführung des Stücks in Osnabrück." *Junge Welt.*
    December 1, 2007.
Leitgeb, Hanna. "Der Verlust der Unschuld. Florian Illies und das Gewissen der Generation
    Golf." *Literaturen* 9 (2001): 26–27.
Lenz, Daniel and Peter Pütz. "'Ich werde versuchen, eine Schriftstellerin zu sein.' Gespräch
    mit Judith Hermann – 21. Mai 1999." *LebensBeschreibungen. Zwanzig Gespräche mit
    Schriftstellern.* Daniel Lenz and Peter Pütz, eds. Munich: Edition Text & Kritik, 2000.
    228–238.
Lenz, Daniel and Peter Pütz. "'Ich muss nicht schreiben, um nicht verrückt zu werden'.
    Gespräch mit Thomas Meinecke – 11. Dezember 1998". *LebensBeschreibungen. Zwanzig
    Gespräche mit Schriftstellern.* Daniel Lenz and Peter Pütz, eds. Munich: Edition Text &
    Kritik, 2000. 145–155.
Link, Jürgen. "(Nicht) normale Lebensläufe, (nicht) normale Fahrten: Das Beispiel des
    experimentellen Romans von Sibylle Berg." *(Nicht) normale Fahrten: Faszinationen eines
    modernen Narrationstyps.* Ute Gerhard et al., eds. Heidelberg: Synchron, 2003. 21–36.
Linklater, Beth. "Germany as background: global concerns in recent women's writing in
    German." *German literature in the age of globalization.* Stuart Taberner, ed.
    Birmingham: Birmingham University Press, 2004. 67–88.
Löfgren, Orvar and Robert Willim. "Introduction: The Mandrake Mode." *Magic, Culture, and
    the New Economy.* Orvar Löfgren and Robert Willim, eds. Oxford/New York: Berg, 2005.
    1–18.
Lottmann, Joachim. "Diese Locken! Alexa Hennig von Lange – die Antwort der Literatur auf
    die Spice Girls". *Die Zeit* (97/1998). http://www.zeit.de/1998/07/Diese_Locken_.
Lottmann, Joachim. "Fulda ist besser. Nahaufnahme: Florian Illies hat das Porträt seiner
    Heimatstadt geschrieben – eine romantische Verklärung der deutschen Provinz." *Der
    Spiegel* 22 (2006). 154.
Lovink, Geert. *Zero Comments: Blogging and Critical Internet Culture.* New York: Routlegde,
    2008.
Lützeler, Paul Michael. "Nomadentum und Arbeitslosigkeit." *Merkur. Zeitschrift für
    europäisches Denken* 9/10 (1998): 908–918.
Lützeler, Paul Michael. "Europäische Identität. Der mühsame Weg zur Multikultur." *Volk –
    Nation – Europa.* Alexander von Bormann, ed. Würzburg: Königshausen & Neumann,
    1998. 227–237.

Lützeler, Paul Michael. *Postmoderne und postkoloniale deutschsprachige Literatur.* Bielefeld: Aisthesis, 2005.

Lyons, Daniel and Daniel Stone: "President 2.0: Obama harnessed the grass-roots power of the Web to get elected. How will he use that power now?" *Newsweek* November 22, 2008.

Macho, Thomas H. "Geistesgegenwart. Notizen zur Lage der Intellektuellen." *Intellektuellendämmerung? Beiträge zur neuesten Zeit des Geistes.* Martin Meyer, ed. Munich: Hanser, 1992. 38–56.

Marx, Friedhelm. "Körper, Kunst, Bildung. John von Düffels Roman *EGO.*" *Familien erzählen. Das literarische Werk John von Düffels.* Stephanie Catani and Friedhelm Marx, eds. Göttingen: Wallstein, 2010. 99–112.

Massey, Doreen. "A Global Sense of Place." *Marxism Today.* June 1991: 24–28.

Matt, Peter von. "Der Chef in der Krise. Zur Inszenierung des Unternehmers in der Literatur." *'Denn wovon lebt der Mensch?' Literatur und Wirtschaft.* Dirk Hempel and Christine Künzel, eds. Frankfurt a.M.: Peter Lang, 2009. 37–48.

Maus, Stephan. "Job fressen Gumbo auf. Joachim Bessing an den Steuerknüppeln der 'Wir Maschine.'" *Neue Zürcher Zeitung.* September 29, 2001.

Maus, Stephan. "Muckibudenzauber. John von Düffels Wellness-Satire *Ego.*" *Frankfurter Rundschau* October 10, 2001. http://www.stephanmaus.de/serendipity/archives/98-John-von-Dueffel-Ego-FR.html#extended.

McCarthy, Margaret. "Somnolent Selfhood: *Winterschläfer* and *Generation Golf.*" *New German Critique* 109 (2010): 53–74.

McCeshney, Robert. "Global Media, Neoliberalism, and Imperialism." *Monthly Review* 52.10 (2001): 1–19.

McLuhan, Marshall. *Understanding Media. The Extensions of Man* (1964). Critical Edition. W. Terrence Gordon, ed. Corte Madera: Gingko Press, 2003.

Mehrfort, Sandra. "Ich-Konstruktionen in der Popliteratur – Christian Krachts *Faserland* (1995), Alexa Hennig von Langes *Relax* (1997) und Benjamin von Stuckrad-Barres *Soloalbum* (1998)." *Individualität als Herausforderung – Identitätskonstruktionen in der Moderne (1770–2006).* Jutta Schlich and Sandra Mehrfort. eds. Heidelberg: Universitätsverlag Winter, 2006. 181–205.

Meier, Albert. "Witzige Erforschung der Heimat. Florian Illies: *Ortsgespräch.*" *Zwischen Globalisierungen und Regionalisierungen. Zur Darstellung von Zeitgeschichte in deutschsprachiger Gegenwartsliteratur.* Martin Hellström and Edgar Platen, eds. Munich: Iudicum, 2008. 157–165.

Mensing, Kolja. "Familiengrab mit Aussicht". *Taz, die tageszeitung.* April 16, 2004 http://www.taz.de/index.php?id=archivseite&dig=2004/04/16/a0286. (March 14, 2010).

Mensing, Kolja. "Blühende Wiesen und Kittelschürzen. Florian Illies unternimmt eine wenig originelle Reise in die deutsche Provinz." *Taz, die tageszeitung.* August 23, 2006 http://www.taz.de/1/archiv/archiv/?dig=2006/08/23/a0140. (July 10, 2011).

Menz, Georg. "*Auf Wiedersehen*, Rhineland Model: Embedding Neoliberalism in Germany." *Internalizing Globalization. The Rise of Neoliberalism and the Decline of National Varieties of Capitalism.* Susanne Soederberg, Georg Menz, and Philip G. Cerny, eds. New York: Palgrave Macmillan, 2005. 33–48.

Merkel, Rainer. *Das Jahr der Wunder.* Roman. Frankfurt a.M.: S. Fischer, 2003 [first publ. 2001].

Mertens, Mathias. "Robbery, assault, and battery. Christian Kracht, Benjamin v. Stuckrad-Barre und ihre mutmaßlichen Vorbilder Bret Easton Ellis und Nick Hornby." *Pop-Literatur.* Heinz Ludwig Arnold, ed. Munich: Edition Text & Kritik (2003): 201–217.

Miersch, Michael. "Sind Blogs die Klowände des Internet?" *Die Welt*. April 1, 2009
    http://www.welt.de/webwelt/article3481382/Sind-Blogs-die-Klowaende-des-
    Internets.html (March 12, 2012).
Milner, Andrew. *Re-Imagining Cultural Studies. The Promise of Cultural Materialism*. London/
    Thousand Oaks: Sage, 2002.
Minkmar, Nils and Volker Weidermann. "Schreiben, später. Judith Hermann und ihr neues
    Buch *Nichts als Gespenster*" (Interview). *Frankfurter Allgemeine Zeitung*. January 19,
    2003.
Mohr, Peter. "Zufall ist Gotteslästerung: Gregor Hens' Roman *Matta verlässt seine Kinder*."
    *Literaturkritik.de* 4 (April 2004).
Mohr, Reinhard. *Zaungäste. Die Generation, die nach der Revolte kam*. Frankfurt: S. Fischer,
    1992.
Morgenroth, Claas and Vera Viehöfer. "Politik im literarischen Museum? Zum Verhältnis von
    Erinnerung und Politik in der Gegenwartsliteratur." *Seminar* 43.2 (May 2007): 100–114.
Moritz, Rainer. "Was kümmern mich die anderen." *Deutschlandradio* August 22, 2007.
    http://www.dradio.de/dkultur/sendungen/kritik/660117.
Mosebach, Kai. "Transforming the Welfare State." *Surviving Globalization? Perspectives for
    the German Economic Model*. Stefan Beck, Frank Klobes, and Christoph Scherrer, eds.
    Dordrecht: Springer, 2005. 133–155
Müller, Agnes C. "Der Schriftstellerberuf als 'Dienstleistung' an der Öffentlichkeit? Gespräch
    mit Matthias Politycki zum Selbstverständnis des Autors im zeitgenössischen
    Literaturbetrieb." *New German Review* 12 (1996/97): 15–25.
Müller, Hans Harald. "Fotografie und Lyrik. Beobachtungen zu medialen
    Selbstinszenierungen Bertolt Brechts." *Autorinszenierungen. Autorschaft und
    literarisches Werk im Kontext der Medien*. Christine Künzel and Jörg Schönert, eds.
    Würzburg: Königshausen & Neumann, 2007. 79–91.
Müller, Heiner. "Fernsehen" (1989). *Die Gedichte. Werke 1*. Frank Hörnigk, ed. 1st ed.
    Frankfurt a.M: Suhrkamp, 1998. 232–233.
Naters, Elke. *Königinnen*. Roman. Cologne: Kiepenheuer & Witsch 1998.
Naters, Elke. *Lügen*. Roman. Cologne: Kiepenheuer & Witsch, 1999.
Naters, Elke and Sven Lager, eds. *POOL. The Buch. Leben am Pool*. 1st ed. Cologne:
    Kiepenheuer & Witsch, 2001.
Negt, Oskar, ed. *Der Fall Fonty. ,Ein weites Feld' von Günter Grass im Spiegel der Kritik*.
    Göttingen: Steidl, 1996.
Nentwich, Andreas. "Die Literatur und ihre Kritik. Mehr Besonnenheit und weniger
    Betriebsamkeit." *Neue Zürcher Zeitung*. January 29, 2002.
Niefanger, Dirk. "Der Autor und sein Label. Überlegungen zur *fonction classificatoire*
    Foucaults (mit Fallstudien zu Langbehn und Kracauer)." *Autorschaft. Positionen und
    Revisionen*. Heinrich Detering, ed. Stuttgart/Weimar: Metzler, 2002. 521–539.
Niefanger, Dirk. "Provokative Posen. Zur Autorinszenierung in der deutschen Popliteratur."
    *Pop Pop Populär. Popliteratur und Jugendkultur*. Johannes G. Pankau, ed. Oldenburg:
    Universitätsverlag Aschenbeck & Isensee, 2004. 85–101.
Niemann, Norbert and Georg M. Oswald. "Aus der Einleitung zur Mitwirkung an diesem
    Heft." *Akzente* 3 (2001). 193.
Niemann, Norbert. "Strategien der Aufmerksamkeit. Eine Umkreisung." *Neue Rundschau*
    113:2 (2002): 156–165.
Nisbet, Matthew C. "The Rebirth of the Independent Bookstore?" August 17, 2010.
    http://bigthink.com/ideas/22874 (August 2011).

Norris, Margot. *Writing War in the Twentieth Century*. Charlottesville: University of Virginia Press, 2000.

Opitz, Sven. *Gouvernementalität im Postfordismus. Macht, Wissen und Techniken des Selbst im Feld unternehmerischer Rationalität*. Hamburg: Argument, 2004.

Oppen, Karoline von: "Introduction." *Local/Global Narratives*. Renate Rechtien and Karoline von Oppen, eds. Amsterdam/New York: Rodopi, 2007. 1–17.

O'Reilly, Tim. "What is Web 2.0? Design Patterns and Business Models for the Next Generation of Software." http://www.oreillynet.com/pub/a/oreilly/tim/news/2005/09/30/what-is-web-20.html (March 2010).

Ostergren, Robert C. and Mathias Le Bossé. *The Europeans. A Geography of People, Culture, and Environment*. 2nd ed. New York/London: The Guilford Press, 2011.

Overath, Angelika. "Das total designte Leben. Rainer Merkels New-Economy-Satire *Das Jahr der Wunder*." *Neue Zürcher Zeitung*. February 21, 2002.

Palfrey, John and Urs Gasser. *Born Digital. Understanding the First Generation of Digital Natives*. New York: Basic Books, 2008.

Pape, Walter. Ed. *1870/71–1989/90. German Unifications and the Change of Literary Discourse*. Berlin/New York: DeGruyter, 1993.

Paulsen, Kerstin. "Von Amazon bis Weblog. Inszenierungen von Autoren und Autorschaft im Internet." *Autorinszenierungen. Autorschaft und literarisches Werk im Kontext der Medien*. Christine Künzel and Jörg Schönert, eds. Würzburg: Königshausen & Neumann, 2007. 257–269.

Perrin, Évelyne. *Chômeurs et précaires, au cœur de la question sociale*. Paris: Dispute, 2004.

Peter, Jürgen. *Der Historikerstreit und die Suche nach einer nationalen Identität der achtziger Jahre*. Frankfurt a.M.: Peter Lang, 1995.

Philippi, Anne and Rainer Schmidt. "Wir tragen Größe 46. Benjamin von Stuckrad-Barre und Christian Kracht wollen mit einer neuen Kombination berühmt werden: Für Mode werben und Bücher schreiben." *Die Zeit*. September 9, 1999. 3.

Plowman, Andrew. "'Was will ich denn als Westdeutscher erzählen?' The 'Old' West and Globalization in Recent German Prose." *German Literature in the Age of Globalisation*. Stuart Taberner, ed. Birmingham: University of Birmingham Press, 2004. 47–66.

Poder, Paul. "Relatively liquid interpersonal relationships in flexible work life." *The Contemporary Bauman*. Anthony Elliott, ed. London/New York: Routledge, 2007. 136–153.

Politycki, Matthias. "Kalbfleisch mit Reis! Die literarische Ästhetik der 78er Generation." *Schreibheft. Zeitschrift für Literatur* 50 (1997): 3–9.

Politycki, Matthias. "Die 78er und der Untergang des Hauses Usher. Was dahintersteckt, wenn sich Kritiker und Lektoren um die neuere deutsche Literatur streiten" (first published in *Frankfurter Rundschau*. April 6, 1996). *Die Farbe der Vokale. Von der Literatur, den 78ern und dem Gequake satter Frösche*. Munich: Luchterhand, 1998. 51–60.

Politycki, Matthias. *Marietta – die Idee, der Datensatz und der Strohhut: Schreiben und Schreiben-lassen im Internet*. Mainz: Akademie der Wissenschaften und der Literatur / Stuttgart: F. Steiner, 2000.

Politycki, Matthias. "Goldene Zeiten für Literatur (IV): Die neue deutsche Plapperprosa ist eine meisterliche Umsetzung des 'Get-up-Prinzips.'" *taz. Die Tageszeitung*. May 25, 2000. 13–14.

Politycki, Matthias. "Simplifizierer und Schubladianer. Es schlägt die Stunde des erhobenen Zeigefingers: Brauchen wir nach dem 11. September wirklich eine andere deutsche Literatur?" *taz, die Tageszeitung*. October 27, 2001.

Politycki, Matthias, Martin R. Dean, Thomas Hettche, and Michael Schindhelm. "Was soll der Roman?" *Die Zeit*. June 23, 2005. http://www.zeit.de/2005/26/Debatte_1.

Porombka. Stephan. "Investieren! Fünf Stellungnahmen zum Scheitern der Hypertextliteratur und ein Vorschlag zu ihrer Rettung." *Literatur.com. Tendenzen im Literaturmarketing*. Erhard Schütz and Thomas Wegmann, eds. Berlin: Weidler, 2002. 10–23.

Porombka. Stephan. "Internet." *Das BuchMarktBuch. Der Literaturbetrieb in Grundbegriffen*. Erhard Schütz, ed. Reinbek: Rowohlt Encyclopädie, 2005. 147–152.

Porombka. Stephan. "Clip-Art, literarisch. Erkundungen eines neuen Formats (nebst einiger Gedanken zur sogenannten 'angewandten Literaturwissenschaft')." *Autorinszenierungen. Autorschaft und literarisches Werk im Kontext der Medien*. Christine Künzel and Jörg Schönert, eds. Würzburg: Königshausen & Neumann, 2007. 223–243.

Porombka. Stephan. "Schriftstellerberuf." *Handbuch Literaturwissenschaft*. Thomas Anz, ed. Vol. 3: Institutionen und Berufsfelder. Stuttgart/Weimar: Metzler, 2007. 283–294.

Posner, Roland. "Kultur als Zeichensystem." *Kultur als Lebenswelt und Monument*. Aleida Assmann, ed. Munich: C.H. Beck, 1991. 37–74.

Poster, Mark. *What's the Matter with the Internet?* Minneapolis/London: University of Minnesota Press, 2001.

Pott, Sandra. "Wirtschaft in Literatur. 'Ökonomische Subjekte' im Wirtschaftsroman der Gegenwart." *KulturPoetik* 4.2 (2004): 202–217.

Preisinger, Alexander. "Ökonomie als Poetologie. Der literarische Realismus des Neuen Kapitalismus." *Literaturkritik.de* 5 (May 2009). http://www.literaturkritik.de/public/rezension.php?rez_id=13089

Rabb, Margo. "I'm Y.A. [Young Adult] and I'm o.k." *New York Times* July 20, 2008. http://www.nytimes.com/2008/07/20/books/review/Rabb-t.html (March 14, 2010).

Radisch, Iris. "Die zweite Stunde Null." *Die Zeit*. October 7, 1994.

Radisch, Iris. "Mach den Kasten an und schau. Junge Männer unterwegs: Die neue deutsche Popliteratur reist auf der Oberfläche der Welt." *Die Zeit*. October 14, 1999.

Radisch, Iris. "Zwei getrennte Literaturgebiete. Deutsche Literatur der neunziger Jahre in Ost und West." *DDR-Literatur der neunziger Jahre*. Heinz Ludwig Arnold, ed. Munich: Text und Kritik IX (2000): 13–26.

Radisch, Iris. "Berliner Jugendstil. In Judith Hermanns frostigen Erzählungen spiegelt sich die Stimmung einer deutschen Zeitenwende." *Die Zeit*. October 14, 2003.

Rädle, Fidel. "Argumentum$_2$." *Reallexikon der deutschen Literatuwissenschaft*. Harald Fricke and Klaus Weimar, eds. 3rd edition. Berlin/New York: De Gruyter, 1997. 132–133.

Reemtsma, Jan Philipp. "Terroristische Gewalt: Was klärt die Frage nach den Motiven?" *Bilder des Terrors – Terror der Bilder? Krisenberichterstattung am und nach dem 11. September*. Michael Beuthner et al., eds. Cologne: Herbert von Halem, 2003. 330–349.

Rehm, Sabine. "Buchhandlung." *Das BuchMarktBuch. Der Literaturbetrieb in Grundbegriffen*. Erhard Schütz, ed. Reinbek: Rowohlt Encyclopädie, 2005. 81–84.

Reich-Ranicki, Marcel. "Das Beste, was wir sein können. Walser, Bubis, Dohnanyi und der Antisemitismus." *Frankfurter Allgemeine Zeitung*. December 14, 1998. 41.

Reinhäckl, Heide. "Literarische Schauplätze deutscher 9/11 Romane." *9/11 als kulturelle Zäsur. Repräsentationen des 11. September 2001 in kulturellen Diskursen, Literatur und visuellen Medien*. Sandra Poppe, Thorsten Schüller, and Sascha Seiler, eds. Bielefeld: Transcript, 2009. 121–31.

Riedel, Manfred. "Bertolt Brecht." Kritisches Lexikon zur deutschsprachigen Gegenwartsliteratur (KLG). http://www.nachschlage.NET/document/16000000073 (November 28, 2011).

Rifkin, Jeremy. *The End of Work. The Decline of the Global Labor Force and the Dawn of the Post-Market Era*. New York: Penguin, 2004.

Rinke, Moritz. *Café Umberto. Szenen*. Mit einem Vorwort von John von Düffel. 3rd ed. Reinbek: Rowohlt Taschenbuch Verlag, 2009.

Ritzer, George. *The McDonaldization of Society*. London: Sage, 1993.

Robertson, Roland. *Globalization: Social Theory and Global Culture*. London: Sage, 1992.

Robertson, Roland. "Globalisation or Glocalisation?" *The Journal of International Communication* I.1. (1994): 33–52.

Robertson, Roland. "Globalization as a problem." *The Globalization Reader*. Frank J. Lechner and John Boli, eds. Oxford: Blackwell, 2004. 93–99.

Röggla, Kathrin. *irres wetter*. Salzburg/Wien: Residenz Verlag, 2000.

Röggla, Kathrin. *really ground zero. 11. September und folgendes*. 2nd ed. Frankfurt a.M.: Fischer Taschenbuch Verlag, 2004 [original publication 2001].

Röggla, Kathrin. Acceptance speech for the Bruno-Kreisky-Prize for the Political Book 2004 [received for *wir schlafen nicht*]. http://www.renner-institut.at/download/texte/roeggla.pdf.

Röggla, Kathrin. „Die Lesbarkeit der Welt in gespenstischen Zeiten. Rede zur Entgegennahme des Solothurner Literaturpreises 2005." http://www.kat.ch.bm/solo10a.htm (October 9, 2006).

Röggla, Kathrin. *junk space*. Premiere Zürich and Graz, October 29. 2004.

Röggla, Kathrin. *draußen tobt die dunkelziffer*. Premiere Volkstheater Wien. June 8, 2005.

Röggla, Kathrin. "die wiedergänger." *Schicht! Arbeitsreportagen für die Endzeit*. Ed. Johannes Ullmaier. 1st ed. Frankfurt a.M.: Suhrkamp, 2007, 291–320.

Rojek, Chris and John Urry. "Transformations of Travel and Theory." *Touring Cultures. Transformations of Travel and Theory*. London/New York: Routledge, 1997. 1–22.

Rosamond, Ben. "Discourses of globalization and the social construction of European identities." *Journal of European Public Policy* 6:4 (1999): 652–668.

Roth, Jürgen. "Schulzerealismus." *Jungle World* 15 (1998). http://jungle-world.com/artikel/1998/15/36445.html.

Roth, Roland and Dieter Rucht. *Die sozialen Bewegungen in Deutschland seit 1945. Ein Handbuch*. Frannkfurt a.M.: Campus, 2008.

Rüdenauer, Ulrich. "Ach, einfach Briefträger sein… Jakob Heins Roman *Herr Jensen steigt aus* besinnt sich etwas zu unaufgeregt aufs Nichtstun." *Frankfurter Rundschau*. May 17, 2006. http://www.fr-online.de/kultur/literatur/ach--einfach-brieftraeger-sein---/-/1472266/3169480/-/index.html.

Rutschky, Katharina. "Wertherzeit: Der Poproman – Merkmale eines unerkannten Genres." *Merkur* 57 (2003): 106–117.

Ryan, Johnny. *A History of the Internet and Digital Future*. London: Reaktion Books, 2010.

Said, Edward W. *Representations of the Intellectual. The 1992 Reith Lectures*. New York: Vintage Books, 1996.

Salomonsson, Karin. "Flexible, Adaptable, Employable. Ethics for a New Labor Market." *Magic, Culture, and the New Economy*. Orvar Löfgren and Robert Willim, eds. Oxford/New York: Berg, 2005. 117–129.

Sassen, Saskia. *The Global City*. 2nd ed. Princeton, NJ: Princeton University Press, 2001.

Scanlan, Margaret. *Plotting Terror: Novelists and Terrorists in Contemporary Fiction*. Charlottesville, VA: University Press of Virginia, 2001.

Schärf, Christian. "Belichtungszeit. Zum Verhältnis von dichterischer Imagologie und Fotografie." *Schriftsteller-Inszenierungen*. Gunter E. Grimm and Christian Schärf, eds. Bielefeld: Aisthesis, 2008. 45–58.

Schediwy, Dagmar. *Sommermärchen im Blätterwald: Die Fußball-WM 2006 im Spiegel der Presse.* Marburg: Tectum Verlag 2008.

Scheel, Kurt. "Da kriege ich doch gleich Wahrnehmungszustände! Was Literatur kann und nicht kann." *Neue deutsche Literatur* 50. 544 (2002): 154–58.

Schenkel, Hubertus. "Buchpreisbindung." *Das BuchMarktBuch. Der Literaturbetrieb in Grundbegriffen.* Erhard Schütz, ed. Reinbek: Rowohlt Encyclopädie, 2005. 88–91.

Schifferes, Steve. "Internet Key to Obama Victories." *BBC News.* June 12, 2008. http://news.bbc.co.uk/2/hi/technology/7412045.stm (March 14, 2012).

Schirrmacher, Frank. "Idyllen in der Wüste oder Das Versagen vor der Metropole. Überlebenstechniken der jungen deutschen Literatur am Ende der achtziger Jahre." *Frankfurter Allgemeine Zeitung.* October 10, 1989. *Maulhelden und Königskinder. Zur Debatte über die deutschsprachige Gegenwartsliteratur.* Andrea Köhler and Reinhard Moritz, eds. Leipzig: Reclam, 1998. 15–27.

Schirrmacher, Frank. "Abschied von der Literatur der Bundesrepublik. Neue Pässe, neue Identitäten, neue Lebensläufe: Über die Kündigung einiger Mythen des westdeutschen Bewusstseins." *Frankfurter Allgemeine Zeitung.* October 2, 1990.

Schirrmacher, Frank, ed. *Die Walser-Bubis-Debatte. Eine Dokumentation*, Frankfurt a.M.: Suhrkamp, 1999.

Schlaffer, Hannelore. "Mit dem entlarvenden Blick einer Göre. Die neue literarische Jugendkultur oder: Ihr Phänotyp Maxim Biller." *Frankfurter Rundschau.* August 29, 1992. ZB4.

Schmelcher, Antje. "Im Schminkkoffer: Elke Naters will alleine baden." *Frankfurter Allgemeine Zeitung.* November 17, 1998: 44.

Schmeling, Manfred, ed. *Literatur im Zeitalter der Globalisierung.* Würzburg: Königshausen und Neumann, 2000.

Schmidt, Thomas E. "Die Wichtigkeit, ernst zu sein – und es nicht zu bleiben! Wie sich im Terrorkrieg die öffentliche Rede entgrenzt." *Neue deutsche Literatur* 50. 544 (2002): 158–163.

Smith-Prei, Carrie. "Kölner Realismus Redux. The Legacy of 1960s Realism in Postunification Literature." *Literatur für Leser* 2 (2008): 81–93.

Schneider, Wolfgang. "Nachrichten aus dem Hinterland." *NZZ Online.* October 25, 2006.

Schneller, Johannes and Gerhard Faehling. *ACTA 2005. Trends in der Internetnutzung und Entwicklung der Online-Medien.* Institut für Demoskopie Allensbach. http://www.acta-online.de/praesentationen/acta_2005/acta_2005_jsgf.pdf (March 2010).

Schoell, Julia. "Entwürfe des auktorialen Subjekts im 21. Jahrhundert. Daniel Kehlmann und Thomas Glavinic." *Das erste Jahrzehnt. Narrative und Poetiken des 21. Jahrhunderts.* Johanna Bohley and Julia Schöll, eds. Würzburg: Königshausen & Neumann, 2011. 279–92.

Schütz, Erhard. "literatur.com. Tendenzen im Literaturmarketing." *Literatur.com. Tendenzen im Literaturmarketing.* Erhard Schütz and Thomas Wegmann, eds. Berlin: Weidler, 2002. 5–9.

Schütz, Erhard. "Literatur – Museum der Arbeit?" *Arbeit – Kultur – Identität. Zur Transformation von Arbeitslandschaften in der Literatur.* Dagmar Kift and Hanneliese Palm, eds. Essen: Klartext, 2007. 13–35.

Schulze, Gerhard. *Die Erlebnisgesellschaft. Kultursoziologie der Gegenwart.* Frankfurt a.M.: Campus, 1992.

Schulze, Ingo. *33 Augenblicke des Glücks. Aus den abenteuerlichen Aufzeichnungen der Deutschen in Piter.* Berlin: Berlin Verlag, 1995.

Schulze, Ingo. *Simple Storys. Ein Roman aus der ostdeutschen Provinz.* Berlin: Berlin Verlag, 1998.

Schulze, Ingo. *Simple Stories. A Novel.* Trans. John E. Woods. New York: Vintage International, 1999.

Schulze, Ingo. "Lesen und Schreiben." *Zuerst bin ich immer Leser. Prosa schreiben heute.* Ute-Christine Krupp and Ulrike Janssen, eds. Frankfurt a.M.: Suhrkamp, 2000. 80–101.

Schulze, Ingo. *Neue Leben. Die Jugend Enrico Türmers in Briefen und Prosa. Herausgegeben, kommentiert und mit einem Vorwort versehen von Ingo Schulze.* Berlin: Berlin Verlag, 2005.

Schulze, Ingo. *Handy. Dreizehn Geschichten in alter Manier.* Erzählungen. Berlin: Berlin Verlag, 2007.

Schumacher, Eckhard. "Omnipräsentes Verschwinden. Christian Kracht im Netz." *Christian Kracht. Zu Leben und Werk.* Johannes Birgfeld and Claude D. Conter, eds. Cologne: Kiepenheuer & Witsch, 2009. 187–203.

Schweizer, Thomas and Michael Schnegg. *Die soziale Struktur der 'Simple Storys.' Eine Netzwerkanalyse* [Talk, May 15, 1998]. http://www.uni-koeln.de/phil-fak/voelkerkunde/alt/simple.html (no longer available online).

Segeberg, Harro, ed. *Vom Wert der Arbeit: Zur literarischen Konstitution des Wertkomplexes Arbeit in der deutschen Literatur (1770–1930).* Tübingen: Niemeyer, 1991.

Sennett, Richard. *The Culture of the New Capitalism.* New Haven/London: Yale UP, 2006.

Sennett, Richard. *The Corrosion of Character: The Personal Consequences of Work in the New Capitalism,* W.W. Norton and Co, 2007.

Shapiro, Andrew L. *The Control Revolution. How the Internet is Putting Individuals in Charge and Changing the World.* New York: Public Affairs, 1999.

Siebert, Horst. *The German Economy. Beyond the Social Market.* Princeton / Oxford: Princeton University Press, 2005.

Sieg, Christian. "Deterritorialisierte Räume. Katharina Hackers *Die Habenichtse* und Terézia Moras *Alle Tage* im Spiegel des Globalisierungsdiskurses." *Weimarer Beiträge* 51.1 (2011): 36–56.

Simanowski., Roberto: *Interfictions. Vom Schreiben im Netz.* Frankfurt a.M.: Suhrkamp, 2002.

Sprang, Stefan. "Textviren zwischen elektronischen Realitätsprogrammen. Wie Literatur am Thema 'Medien' ihre Gegenwärtigkeit beweisen kann." *Deutschsprachige Gegenwartsliteratur. Wider ihre Verächter.* Christian Döring, ed. Frankfurt a.M.: Suhrkamp, 1995. 49–81.

Spreckelsen, Tilman. "Loft der Abenteuer. Rainer Merkels Debüt aus der Werbewelt." *Frankfurter Allgemeine Zeitung.* October 20, 2001.

Staffel, Tim. *Terrordrom.* Roman. Zürich: Ammann, 1998.

Stahl, Enno. "New Economy und Literatur." *Arbeit – Kultur – Identität. Zur Transformation von Arbeitslandschaften in der Literatur.* Dagmar Kift and Hanneliese Palm, eds. Essen: Klartext, 2007. 85–97.

Standing, Guy. *The Precariat. The New Dangerous Class.* London: Bloomsbury Academic, 2011.

Stein, Hannes. "Wie altmodisch, Herr Biller! Porträt eines konservativen Schriftstellers." *Aufgerissen. Zur Literatur der 90er.* Thomas Kraft, ed. Munich, Zürich: Piper, 2000. 117–126.

Steinfeld, Thomas. "Gumborama. Auch Joachim Bessing verschärft die Frage nach dem Stil." *Süddeutsche Zeitung.* November 8, 2001.

Steinfeld, Thomas. "Liebst du mich? Judith Hermanns Erzählband *Nichts als Gespenster.*"
  *Süddeutsche Zeitung.* January 31, 2003.

Steinhoff, Eirik, ed. *New Writing in German. Chicago Review* 48.2/3 (2002).

Stephan, Inge. "Undine an der Newa und am Suzhou River. Wasserfrauen-Phantasien im
  interkulturellen und intermedialen Vergleich." *Zeitschrift für Germanistik* 12.3 (2002):
  547–563.

Stolz, Matthias. "Generation Praktikum." *Die Zeit.* March 21, 2005. http://www.zeit.de/2005/
  14/Titel_2fPraktikant_14.

Streisand, Lea. "Tu was, tu nix. Jakob Hein schreibt einen Hartz IV-Roman." *Der
  Tagesspiegel.* March 15, 2006. http://www.tagesspiegel.de/kultur/tu-was-tu-nix/
  693326.html (July 2, 2011).

Stricker, Armin. "Wir kehren immer wieder zum Wasser zurück." *Paradoxien der
  Wiederholung.* Robert Andre and Christoph Deupmann, eds. Heidelberg: Winter, 2003.
  137–156.

Sullivan, Robert. "Dreamcatcher. How did a suburban mother of three become the next big
  thing in publishing with her chaste-but-erotic Twilight series? Robert Sullivan meets
  Stephenie Meyer." *Vanity Fair.* March 2009. http://www.style.com/vogue/feature/2009_
  March_Stephenie_Meyer/.

Szeman, Imre. "Cultural Studies and the Transnational." *New Cultural Studies. Adventures in
  Theory.* Gary Hall and Claire Birchall, eds. Athens: University of Georgia Press, 2006.
  200–219.

Taberner, Stuart. *German Literature of the 1990s and Beyond. Normalization and the Berlin
  Republic.* Rochester: Camden House, 2005.

Taberner, Stuart. "Introduction: German literature in the age of globalization." *German
  literature in the age of globalization.* Stuart Taberner, ed. Birmingham: Birmingham
  University Press, 2004. 1–24

Tabert, Nils. "Gespräch mit John von Düffel." *Playspotting 2. Neue deutsche Stücke.* Nils
  Tabert, ed. Berlin: Rowohlt Taschenbuch Verlag, 2002. 249–262.

Tabert, Nils. "Gespräch mit Sibylle Berg." *Playspotting 2. Neue deutsche Stücke.* Nils Tabert,
  ed. Berlin: Rowohlt Taschenbuch Verlag, 2002. 9–22.

Tacke, Alexandra and Björn Weyand, eds. *Depressive Dandys. Spielformen der Dekadenz in
  der Pop-Moderne.* Cologne: Böhlau, 2009.

Terkessidis, Mark. "Das klaustrophobische Subjekt. Neue Romane von der Popfraktion."
  *Die Zeit* 41. October 5, 2000. 63.

Thomalla, Ariane. *Die "femme fragile." Ein literarischer Topos der Jahrhundertwende.*
  Düsseldorf: Bertelsmann Universitätsverlag, 1972.

Thomas, David. "Über die Gegenwart nachdenken. Michael Kumpfmüller und Ulrich Peltzer
  im Gespräch über die Aktualität des Politischen in der Literatur." *Neue Zürcher Zeitung
  Online.* April 26, 2008.

Thiel, Christian. "Eine mußte es ja machen. Literatur zwischen Provinz und Metropole.
  Koobooks-Verlegerin und Autorin Daniela Seel macht mit ihrem Verlag seit zwei Jahren
  wunderschöne Bücher." *Frankfurter Allgemeine Zeitung.* June 30, 2005. 39.

Todorow, Almut. "Das Feuilleton im medialen Wandel der Tageszeitung im 20. Jahrhundert.
  Konzeptionelle und methodische Überlegungen zu einer kulturwissenschaftlichen
  Feuilletonforschung." *Die lange Geschichte der kleinen Form. Beiträge zur
  Feuilletonforschung.* Kai Kaufmann and Erhard Schütz, eds. Berlin: Weidler, 2000.
  15–30.

Tollmann, Verena and Stephanie Wurster: "Dreifache Verpflichtung. Arbeiten im 'neoliberalen Wertekorsett.' Interview mit Katrin Röggla." *Fluter.de*. April 19, 2004. http://www.fluter.de/de/wirtschaft/lesen/2851/?tpl=86.

Tomlinson, John. *Globalization and Culture*. Chicago: University of Chicago Press, 1999.

Trojanow, Ilija. "Döner in Walhalla oder Welche Spuren hinterläßt der Gast, der keiner mehr ist?" *Döner in Walhalla. Texte aus der anderen deutschen Literatur*. Trojanow, Ilija, ed. Cologne: Kiepenheuer & Witsch 2000, 9–15.

Trommler, Frank. "Forum: German Studies and Globalization." *The German Quarterly* 78.2 (Spring 2005): 240–242.

Ullmaier, Johannes. *Von Acid nach Adlon und zurück. Eine Reise durch die deutschsprachige Popliteratur*. Mainz: Ventil-Verlag, 2001.

Ullmaier, Johannes, ed. *Schicht! Arbeitsreportagen für die Endzeit*. Frankfurt a.M.: Edition Suhrkamp, 2007.

Ujma, Christina. "Vom 'Fräuleinwunder' zur neuen Schriftstellerinnengeneration. Entwicklungen und Tendenzen bei Alexa Hennig von Lange, Judith Hermann, Sibylle Berg und Tanja Dückers." *Zwischen Inszenierung und Botschaft. Zur Literatur deutschsprachiger Autorinnen am Ende des 20. Jahrhunderts*. Ilse Nagelschmid, Lea Müller-Dannhausen, and Sandy Feldbacher, eds. Berlin: Frank & Timme, 2006. 73–87.

Ungerer, Klaus. "Schlimme, fette Welt, Arbeitslosenabwicklung: Joachim Zelter erzählt vom Elend." *Frankfurter Allgemeine Zeitung*. March 20, 2007. 34.

Urry, John. *Consuming Places*. London and New York: Routlegde, 1995.

Urry, John. *Sociology beyond Societes. Mobilities for the twenty-first century*. London/ New York: Routledge, 2000.

Urry, John. *Mobilities*. Cambridge/Malden: Polity, 2007.

Vaihinger, Dirk. "Verleger." *Das BuchMarktBuch. Der Literaturbetrieb in Grundbegriffen*. Erhard Schütz, ed. Reinbek: Rowohlt Encyclopädie, 2005. 374–377.

Varna, Sascha. "Würdest du bitte endlich die Fresse halten, bitte! Joachim Bessings Roman-Debüt." *Die Zeit*. October 4, 2001.

Vinokur, A.D. and Y. Schul. "The Web of Coping Resources and Pathways to Reemployment Following a Job Loss." *Journal of Occupational Health Psychology* 7 (2002): 68–83.

Vogl, Joseph. *Kalkül und Leidenschaft. Poetik des ökonomischen Menschen*. Munich: Sequenzia, 2002.

Vormweg, Heinrich. "Literaturzerstörung." *Vergangene Gegenwart – gegenwärtige Vergangenheit. Studien, Polemiken und Laudationes zur deutschsprachigen Literatur 1960 bis 1994*. Jörg Drews, ed. Bielefeld: Aisthesis, 1994. 42–60.

Wadhwani, Anita N. "'Bollywood Mania' Rising in United States. US State Department." http://www.america.gov/st/washfile-english/2006/August/20060809124617nainawhdaw0.8614466.html (August 6, 2011).

Wagner, David. "Verdammt zum ewigen Klassentreffen." *Die Welt*. August 13, 2006 http://www.welt.de/print-wams/article145982/Verdammt_zum_ewigen_Klassentreffen.html (July 11, 2011).

Walser, Martin. *Über Deutschland reden*. Frankfurt a.M.: Suhrkamp, 1990;

Walser, Martin. "Die Einheit mißlingt nicht. Wider die Verdrossenheit der Medien: Ein Stimmungsbericht zum Stand der deutschen Dinge." *Frankfurter Allgemeine Zeitung*. February 11, 1994.

Walser, Martin. *Erfahrungen beim Verfassen einer Sonntagsrede. Friedenspreis des Deutschen Buchhandels 1998*. Frankfurt a.M.: Suhrkamp, 1998.

Waltz, Matthias. "Zwei Topgraphien des Begehrens: Pop/Techno mit Lacan." *Sound Signatures. Pop-Splitter*. Jochen Bonz, ed. Frankfurt a.M.: Suhrkamp, 2001. 214–231.

Weber, Max *Die protestantische Ethik und der Geist des Kapitalismus* (1904). Vollständige Ausgabe. Munich: C.H. Beck, 2004.

Weidermann, Volker. "Als der Turm noch ein Türmchen war. Der Nationalpreisträger Uwe Tellkamp warnt die Welt vor seinem Romandebüt. Er weiß, warum." *Frankfurter Allgemeine Sonntagszeitung*. June 7, 2009. 28.

Weigel, Sigrid. *Genea-Logik. Generation, Tradition und Evolution zwischen Kultur und Naturwissenschaften*. Munich: W. Fink, 2006.

Weingart, Brigitte. "Judith Hermann: *Sommerhaus, später*." *Meisterwerke. Deutschsprachige Autorinnen im 20. Jahrhundert*. Claudia Benthien and Inge Stephan, eds. Cologne, Weimar, Vienna: Böhlau, 2005. 148–175.

Wellershoff, Marianne. "Die neue Vorschusspanik." *Der Spiegel*. December 4, 2000. http://www.spiegel.de/spiegel/print/d-17976954.html.

Werber, Nils. "Der Teppich des Sterbens. Gewalt und Terror in der neusten [sic] Popliteratur." *Weimarer Beiträge* 1 (2003): 55–69.

Widmer, Urs. *Top Dogs*. 12th ed. Frankfurt a.M.: Verlag der Autoren, 2006.

Wilke, Sabine. "The Expulsion of Morals Out of Politics. East and West German Intellectuals Discuss Politics." *Germany Reunified. A Five- and Fifty-Year Retrospective*. Peter M. Daly et al., eds. New York: Peter Lang, 1997. 3–18.

Wilke, Sabine. "Die Akademie im Zeitalter der Globalisierung: Zur Rolle von Literatur und Kulturwissenschaften." *Literature (Literatura)* 50.5 (2008): 104–111.

Wille, Franz. "Neue Arbeit. Ein Gespräch mit Moritz Rinke über *Café Umberto* und zwei Arten, kein Geld zu haben." *Theater Heute* 8/9 (2005): 68–71.

Winkels, Hubert. "Der unglückliche Studiogast. Über Literatur im Fernsehen." *Leselust und Bildermacht. Über Literatur, Fernsehen und neue Medien*. Cologne: Kiepenheuer & Witsch, 1995. 29–61.

Winkels, Hubert. "Der verhinderte Attentäter." *Die Zeit*. May 8, 2002.

Winkels, Hubert. "Literarische Weltinnenpolitik. Gregor Hens' Novelle *Matta verlässt seine Kinder*." *Die Zeit* 20 (2004).

Winkels, Hubert. "Zwischen Kind und Krieger. Annette Pehnts *Mobbing* ist ein kluger, kompakter Roman über unsere Arbeitswelt." *Die Zeit*. October 5, 2007. http://www.zeit.de/2002/20/Der_verhinderte_Attentaeter.

Wittstock, Uwe. "Ab in die Nische? Über neueste deutsche Literatur und was sie vom Publikum trennt." *Neue deutsche Rundschau*. Heft 3.104 (1993). *Maulhelden und Königskinder. Zur Debatte über die deutschsprachige Gegenwartsliteratur*. Andrea Köhler and Reinhard Moritz, eds. Leipzig: Reclam, 1998. 86–104.

*Women in Bangladesh*. Country Briefing Paper. Asian Development Bank 2001. http://www.adb.org/Documents/Books/Country_Briefing_Papers/Women_in_Bangladesh/default.asp (June 28, 2011).

Wojcik, Nadine. "Der Literaturbetrieb in Deutschland." *Bücherwelt. Deutsche Welle*. July, 24, 2010. Radio.

Wolf, Christa. *Was bleibt*. Erzählung. Munich: Luchterhand, 1990.

Wozniak, Nathalie. "George Orwell lässt grüßen: Joachim Zelters bitterböse Satire auf den Neuen Kapitalismus." *Märkische Allgemeine Zeitung*. March 10, 2007.

Yeşilada, Karin E. "'Nette Türkinnen von nebenan' – Die neue deutsch-türkische Harmlosigkeit als literarischer Trend." *Von der nationalen zur internationalen Literatur*.

*Transkulturelle deutschsprachige Literatur und Kultur im Zeitalter globaler Migration.* Helmut Schmitz, ed. Amsterdam/New York: Rodopi, 2009. 117–142.

Zank, Wolfgang. "Vom Globus an sich zum Globus für sich. Geschichte der Globalisierung. *Die Globalisierung im Spiegel der Reiseliteratur.* Ernst-Ullrich Pinkert, ed. Munich: Fink, 2000. 15–26.

Zarkirova, Laylo. "What Micro Loans Mean to Women." *Voices from Eurasia.* United Nations Development Programme in Europe and CIS. http://europeandcis.undp.org/blog/2011/07/13/what-micro-loans-mean-to-women/ (July 24, 2011).

Zelter, Joachim. *Schule der Arbeitslosen. Ein Roman.* 4th ed. Tübingen: Klöpfer und Meyer, 2010.

# Index

www.ingramcontent.com/pod-product-compliance
Lightning Source LLC
Chambersburg PA
CBHW070028100426
42740CB00013B/2629